Psychoanalysis, Literature and War

Hanna Segal, pioneer in psychoanalytic thought, has made many original contributions to her field of study. This volume of her most recent papers revisits the themes elaborated in her earlier work and brings new insights into their relevance to our understanding of the external world as well as to clinical practice. The two themes which act as connecting strands and give the book its unity are the clinical usefulness of the concept of the death instinct and the relationship between phantasy and reality.

The author is a past master at capturing the vitality of the clinical session on the page, and the clinical papers in this volume deal with a variety of topics. These include symbolism; a delusional system as defence against the re-emergence of a catastrophic situation; early infantile development as reflected in the psychoanalytic process; emergence from narcissism; the Oedipus complex today; paranoid anxiety and paranoia; termination; and the use and abuses of counter-transference.

The papers on literature deal with Joseph Conrad and Salman Rushdie, while those on politics deal with problems of war and disarmament. Segal shows how the same conflicts between life and death instincts, phantasy and reality, experienced in the consulting room, are reflected in literature and played out by nation and individuals in their attitudes to war.

Sympathetically edited and set in context by John Steiner, this collection of writings by an exceptional analyst provides a rich source of clinical insights and challenging theory for others.

Hanna Segal is a member, Training Analyst and former president of the British Psycho-Analytical Society. She has also served as Freud Professor of Psychoanalysis in the University of London and as Vice President of the International Psychoanalytical Association.

John Steiner is a member and Training Analyst of the British Psycho-Analytical Society, a former Consultant Psychotherapist at the Tavistock Clinic, London, and author of *Psychic Retreats*.

THE NEW LIBRARY OF PSYCHOANALYSIS

The New Library of Psychoanalysis was launched in 1987 in association with the Institute of Psycho-Analysis, London. Its purpose is to facilitate a greater and more widespread appreciation of what psychoanalysis is really about and to provide a forum for increasing mutual understanding between psychoanalysts and those working in other disciplines such as history, linguistics, literature, medicine, philosophy, psychology and the social sciences. It is intended that the titles selected for publication in the series should deepen and develop psychoanalytic thinking and technique, contribute to psychoanalysis from outside, or contribute to other disciplines from a psychoanalytical perspective.

The Institute, together with the British Psycho-Analytic Society, runs a low-fee psychoanalytic clinic, organizes lectures and scientific events concerned with psychoanalysis, publishes the *International Journal of Psycho-Analysis* (which now incorporates the *International Review of Psycho-Analysis*), and runs the only training course in the UK in psychoanalysis leading to membership of the International Psychoanalytical Association – the body which preserves internationally agreed standards of training, of professional entry, and of professional ethics and practice for psychoanalysis as initiated and developed by Sigmund Freud. Distinguished members of the Institute have included Michael Balint, Wilfred Bion, Ronald Fairbairn, Anna Freud, Ernest Jones, Melanie Klein, John Rickman and Donald Winnicott.

Volumes 1–11 in the series have been prepared under the general editorship of David Tuckett, with Ronald Britton and Eglé Laufer as associate editors. Subsequent volumes are under the general editorship of Elizabeth Bott Spillius, with, from Volume 17, Donald Campbell, Michael Parsons, Rosine Jozef Perelberg and David Taylor as associate editors.

ALSO IN THIS SERIES

To the memory of Paul, my husband

'Though lovers be lost, love shall not,
And death shall have no dominion.'
Dylan Thomas

NEW LIBRARY OF PSYCHOANALYSIS
27

General editor: Elizabeth Bott Spillius

Psychoanalysis, Literature and War

PAPERS 1972–1995

HANNA SEGAL

London and New York

First published 1997
by Routledge
11 New Fetter Lane, London EC4P 4EE

Simultaneously published in the USA and Canada
by Routledge
29 West 35th Street, New York, NY 10001

Typeset in Times by LaserScript, Mitcham, Surrey
Printed and bound in Great Britain by
Clays Ltd, St Ives, PLC

British Library Cataloguing in Publication Data
A catalogue record for this book is available from the British Library

Library of Congress Cataloguing in Publication Data
Segal, Hanna.
Psychoanalysis, literature and war: papers 1972–1995/Hanna Segal
edited and introduced by John Steiner.
p. cm. – (New library of psychoanalysis: 27)
Includes bibliographical references and index.
1. Psychoanalysis. I. Steiner, John, 1934–   . II. Title.
III. Series
BF109.S42A25   1996
150.19′5 – dc20   96-7559

ISBN 0–415–15328–x (hbk)
ISBN 0–415–15329–8 (pbk)

Contents

Acknowledgements

Throughout the twenty years that the papers in this collection were written I have benefited greatly from the writing of other psychoanalysts as well as from discussion with colleagues and students, too many to mention. My indebtedness to Wilfred Bion will be evident in several of the papers. Betty Joseph saw a number of my papers in manuscript and I was greatly helped by her comments. For the work on this book I am particularly grateful to John Steiner who undertook the arduous task of collecting all my papers many of them unpublished, selecting and editing them. I also wish to express my thanks to him and to Deborah Steiner for reading the proofs and constructing the index.

The following kindly gave permission to use previously published material: *The International Journal of Psychoanalysis*, The Psychoanalytic Study of the Child, Common Knowledge, The International Universities Press and Routledge.

(1993) 'On the clinical usefulness of the concept of the death instinct', *International Journal of Psychoanalysis*, 74, 55–61. Copyright © Institute of Psycho-Analysis.

(1994) 'Phantasy and reality', *International Journal of Psychoanalysis*, 75, 359–401. Copyright © Institute of Psycho-Analysis.

(1978) 'On symbolism', *International Journal of Psychoanalysis*, 55, 315–319. Copyright © Institute of Psycho-Analysis.

(1972) 'A delusional system as a defence against the re-emergence of a catastrophic situation', *International Journal of Psychoanalysis*, 53, 393–401. Copyright © Institute of Psycho-Analysis.

(1982) 'Early infantile development as reflected in the psychoanalytical process: steps in integration', *International Journal of Psychoanalysis*, 63, 15–22. Copyright © Institute of Psycho-Analysis.

(1983) 'Some clinical implications of Melanie Klein's work. Emergence from Narcissism', *International Journal of Psychoanalysis*, 64, 269–276. Copyright © Institute of Psycho-Analysis.

(1994) 'Paranoid anxiety and paranoia', in *Paranoia – New Psychoanalytical Perspectives*, J.M. Oldham and S. Bone (eds), Madison: International Universities Press.

(1988) 'Sweating it out', *Psychoanalytic Study of the Child*, 43, 167–175.

(1984) 'Joseph Conrad and the mid-life crisis', *International Review of Psychoanalysis*, 11, 3–9.

(1994) 'Salman Rushdie and the sea of stories', *International Journal of Psychoanalysis*, 75, 611–618. Copyright © Institute of Psycho-Analysis.

(1987) 'Silence is the real crime', *International Review of Psychoanalysis*, 14, 3–12.

(1992) 'The achievement of ambivalence', *Common Knowledge*, 1, 92–104.

(1995) 'Hiroshima, the Gulf War, and after', in *Psychoanalysis in Contexts: Paths between theory and modern culture*, A. Elliot and S. Frosch (eds), London: Routledge.

Introduction

JOHN STEINER

Hanna Segal qualified as a psychoanalyst in 1945 at the age of 27 and went on to train as a child analyst at a time of immense creativity and controversy in the British Psycho-Analytical Society. The controversial discussions (King and Steiner, 1991) had revealed tensions within the Society but had also led to the clarification of Melanie Klein's new ideas which were continuing to develop. This was the period when Klein had just published her pioneering paper, 'Notes on some schizoid mechanisms' (1946), which opened up a new approach to the treatment of psychotic, schizoid and borderline patients. The revolutionary impact of this paper is in my view not always recognized. Although Freud had introduced the idea of splitting of the ego, he did this chiefly to explain how two contradictory attitudes could co-exist in the mind, and, for the most part, he thought of the ego as a unitary structure. The ego struggled to resolve the pressures of the id on the one hand and the superego on the other and under these pressures Freud thought of the ego as undergoing deformations as if it were a rubber ball. For Klein the ego was conceived of as capable of being split, perhaps like a piece of granite with natural lines of cleavage. This splitting was sometimes between good and bad parts of the self and was accompanied by a parallel split in the object, but at other times, under the pressure of severe anxiety, pathological splitting led to fragmentation into minute particles. Moreover, such splitting was followed by projection of split-off elements of the self and led to complex identifications both projective and introjective. The idea of an internal world which included the self in relation to objects and an external world with which the subject interacted by repeated introjection and projection emerged from these mechanisms. It was a world in which projective and introjective mechanisms profoundly altered the state of the ego as well as the perception of objects and had far-reaching consequences. For example, it enabled the world of the schizoid and psychotic patient to be understood in a new way. It led to a redefinition of

1

clinical development in terms of a move towards a more integrated state which Klein later formulated as a move from the paranoid-schizoid to the depressive positions. It helped Hanna Segal herself to formulate a new understanding of symbolic function and of concrete thinking, to which I will refer later. And it led to a reformulation of the aim of psychoanalysis in terms of helping patients regain elements of their ego which had been lost through fragmentation and projective identification.

These ideas were enormously stimulating and led to an atmosphere of pioneering optimism about the potential of psychoanalysis. In 1947 Herbert Rosenfeld read a paper, 'On the analysis of a schizophrenic state with depersonalisation', in which he described a borderline patient who developed a transference psychosis. In 1949 Hanna Segal followed with her membership paper entitled, 'Some aspects of the analysis of a schizophrenic', which is probably the first account of the treatment by unmodified psychoanalysis of a patient who was schizophrenic at the time of referral. Bion, whose membership paper followed in 1950, was the third of Klein's analysands to break new ground by working with psychotic and borderline patients. While each of this new generation of Kleinian analysts made their own unique contribution, they undoubtedly influenced one another greatly, and an extraordinarily creative period was ushered in which continued after Klein's death in 1960.

Quite soon after she qualified, Hanna Segal began teaching students at the Institute of Psycho-Analysis and quickly became the leading exponent of Melanie Klein's ideas. Her first book, published in 1964, was the justly influential *Introduction to the Work of Melanie Klein*, in which Klein's ideas were clarified and illustrated through clinical material from Segal's own patients. In this way the reader gains a view of how Klein's ideas can be put to clinical use by an analyst, profoundly influenced by her personal analysis and reading, but retaining her own identity and giving the concepts a personal interpretation. It is no surprise to find that this book was developed from Segal's lecture notes, since it shows the thorough working over which is the hallmark of a great teacher. But it also shows Hanna Segal's unusual capacity to understand Klein's ideas and to tune in with them in a natural way.

Her second book, *Klein*, in the Fontana Modern Masters series (Segal, 1979), was also a homage to her predecessors Freud and Klein, but had a different purpose and style. This series was intended for a popular audience, and Segal recognized that she would have to put Klein's work in its context by reviewing Freud's contribution and showing how Klein built on this and extended it. Here, in addition to giving a brief account of Klein's life, she used Klein's clinical material as illustration, particularly in the chapter on her work with Richard which led to the *Narrative of a Child Analysis* (Klein, 1961).

2

In 1952 she became a training analyst and quickly built up an active psychoanalytic practice with a variety of patients, including candidates in training, psychotic patients, and also some artists who sought help because of a blockage of creativity. This enabled her to make use of her interest in creativity, art and literature and led to her now famous paper on aesthetics which remains perhaps the most original attempt at a psychoanalytical understanding of creativity. In this paper Hanna Segal did not restrict herself to a study of the psychology of the artist. She showed how psychoanalysis can also contribute to the understanding of aesthetic questions about the nature of art and the nature of the distinction between good and bad art.

It was during this period that Hanna Segal wrote her seminal paper on symbolism, in which the distinction between true symbolic function and a concrete use of symbols, which she called symbolic equations, is made. Based on an earlier paper by Klein, it fundamentally extends her concepts by showing that a true symbol has to be distinguished from the thing symbolized, and that this distinction is impaired if there is a failure to distinguish self from object as a result of excessive projective identification. It is interesting that Segal's development of this theme has continued over the years, and in Chapter 3 of the present volume a further extension of her work is found in which Bion's ideas about the relationship between the container and the contained are seen to deepen and in some ways complicate the theory.

Many of the papers written in this highly productive period were reprinted in her third book, *The Work of Hanna Segal* (1981), which collected together papers from the years 1950–78. Subsequently her work has evolved under a variety of influences, but I think it would be fair to say that it did not greatly depart from the lines laid down in that early period which established her areas of interest in basic psychoanalytic technique, in the mental mechanisms underlying psychotic and borderline conditions, in symbol formation, and in the application of psychoanalysis to art and literature. Thus her friendship and collaboration with Betty Joseph led to an appreciation of Joseph's attention to the fine grain of the interaction between patient and analyst in the session. Over the years this influenced her technique without fundamentally changing it, so that her style remained her own.

Her fourth book, entitled *Dream, Phantasy and Art*, appeared in 1991. She begins by exploring afresh the interpretation of dreams and via this route proceeds to a discussion of phantasy and symbolism. Freud's view that the interpretation of dreams is the 'Royal road to the unconscious' is endorsed and illustrated. Then Klein's contribution through her work on phantasy as elaborated by Susan Isaacs is developed and linked to symbolism as it appears in both phantasy and dreams. But Segal's particular contribution to this theme is important and original. In the chapter called 'Dreams and the ego' she suggests that in psychotic and borderline patients the dream-work required to express unconscious phantasy symbolically may be interfered with by psychotic processes so that the dream takes on other functions. For example, she shows how dreams may be concretely used to evacuate mental contents, to seduce, to attack or to act out in other ways. It is therefore not sufficient to attend to the content of a dream; the analyst must consider the way it is recounted and the function it performs in the session. She stressed that we must analyse the dreamer and not simply the dream. In the final section Hanna Segal returns to the themes opened up in her original paper on aesthetics and discusses art and literature and its relation to phantasy and play.

Unlike the previous book, *Dreams, Phantasy and Art* is not a collection of published papers even though it was based on papers which Segal was working on at the time. Many of these papers are collected in the present volume, which enables the reader to see more clearly how the themes in *Dreams, Phantasy and Art* developed. In the papers she was able to explore individual themes in greater depth than she could in a book, and, in my view, they not only clarify some of the ideas presented there but extend them in several areas.

This, her fifth book, will therefore be of interest to those who have studied *Dreams, Phantasy and Art*, as well as to those who come afresh to the subject. Many of the themes that were elaborated in Hanna Segal's earlier work return in the present volume, which is divided into two sections: Part One, 'Clinical psychoanalysis', and Part Two, 'Literature and politics'. In my view two themes, elaborated in Chapters 1 and 2, act as connecting strands to integrate all of the subsequent chapters and give the book an impressive unity. These themes – namely that of *The clinical usefulness of the concept of the death instinct*, and that of *the relationship between phantasy and reality* – are given a highly original treatment which is very characteristic of Hanna Segal and which helps us to understand many of her other ideas. They are also related to each other since the balance between recourse to omnipotent phantasy on the one hand and the tolerance of reality on the other is closely related to the balance between the death instinct and the life instinct. As Hanna Segal makes clear, one of the important ways the death instinct becomes manifest is as an intolerance and a hatred of reality.

The importance of the death instinct was repeatedly emphasized by Freud and was taken up against contemporary trends by Klein. Now Segal brings out its clinical importance by showing that its manifestations are observable in the patient's material as a pull towards death and a hatred of reality, but always in a struggle with the life instinct. To my mind this rectifies an oft-held notion, supported in part by Freud's early writing, that the death instinct is primarily a theoretical idea.

This hatred of reality and its replacement by omnipotent phantasy is clarified by Hanna Segal in her discussion of the two possible reactions to states of need. One is life seeking and object seeking, leading to an attempt to satisfy those needs in the real world, even when necessary by aggressive striving. The other has as its aim to annihilate experience of need and the mental pain which goes with it. Here the self or that part of the self capable of experiencing pain is attacked and also the object which gives rise to the awareness of need. Instead of a reliance on reality, the patient turns to omnipotent phantasy as a solution. Segal emphasizes that both types of reaction to need are present in all of us but the balance varies and represents to her the conflict between life and death instincts. This theme is illustrated by the first patient described in Chapter 1, who found life a perpetual torture and whose reaction to mental pain was to wish to make it disappear. In connection with the threat of nuclear war she spoke about her concern as to 'Whose finger was on the button', and, when her sense of fragmentation and persecution related to the approaching break was interpreted, she replied, 'I hate last sessions – I cannot stand them. I wish I could just press a button and make it disappear.' This enabled an understanding to develop of her intolerance of pain and how it was her own finger on the button which constantly threatened annihilation as a delusional way of finding relief.

While it remains true that the concept of the death instinct has a theoretical importance, touching on the deepest sources of human motivation, the theoretical aspect has always been of secondary interest to Hanna Segal. What she makes clear is that, clinically, the death instinct only has meaning in relation to and in its perpetual conflict with the life instinct. Not only are these two great primordial forces in opposition to each other but they also stimulate each other, and if ever one gains too dominant an advantage, the other is provoked into action. The theoretical links with forces of integration and disintegration, anabolism and catabolism, and creation and destruction are obvious. I have always been impressed by the idea that structure and information created in living organisms is the fundamental basis of life and that it is in the process of ageing, illness and death that such structures gradually decay until we return to the dust of inanimate matter. Reproduction, growth and integration can in this way be thought of as representatives of the life instinct in a constant conflict with forces leading to disintegration.

Hanna Segal's vitality and intelligence seems to be a testament to the fact that an awareness of the death instinct in everyday life and in the consulting room does not lead to a pessimistic attitude. Indeed, in her discussion of the quotation from Jack London's *Martin Eden* with which she begins Chapter 1, she shows how even the suicidal impulse comes up against the life instinct which presents itself as an obstacle to the longing for death. In this context Segal points out that 'All pain comes from living', and it is indeed this pain which may become unbearable and lead to the wish to die. While being particularly concerned to illustrate the conflict and mutual interaction between the two basic instincts, Segal is also aware of the ways the death instinct becomes manifest as a terrible negativity, an almost tangible deadliness which can pervade an individual's life and become manifest in an analysis as a state of awful despair. Another patient described in Chapter 1 actually had the experience of feeling cold and invaded by death in connection with the prospect of ending his analysis. He had a feeling of paralysis as though he had no limbs, no eyes and no mouth, like an unformed embryo. Hanna Segal points out that we are familiar with the way an individual deals with the dread of annihilation by projecting it outwards into objects, but sometimes on the contrary, as in this case, the patient projects his life instincts into the analyst, and feels himself to be invaded by death, leaving the matter of survival in the analyst's hands. Joseph (1982) has described this type of manifestation in her work on 'addiction to near death', and Rosenfeld (1971) demonstrated the way we can observe the pull towards death in self-destructive patients who wish to annihilate all experience of living and to find a state without pain or pleasure. Segal points out that such states can be idealized as havens of peace similar to the states which Freud described in relation to his Nirvana Principle which, in his later writings, he too associated with the operation of the death instinct.

In Chapter 2, on phantasy and reality, Hanna Segal brings Freud's early distinction between the reality and pleasure principles up to date. Why is it, she asks, that despite our innate capacity to perceive reality accurately, there are so many distortions and misrepresentations which tilt perception in the direction of the pleasure principle? She suggests that we are born with innate preconceptions of the basic grammar of object relations which comprise a deep structure for the mind similar to that which Chomsky postulates for language. However, when reality is unbearable we are drawn to an alternative system of beliefs based on omnipotent phantasy, and dominated by the pleasure principle.

Money-Kyrle (1968) suggested that it is the perception of the reality of difference which is so difficult for the individual to tolerate, and he describes three aspects of reality which are so fundamental that he refers to them as the 'Facts of Life'. These are represented by differences between self and object, differences between the sexes and between the generations, and finally the reality of the passage of time. It is this latter which comes to represent the difference between the present, the past and the future and to have associated with it the fact that all good things must end, including life itself. The reality of ageing and death are parts of life and give meaning to the structure and organization which constitute life itself. It is death which gives meaning to life and this is why the gods who are immortal have been held to understand life so little (Vellacott, 1991).

It is in such areas that we can see the intimate connection between the conflict between phantasy and reality and that between the life and death instincts. It is the attack on structure which is the hallmark of the death instinct and it is why its activity is often most clearly conceptualized as envy that attacks any expression of difference, of organization and of structure. Here we begin to see how these theoretical concepts begin to have a clearer clinical relevance. Anything which emphasizes difference is an expression of structure, and the ultimate goal of the death instinct is the achievement of randomness, of chaos, and of a structureless state in which nothing exists which can give rise to envy.

Segal, like Klein, emphasizes the fact that *envy* is suffused with the death instinct. One corollary of this connection is that clinical improvement so often leads to a negative therapeutic reaction in which envy dominates. However, Segal is not a fatalist and, although she recognizes the importance of constitutional factors in instinct, she repeatedly stresses how the real nature of the environment crucially affects the process. Envy cannot be evaded, but if it can be understood and worked through the patient is less compulsively forced to deal with it by evacuative projection and can integrate it in his personality where it can be modified by constructive elements associated with the life instinct. Moves towards integration can be thought of to represent the life instinct and are opposed by fragmentation in the service of the death instinct. This emphasis forces us to recognize that disintegration and fragmentation are as much part of life as are the opposing tendencies to create structure and difference.

Not all phantasy is omnipotent, and Hanna Segal discusses those factors which enable phantasy to co-exist with a perception of reality without being in conflict with it. The distinction is based on a recognition of the symbolic nature of phantasy and the view that it consists of a set of primitive hypotheses about the nature of the object and the world. Perception is an active process in which these hypotheses are tested in relation to reality both through action and through imagination. Freud considered thought to be an experimental action, and Segal suggests that phantasy is tested against reality partly by action and partly in the imagination as the individual plays through different imagined actions and their consequences. This leads to the consideration of 'What would happen if . . .' which enables even wildly surrealistic scenarios to be imagined in a non-delusional manner. There is, of course, a close relationship between freedom of the imagination and artistic creativity, but what Segal stresses is that it is their craft which anchors artists to reality, so that their imagination can run free in a non-delusional way.

In Chapter 2 Hanna Segal also discusses some of the consequences of a failure to develop symbolic function adequately. Such a failure, she suggests, leaves the subject at the mercy of an omnipotent phantasy which is compulsive and repetitive, requiring action as the only form of expression available. She relates this to the compulsive acts of violence seen in some murderers and also to the repetition compulsion and rigidity of structures when they are based on concrete thinking.

Although these themes are discussed in detail in these first two chapters, they appear in one form or another in most of the other chapters in the book. Chapter 3, 'On symbolism', begins with a review of Segal's classic 1957 paper, 'Notes on symbol formation', which is one of her most important and original contributions. Here she introduced the distinction between symbolism proper and the concrete types of symbol which she termed 'symbolic equations'. The latter result from the excessive use of projective identification, which leads to a failure to recognize a separateness between self and object. Part of the ego becomes identified with the object and, as a consequence, the symbol is equated with the thing symbolized. The symbol does not represent the object, but is treated as though it was the object, and is used to deny the reality of loss. By contrast, in symbolism proper the object is given up and mourned and the symbol is established as representing the object, but not equated with it.

Segal ceased to be completely satisfied with this model despite its elegance and evident clinical relevance. She came to believe that it was not simply projective identification which gave rise to symbolic equations, and that, in particular, the relationship between projective identification and the capacity of the object to deal with it was crucial. Rosenfeld's work on destructive narcissism and especially Bion's ideas on container and contained became relevant for her, and led to the notion that concrete symbolism was particularly prominent in those cases where a bad relation between container and contained dominated. In this chapter she describes the type of clinical observation which led to these views, and when she introduces the critical role of envy the link with the death instinct becomes clear.

Chapter 4, 'A delusional system as a defence against the re-emergence of a catastrophic situation', presents an earlier paper of 1972 which, for clinical reasons, could not be included in a previous collection of her papers. It is one of the first descriptions of a pathological organization based on a delusional system in which the interplay of omnipotent phantasy and reality is traced out in clinical detail. The patient's fear of a catastrophe was linked to an uncontrollable destructiveness which the delusional system was designed to control and bind.

In Chapter 5, 'Early infantile development as reflected in the psychoanalytical process: steps in integration', Segal describes the way early infantile situations are relived in the transference in adult patients.

Two patients are discussed in detail, and both relive early experiences in relation to the breast and the defences associated with them. She shows how in the process of analysis these early experiences, previously split off, can be re-integrated into the personality, and she illustrates how development is reflected in steps towards integration while regression involves disintegration. Again it is clear that this has a parallel with the way life and death instincts are associated with these processes.

In Chapter 6, 'Some clinical implications of Melanie Klein's work: emergence from narcissism', Segal discusses Klein's approach to narcissism and adds her own view that all persistent narcissism is rooted in the death instinct even when it is based on the internalization of and identification with good objects. This is clear from the way the object is controlled and its goodness appropriated. Emergence from such narcissistic structures gives rise to an experience of separateness, and necessitates the analysis of primitive object relations in which envy is dominant.

Chapter 7, 'The Oedipus complex today', is not simply a re-statement of Melanie Klein's views on the Oedipus complex, since it enlarges the ideas she has put forward and links them with what are often thought of as pre-Oedipal situations but in fact involve primitive part-object versions of the complex. She shows how these result from a splitting of the object into an object of desire and a usually hostile observing object containing the split-off bad parts of the self. Here she is in accord with developments in theory and technique made by her students and colleagues whom she has profoundly influenced (e.g., Britton *et al.*, 1989).

We can now conceive of the Oedipus complex as the individual's particular method of negotiating the Oedipus situation, which arises first as a result of splitting but becomes attached to all the many triangular situations which the developing child confronts. An important step in the development of the child has to do with the recognition of the father as a person in his own right, with his own characteristics and his own functions different from those of the infant and of the mother. He can then exercise the vital function of protecting the mother and the child from a stream of mutual projective identifications, in phantasy and in reality, and help to establish the mother's right to separateness. The father is also seen as a provider of goodness for the mother of a kind that the infant cannot provide. We can see how this is an essential part of the early establishment of the capacity to differentiate between the generations and between the sexes which is so important for healthy development, and which is one of the structural factors provoking attacks linked with the death instinct.

This theme emerges in material from a patient who became very anxious as he was going past Hanna Segal's consulting-room door to the waiting room, because the thought occurred to him that there was no guard at the door and nothing to stop him from getting into the consulting room and interfering with the session of another patient. This led to further material connected with omnipotent phantasies of doing whatever he wanted because, without a guard on the door representing her husband, the analyst was unprotected and undifferentiated from himself. In the absence of the father, at a part-object level the penis in the vagina, there was nothing to stop him from unrestrained projective identification with her, leading to a loss of boundaries, confusion and panic.

A further theme which Hanna Segal develops is that of the relationship between the early Oedipal situation and processes of symbolization and thinking. Her previous work established that symbolization depends on the working-through of the depressive position and on the differentiation between external and internal realities, and in this chapter she clarifies the way a recognition of the reality of the father and of the Oedipal couple is essential in this process.

The main theme of Chapter 8, 'Paranoid anxiety and paranoia', is to show how similar and yet how crucially different these two conditions are. The concrete thinking of the psychotic makes it much less amenable to reality testing even though it may be based on similar mechanisms deep in the personality. Segal uses cases discussed in detail elsewhere in the book to illustrate these themes and to link them to Bion's ideas of Beta elements and the relationship between the container and the contained. In this way she shows how the capacity of the analyst to understand the nature of the patient's experience may play a crucial role in their capacity to stay in touch with reality.

Chapters 9 and 10 deal more directly with psychoanalytic technique. Chapter 9, 'Termination: sweating it out', is essentially a description of the ending of an analysis, in the course of which the criteria for termination and the issue of what patient and analyst expect from an analysis are discussed. Segal illustrates the way continuous movements occur throughout an analysis between development and integration, on the one hand, and regression and fragmentation, on the other, and she confirms the well-recognized fact that towards the end of an analysis regression is common. This should not inevitably be seen as a reason for prolonging the treatment, and a careful judgement and recognition of realistic and not idealized goals is required.

Chapter 10, 'The uses and abuses of counter-transference', is an important corrective to the misuse of this concept, which is sometimes seen in analysts who themselves have a propensity to think concretely and who misunderstand the way projective identification functions. An important advance in the understanding of counter-transference came as projective identification was understood not simply as a phantasy on the part of the patient as Klein herself saw it, but also as an enactment in the transference, which had a profound effect on the experience and behaviour

10

of the analyst. This led to the idea that it is the projection into the analyst which gives rise to counter-transference and to a very misleading shorthand in which states of mind in the analyst were attributed to the projections of the patient almost as if the analyst believed in the omnipotent transfer of phantasy from one mind to the other. We recognize the situation to be more complex, and that the patient, sometimes through subtle communications and actions, helps to create or to connect up with a state of mind in the analyst which is of course always the analyst's and not the patient's. Patients may come to believe that this state was produced by their omnipotence in accordance with their aims, which may include evacuation, control and sometimes communication.

If analysts recognize their propensity to develop particular states of mind, and if they are sensitive to their own experience, the counter-transference can give a clue about something which their patients are also experiencing and going through. However, it is only a clue and has to be supported by further observation of the patient's material which still has to be understood. This led Segal to emphasize in words well-remembered by her students: 'We must always remember that counter-transference is the best of servants, but it must remain a servant because it is absolutely the worst of masters.'

Finally, in Part Two, 'Literature and politics', the topics deal with the fundamental issues of ageing and the mid-life crisis, of the conflict between life and death, and the theme to which she devoted so much of her recent energy, the understanding of the nature of nuclear war and our seeming inability to take its dangers seriously.

Chapter 11, 'Joseph Conrad and the mid-life crisis', presents a sensitive treatment of three of Conrad's outstanding stories and links his creative crisis with the conflicts of mid-life. Although it is primarily intended to help us understand psychoanalytic ideas, I believe it also illuminates the works she studies. Her affinity for Conrad is undoubtedly connected with her own Polish origins and her own passage via Geneva and Edinburgh to settle finally in England. She admires him as a writer and makes connections with psychoanalytical ideas, in this case using Elliot Jaques' notion of the mid-life crisis (1965). What Jaques pointed out was that mid-life puts the individual in touch with the passage of time and with the often painful facts of ageing and personal death. In all individuals, but perhaps most sharply in creative ones, this recognition takes the form of a crisis, and some fail to surmount it and cease to work creatively. Others are propelled into new phases of development of a mature kind.

If earlier infantile anxieties have not been worked through, death is imbued with paranoid-schizoid terrors of fragmentation and persecution, and the prospect of death cannot be faced. Again we see the connection with the conflict between the life and death instincts. One could say that maturity involves acknowledging the reality of death and in a sense being able to mourn not only the loss of one's objects but ultimately the loss of ones own life and the things dear to us. Segal believes that it depends on the acceptance of one's personal mortality.

A similar issue of the struggle between life and death, between light and darkness, good and evil is found in Salman Rushdie's children's book, *The Sea of Stories*. In Chapter 12, Segal describes the themes with relatively little comment and shows how a narrative meant for children can address such deep and disturbing issues in a humorous way.

With Chapters 13 and 14 we see another side of Hanna Segal, the politician, the fighter and even perhaps the idealist, who is not afraid to have and struggle for ideals, perhaps because she can distinguish between ideals and idealizations. This made her aware of the terrible madness of our attitude to nuclear war and she was convinced that psychoanalysts had something special to contribute to our understanding of it. In 1983, together with Moses Laufer, she helped to found PPNW (Psychoanalysts for the Prevention of Nuclear War), which functioned both as a political pressure group within the British Psycho-Analytical Society, and as a forum for the study of nuclear war and its prevention by psychoanalysts and others. And she began a series of papers on this subject, of which two are presented here.

In Chapter 13, 'Silence is the real crime', she argues that it is only insight into our motives and into the consequences of our action which can allow the individual to modify destructive and self-destructive drives. Psycho-analysts know that powerful resistance against such knowing exists and she elaborates the way such resistance operates in relation to nuclear war. The fact that it is even more powerful when group processes come to bear on it relates directly to ideas put forward by Fornari (1975), who described wars as a paranoid defence against depressive anxiety, as well as to those of Bion arising from his study of group behaviour.

Again the conflict between life and death instincts plays a central role in Segal's orientation, and here she clarifies Lifton's (1982) distinction between death and aggression which forms part of life and which allows the possibility of symbolic survival, and nuclear annihilation which leaves nothing behind. In this chapter Segal herself summarizes this point as follows:

> In natural death or even in conventional war, men die, or at least those who have acquired some maturity die, with some conviction of symbolic survival in their children, grandchildren, in their work or in the civilisation itself of which they were part. Coming to terms with the prospect of one's own personal death is a necessary step in maturation and in giving full meaning to life.
>
> (Jaques, 1965; Segal, 1952, 1958)

12

The existence of nuclear weapons and the prospect of nuclear war makes difficult a growing acceptance of death and symbolic survival. The prospect of death in atomic warfare leaves an unimaginable void and produces terror of a different kind. Those of us who work with psychotics get an inkling of this kind of terror.

In Chapter 14, 'From Hiroshima to the Gulf War and after: socio-political expressions of ambivalence', Segal continues her discussion by relating it to the theme of ambivalence, in which love and hate are directed to the same object and which leads to the awareness of inevitable conflict. We cannot avoid destructiveness and conflict, but the achievement of knowing one's ambivalence, accepting it and working through it is considerable. These ideas are applied to the issues of nuclear war and in this chapter in particular to the factors which give rise to outbreaks of war, using the Gulf War as an example. Segal argues that following perestroika and the collapse of the Soviet Union, the West was faced with the lack of an enemy, and that the Gulf War was a striking instance in which an enemy was found or created to fill this vacuum.

One of the reasons an enemy is needed is to sustain a paranoid attitude when the guilt and pain of depression cannot be faced. Segal argues that this guilt is based, in part, on the nuclear mentality as a whole, but includes the specific guilt of the various wars we have engaged in, most particularly the Vietnam War and the Gulf War, and their consequences. Unless we can admit our part in those devastating events, the old way of paranoia and fragmentation will increase all the dangers.

Throughout her life Hanna Segal has worked tirelessly, gaining an enormous respect as a clinician and as a teacher, at home, in Europe, in South America and in the United States. Her writings on political themes, while sufficiently polemical to reveal her passionate beliefs, remain intelligent and rooted in a psychoanalytical approach. Her devotion to the fundamental tenets of psychoanalysis has been unyielding but she has remained open and receptive of new ideas. While she had an enormous influence on her analysands and supervisees, who owe her a great debt, she was at the same time open minded and able to encourage her students to do original work and to be influenced by their contributions. Recent writings, such as *Melanie Klein Today* (Spillius, 1988), *The Oedipus Complex Today* (Britton *et al.*, 1989), *Clinical Lectures on Klein and Bion* (Anderson, 1991) and *Psychic Retreats* (Steiner, 1993), are testaments to her importance both as a clinician and theoretician.

PART ONE

Clinical psychoanalysis

1

On the clinical usefulness of the concept of the death instinct[1]

At the end of Jack London's *Martin Eden*, Martin commits suicide by drowning. As he sinks he automatically tries to swim.

> It was the automatic instinct to live. He ceased swimming, but the moment he felt water rising above his mouth his hands struck out sharply with a lifting movement. 'This is the will to live,' he thought, and the thought was accompanied by a sneer.

London brings out vividly the hatred and the contempt Martin feels for that part of him that wishes to live. '"The will to live," he thought disdainfully.' As he drowns he has a tearing pain in his chest. '"The hurt was not death" was the thought that oscillated through his reeling consciousness. It was life – the pangs of life – this awful suffocating feeling. It was the last blow life could deal him.'

All pain comes from living. Freud described the death instinct first in *Beyond the Pleasure Principle* (Freud, 1920). He linked it with the drive to return to the inorganic – the organism reacting to any disturbance to the status quo.[2] He postulated that the life instinct aims at combining elements into bigger units; it aims at life and propagation. (Hence, sexuality is part of it.) The death instinct aims at destructuralization, dissolution, death.

I think that Freud emphasizes the biological aspect which later allowed others, and sometimes himself, to describe his ideas about the death instinct as a biological speculation, partly defensively; he expected that his new idea would be found shocking and meet with great resistance, which, indeed, it did. We must not forget, however, that he was motivated in those speculations by purely clinical considerations about the repetition-compulsion, the nature of masochism, the concept of the death instinct, the murderousness of the melancholic superego, and so on. In *The Ego and the Id* (Freud, 1923) he makes clear the psychological aspect of the death instinct and the relevance of the concept, not only to melancholia and masochism, but to neuroses in general. 'Defusion and a marked emergence of the death instinct are amongst the most noteworthy effects of many severe neuroses.'

One could formulate the conflict between the life and death instincts in purely psychological terms. Birth confronts us with the experience of needs. In relation to that experience there can be two reactions, and both, I think, are invariably present in all of us, though in varying proportions. One, to seek satisfaction for the needs: that is life-promoting and leads to object seeking, love, and eventually object concern. The other is the drive to annihilate: the need to annihilate the perceiving experiencing self, as well as anything that is perceived.

Sometimes Freud refers to this rejection of disturbance as the nirvana principle. Originally he thought that the nirvana principle was part of the pleasure-pain principle since it is a search for constancy, which he originally thought of as part of the pleasure principle. But later he equated it with the death instinct – the drive to return to the inorganic, that is death. The organism defends itself against the death drive by deflecting it so that it becomes aggression. The term 'nirvana principle', however, carries an implicit idealization of death, linked with some idealized fusion like the oceanic feeling. Nevertheless it is destructive since it aims at destroying all life, and Freud mainly emphasizes its destructiveness in such manifestations as repetition-compulsion, sado-masochism and the murderousness of the melancholic superego.

I think that the destructiveness towards objects is not only a deflection of self-destructiveness to the outside, as described by Freud – important though it is – but that also from the very beginning the wish to annihilate is directed both at the perceiving self and the object perceived, hardly distinguishable from one another. I shall return to this point later.

Freud says that the death instinct mostly operates silently within the body and that we can never see its pure manifestations – only manifestations in fusion with the libido. But he also speaks of defusion. I think that now with new technical developments, we have become more adept at teasing out the components belonging to the death instinct in the fusion. Also, with our access to more disturbed patients, we can often detect the operation of the death instinct in an almost pure form in conflict with the life forces, rather than in fusion, and that not in the psychotic only.

Mrs A is not psychotic. She is intelligent, sensitive, perceptive and capable of affection. She is, however, fragile. Her life, in some ways, was a perpetual torture. She was troubled by widespread feelings of persecution, subject to tormenting persecutory guilt and a variety of psychosomatic and hypochondriacal, forever shifting, fears. She was very inhibited in constructive external aggression. Her phantasy and emotional reactions to any stimulus of deprivation, anxiety, jealousy or envy were of extreme violence. 'I want him dead. I want to kill all of them', and so forth, was an almost immediate reaction to discomfort, and was genuinely and strongly felt. But more than that, there was constant violence against herself. She really came close to believing that the only immediate cure to the slightest headache was to cut one's head off. She was constantly wishing to get rid of her limbs, her organs, in particular her sexual organs, not to experience any perception or impulse which could lead to frustration or anxiety. These attacks on herself, clearly going beyond attacks on internal objects, gave rise to somatic manifestations such as partial anaesthesia of sexual organs, migraines, and so on, as well as to constant hypochondriacal anxiety.

We had of course analysed various situations leading to her aggression, to projections into the objects – accounting for persecution and the re-internalization of persecutory objects – giving rise to persecutory guilt, and so on. We also analysed often her attacks on her perceptual apparatus, physical and mental. But one session seemed to have brought it together in a simple way, which she found particularly convincing and which I think led to a real shift in her functioning. Mrs A is of mixed East-European and English descent. She is often preoccupied with the East–West conflict and the dread of a nuclear war. The session I wish to report was last but one before a break. She had started the session by referring to a CND meeting which she wanted to go to, but didn't, and complained of her own passivity and her inability to get herself together to do things she wants to do or things that she thinks are right. She then spoke briefly about her fears of nuclear warfare, in particular of the question of whose finger was on the button. At that time there was particular preoccupation about American control over nuclear weapons sited in England. One of the reasons why she did not go was that she did not want to ring a friend whom she suspected of looking down on her, and from then on she went on to some other diffuse persecutory fears, obviously involving, in greater or lesser measure, all her objects. I felt as though the analytic space was getting filled with persecutory objects of a very fragmentary kind.

I felt it pointless to follow individual bits of projection and persecution, and was more concerned by two elements in the session. One, that she felt unable to confront and counteract something she disapproved of (represented by not being able to attend a discussion meeting of the CND); and the second, that there was no reference to the approaching end of term. I thought that the increase of fragmentation and persecution was related to the approaching break. I mentioned that to her. Her reaction was immediate and violent. She said: 'I hate last sessions – can't stand them. I wish I could just push a button to make it disappear.' I reminded her of the beginning of the session – and said that now we knew whose finger was on the button. She relaxed and the whole atmosphere of the session changed. She said she knew that she wouldn't mind a nuclear war. In fact, she might

19

wish for it if she could be sure that she and her child would die immediately. What she couldn't bear was the thought of surviving in a post-nuclear-war world – perpetual fall-out and all. I pointed out to her that she was alive and looked devotedly after her child. She was in fact surviving; there was a living part of her wishing herself and her child to survive or she wouldn't be here. But it seemed that after pushing the 'mental button', as she frequently does, she often felt as though she was living in a mental post-war situation and subjected to a perpetual fall-out. The diffuse experience of persecution in a large part of the session was like the fall-out.

Her associations to pushing a button and to the fall-out threw a vivid light on how she dealt with her death drive. Pushing the button was an expression of the death instinct, but combined with immediate projection, so that the threat of death was felt to come from outside – the fall-out. I think that in that session she got in touch with an almost direct experience of her own wish for total annihilation of the world and herself. The interpretation on these lines immediately lessened the persecution and put her in touch with the psychic reality of her own drives. The impact of that realization and subsequent relief were very striking and lasting. It did not do away with her problems, of course, but the intensity of destructiveness and anxiety was much diminished.

A confrontation with the death instinct, in favourable circumstances, mobilizes the life instinct as well. This was vividly demonstrated by Mr B.

Mr B was facing the prospect of having to end his analysis. This patient normally manifested little anxiety and generally little feeling. Soon after facing that prospect he came to a Monday session feeling shattered. He said he had had an experience on Sunday which was deadly. He was walking in the park with his family and suddenly he felt all cold and totally invaded by death. He didn't actually feel anxious, just physically and mentally cold and progressively paralysed. He didn't know if he could reach his car. He reached it and felt a bit safer inside it. He was sure he would die or else was dead, and the only way he could think of getting rid of this deadness inside was to come and to kill me. When he got home and felt a little better he tried to think whether he wanted to kill me out of hatred or as a punishment for having brought him to this pass. But it didn't seem to feel right. All he knew was that that was the way for him to get rid of the deadness. The experience not only made a shattering impact on him; it had a strong impact on me. One could dismiss it as a simple agoraphobic attack, but I had no doubt in the session that we were dealing with life-and-death forces.

Later in the week, as we were analysing the event, he asked me for a replacement session the following week. He had had a fairly long notice that that week I was having to be away on the Monday. He said he couldn't face a short week and asked if I would see him on Saturday instead. I agreed, and he had an unusually strong emotional reaction. He cried, and said he had never in his life asked for anything meaningful from anyone and had not expected to get it. Later it appeared that part of his experience of paralysis in the park was that he felt as though he had no limbs, no eyes, no mouth, and it struck me that he was describing something like a yet-unformed embryo. In subsequent sessions he told me that when he asked for the replacement session he felt as though he now had arms that could reach, eyes that could cry and a mouth that could ask. Soon after, object concern appeared. He was horrified at the thought of what it would have done to me if he had had a spectacular breakdown or died towards the end of his analysis. He also said that he always knew he was self-destructive, but not how self-destructive; he did not know he actually wanted to die, but having experienced what it feels like to be invaded by death he knew now that he didn't really want it.

This patient had always had an enormous resistance against any idea of separateness. He could not conceive of separateness or separation otherwise than as a catastrophic birth. His reaction to the prospect could be seen as a wish to return to the womb. But once there is a taste of life the return to the womb is a violent, mutilating procedure: to become an unformed embryo he had in his phantasy to chop off his limbs and his senses – not a benign return to the womb but a violent expression of the death instinct.

The experience of the real consequences of giving in to this death drive mobilized his life forces in opposition. His later phantasy of acquiring limbs and senses was under the aegis of the life instinct; it was an acknowledgement of needs, of the wish to live and a hopeful reaching for a satisfying object. In those sessions, and subsequent ones, he could feel need, love, gratitude and anger with a strength and depth never experienced by him before.

Freud said that the death instinct is dealt with by deflection and turned against objects. My patient's impulse to come and kill me, as the one way of dealing with the death within, seems almost like a textbook example. Klein's view, as I understand it, is that this deflection is not only a conversion into aggression, but predominantly a projection. At the same time, the death instinct inside becomes aggression (Freud's deflection) directed to the bad object created by the original projection. It is a projection that accounts for Mrs A living in the fall-out.[3] In the analytical situation the projection of the death instinct is often very powerful and affects the counter-transference. It can take many forms. For instance, with Mr B, I was often invaded by paralysis and a sense of deadness; with other patients, pessimism and despair. Sometimes the projection stimulates aggression. Both A and B were past masters at stimulating aggression in others and getting themselves into situations where they were misunderstood, misjudged, exploited and persecuted. The analyst was constantly pushed and pressed to become a persecutory superego.

Sometimes, on the contrary, the patient projects his life instincts into the analyst, leaving the matter of survival in the analyst's hands, and stimulates excessive protectiveness and concern. Mrs A's fragility and refusal to fight for herself could have that effect. It is important in the session to be aware of those projections or the analysis may become very static, or the analyst is pushed into an acting-out of their protective impulses.

There is always a great deal of pain involved in the operation of the death instinct. The question arises: if the death instinct aims at not perceiving, not feeling, refusing the joys and the pain of living, why is the operation of the death instinct associated with so much pain? I think the pain is experienced by the libidinal ego originally threatened by the death instinct. The primary source of pain is the stirring of the death instinct within, a dread of annihilation. As the instinct is projected it becomes the dread and pain of persecution and guilt. Freud described the superego of the melancholic as 'a pure culture of the death instinct'. In *Civilization and its Discontents*, Freud (1930) had come to the conclusion that, in depth, all guilt feeling arises from the operation of the death instinct. For Klein both anxiety and guilt have their origins in it. In *Inhibitions, Symptoms and Anxiety*, Freud (1926) says that the first fear is a fear of annihilation. This seems in conflict with his statement that the child has no concept of death. But maybe the two statements are not as contradictory as they seem. I came to the view that death wishes and fear of death, with the possibility of symbolic survival, are a later and different experience from the primitive dread of annihilation and the terrors associated with it.

So the operation of the death instinct produces fear, pain and guilt in the self that wishes to live and be undamaged. But there is also the problem of the pleasure in the experience of pain. This is the problem that exercised Freud in his consideration of masochism. I think the pleasure in the pain is a complicated phenomenon. Partly, it is the sheer satisfaction of an instinct. The death instinct, like the life instinct, seeks satisfaction, and the satisfaction of the death instinct, short of death, is in pain.

Mr C had the following dream. He was in a deep, dark, wet cave, extremely gloomy and oppressed. In the dream he asked himself, 'Why do I want to stay here?' This type of gloomy dream was not new and we had often had occasion to analyse his melancholic identification with his father, a miner who had died in a mining accident. What was new in the dream was the question not 'Why do I have to stay here?' but 'Why do I *want* to be here?'. This dream brought the patient great insight into his unconscious primary masochism. As with Mr B, there were of course womb elements in the dream, but it was a death womb, preferable to a life womb because a life womb implied the possibility of birth and life.

In enjoying pain there is also the satisfaction of triumph of the death-dealing part over the wish to live. Martin Eden thinks of his wish to live with a sneer. This sneer of triumph, conscious or unconscious, is an important component in the negative therapeutic reaction – not only the sadistic pleasure of triumph over the defeated analyst but also the masochistic pleasure of the triumph over that part of oneself that wishes to live and to grow.

The pleasure in pain arises also because of the invariably present libidinization and sexualization. Mr D is very self-destructive and used to spend his life in an endless and fairly successful pursuit of uninterrupted sexual pleasure. His libido is used to make acceptable, and cover up, a sadism and masochism which, prior to his analysis, were completely unconscious. The conscious, sensuous pleasure masks the fact that the deeper pleasure is inflicting pain and destruction on others and oneself. Generally, except in overt perversions, the pleasure in the pain, and the active seeking of pain, is deeply unconscious. To Mr C the fact that he wanted the pain was a revelation.

Libidinization is always present as part of fusion of the life and death instincts. But fusion can take many different forms. In healthy development the fusion of the life and death instinct is under the aegis of the life instinct, and the deflected death instinct, aggression, is at the service of life. Where the death instinct predominates the libido is at the service of the death instinct. This is particularly evident in perversions. A delicate balance is established between the life and death forces and a disturbance of this balance in the process of analysis is perceived as a great threat.

Mr D had the following dream:

> There was an area in which everything and everybody was immobile and nearly dead. Around that area, at regular intervals, there were nuclear weapons facing outwards. If anybody approached the area the weapons would automatically trigger off. Amongst the near-dead people in the area were his parents.

That dream illustrates vividly those states of mind described by Betty Joseph (1982) as near death, in which life is allowed to continue only just so long as nothing is really alive and functioning. The dream is meant to warn the analyst that approaching this area, which would disturb the deathly balance, would mobilize unbound destructiveness.

Since the publication of Klein's *Envy and Gratitude* (1957), the problem of the interrelation of death instinct and envy has preoccupied many analysts. Klein had noticed that envy and the death instinct have a main common feature. They attack life and sources of life. Klein, however, simplified the relation, saying that envy is the outward manifestation of the death instinct. Envy is necessarily an ambivalent feeling, since it is rooted, as she herself noticed, in need and admiration. But like all ambivalent feelings there may be a predominance of libidinal or destructive forces. The primitive envy she describes is suffused by the death instinct. There is an intimate link between the death instinct and envy. If the death instinct is a reaction to a disturbance produced by needs, the object is perceived both as disturbance, the creator of the need, and as the unique object, capable of disturbance removal. As such, the needed breast is hated and envied. And one of the pains that has to be avoided by self–annihilation and object–annihilation is the pain caused by the awareness of the existence of such an object. The annihilation is both an expression of the death instinct in envy and a defence against experiencing envy by annihilating the envied object and the self that desires the object. But envy is of course not the only expression of the death instinct.

Mr D, very narcissistic and envious, has made considerable progress at a certain point in his analysis, particularly in his ability to work creatively. He was very aware that this was the result of his analysis. Such situations always mobilized in him a frantic envy, in conflict of course with other feelings, but powerful and very dangerous for him, bringing him to the verge of a psychotic breakdown and sometimes over the edge, though he had not had certifiable psychotic breakdowns for several years now. This time the improvement was followed by the withdrawal of love, putting me and analysis on ice, as he described, and by anal attacks in which his faeces were both idealized and used as weapons against me. In one dream, for instance, he was in the session. I was talking but he was sitting on a high commode, as on a throne, shitting enormous stools and not listening. After a couple of weeks of great resistance, he brought the following dream:

> In a house a man sat on a a bucket covered with ice. He knew that the ice would break and the man fall into the bucket and die. The man was trying to pull the patient with him. The patient struggled and he wanted to strangle the man, but he could not because of course when he lost his breath the patient's hands would naturally fall away.

He associated the bucket and the ice to the material of previous sessions, and added that probably the man was a shitty, envious part of himself. But he was puzzled as to why he could not strangle the man. It is characteristic of this patient that he shows a kind of insight or pseudo insight, apparently recognizing his envious side, but he misses the obvious. I had to point out to him that it is one's self one could not strangle for the reason given in the dream. He laughed with great relief and said, 'But of course, we were talking with friends about that only a few days ago.' That is what I mean about his pseudo insight. He associates freely to the man on the bucket as part of himself but does not truly believe it, or he would not be so puzzled as to why he cannot strangle him. But there is also a kind of perverse situation: to kill his destructive and suicidal self he thinks in the dream that he has to kill himself. The whole situation is so suffused with death drive

24

that the only way he can think of to avoid suicide is to commit suicide. The physiological impasse in the dream, one cannot strangle oneself, represents also a psychological impasse: one cannot avoid suicide by committing suicide.

An objection to the concept of the death instinct which is often put forward is that it ignores the environment. This is certainly incorrect, since the fusion and the modulations of the life and death drives which will determine the eventual development are part of developing relationships to the early objects and, therefore, the real nature of the environment will deeply affect the process.

In this paper I am not propounding anything new or adding anything to what has been stated by Freud and Klein. What I wish to do is to demonstrate that the concept of the death instinct is, to my mind, indispensable to clinical work. Beyond the pleasure principle, beyond ambivalence, aggression, persecution, jealousy, envy and so on, there is a constant pull of the self-destructive forces, and it is the task of the analyst to deal with them.

Summary

Freud's concept of the death instinct is often considered as a purely biological speculation, and very few psychoanalysts consider it useful in clinical work. Yet Freud was led to it by purely clinical problems. Klein used Freud's concept of the duality of instinct in her clinical work, but mainly she addressed herself to the conflict between love and hatred of the object, considering hatred as an expression of the deflected death instinct.

I contend that the death instinct from the beginning is directed at both the perceived object and the perceiving self, resulting in such phenomena as pathological projective identification, described by Bion.

The defences against the death instinct create vicious circles leading to severe pathology. I try to show in some clinical examples how analysing those vicious circles, and confronting the death instinct in the stable setting of analytic work, can lead to a mobilization of the life forces in the patient.

Notes

1 This chapter has been published previously (Segal, 1993). It was initially read as part of lectures given for the Freud Chair at University College, London, in 1986.
2 I have always disagreed with the translation of Trieb as 'instinct'. I agree with

Bettelheim that the best translation is the French 'pulsion'. The nearest in English would be 'drive'.

3 At this point, I shall not go into the problem of the contribution made by the environment.

2

Phantasy and reality[1]

In this paper I shall address myself to the interplay between phantasy and reality which I believe moulds our view of the world. It profoundly affects our personality, it influences our perceptions and it plays a large part in determining our actions. According to Freud (1911a), the basic function of phantasy is to fill the gap between desire and satisfaction. Initially this gap is filled by omnipotent phantasy, sometimes by hallucination, but Freud argued that, at some point, the infant discovers that omnipotence does not satisfy his needs, and that a picture of reality has to be formed. At this point the pleasure–pain principle gives way to the reality principle. But at what point, and by what mechanisms, is this transition achieved? Why does it sometimes fail? And what form does the struggle take?

This struggle between omnipotent phantasy on the one hand and the acceptance of reality on the other exists from birth and reaches its culmination in the depressive position in which, in Klein's definition, infants recognize their mother as a real, whole and external object, and simultaneously recognize the reality of their own ambivalent feelings. Phantasy is thus modified by experience, and becoming less omnipotent is more able to guide actions without distorting the perception of reality. Nevertheless regression to omnipotence constantly threatens the perception of reality and leads to misconceptions and misperceptions which underlie much of clinical pathology (Money-Kyrle, 1968).

Such misconceptions become manifest in the perception of the analyst, and their study has been recognized as the crucial task of analysis ever since Freud discovered transference. In the transference relationship an image is formed of the analyst and the analysis of this image helps the patient gradually to differentiate between realistic perceptions and misperceptions. For instance, reacting to the analyst as though he or she were a figure of the past is a misperception of the current relationship and, when this is corrected, the past is also revised. In this way the misperceptions in relation

27

to the original figures can also be corrected, because, as we have discovered, transference is not a simple phenomenon of projecting the figures of the parents onto the analyst. It is internal figures, sometimes part-objects, which are projected, and these internal objects have themselves a history in which the conflict between phantasy and reality has led to distortions. In fact, the internal models on which we base our attitudes to one another not only fail to correspond to current reality; they are also, to a varying extent, a misrepresentation of past reality.

Recent psychoanalytic work has led to a better understanding of perception and misperception. I think this may partly be because perception is particularly subject to distortion through excessive and pathological projective identification, and, through recent work (Bion, 1962; Rosenfeld, 1971; Money-Kyrle, 1968), projective identification itself has been much better understood. When omnipotent phantasy dominates, the desired state of affairs in accordance with the pleasure principle predominates over the realistic. Reality testing has failed as omnipotent projective identification comes to distort the object and the subject's relationship with it.[2]

The important reality for infants is the reality of their needs, desires and fears in relation to their primary objects, and it is in the struggle to satisfy these needs that the conflict between the two principles takes place. Money-Kyrle (1968) suggests that the child has an innate predisposition to relate to objects in a realistic way that is based on inborn mental structures which become activated at various stages of maturation. In my view these structures, which Bion refers to as preconceptions (Bion, 1963), are associated with phantasies of the self and its basic relation to primary objects. Freud had postulated inborn phantasies of this kind which arise out of our common prehistoric past, and Klein (Isaacs, 1948) related them to the operation of instincts. I believe that a biologically based inner perception of our instinctual needs, both physical and emotional, leads to an unconscious phantasy of a need-satisfying object. Money-Kyrle (1968) also assumes, and I agree with him, that there is, in addition, an innate phantasy of a satisfying relationship between two other objects, which serves as the basis of the Oedipus complex.

What I am saying here parallels Chomsky's view of the development of language (Chomsky, 1968), which always struck me as very close to a psychoanalytical viewpoint. For instance, he emphasizes that language is not a habit or a skill to be taught and learned, but that it is always a creative act. He assumes, and indeed demonstrates, that there is an inborn grammatical structure which does not need to be learned, but which, meeting the external world which provides a vocabulary and grammatical forms, interacts with them to create a language. Having an inborn grammatical structure, and yet being able to acquire the different grammars of different languages, is like our view that the Oedipus complex is an inborn structure but that its actual realization will vary in different cultures, and in different individuals within a culture.

Sometimes it is possible to observe the way individual patients can recognize basic mental structures and are also aware of their hatred and prejudice against the recognition of the reality which this structure represents. Mrs A's material illustrates my point. She started the session by telling me that she had two very tiny fragments of a dream. In one, she saw me surrounded by middle-aged, stupid, altogether despicable men. Of the second fragment she could remember only that it had something to do with African land and African people. The first dream seemed pretty obvious to both of us, and connected to an impending long weekend. But the other, hardly remembered, fragment brought surprisingly rich associations. To begin with, she expressed her horror of racial prejudice from which she cannot free herself, and yet detests. That seemed to provide a link between the first dream of the men with whom I may be spending my weekend and the second about the Africans.

The patient, who was a teacher in charge of a class of young children, started to speak about a child's difficulty in learning any grammar, particularly foreign grammar. She thought that Africa might represent this child's feeling that grammar was totally exotic and incomprehensible. This girl, she said, was quite clever, but very disjointed. She seemed unable to make certain connections, something which was particularly obvious in her total inability to grasp the rules of grammar. After all, grammar, with the sort of patterns it describes, should come more naturally. Then she laughed, and said, 'Maybe to her grammar is as foreign and exotic as parents in intercourse must appear to a child – beyond reach, incomprehensible, exotic, foreign.' This patient was often preoccupied and disturbed by very primitive phantasies of the primal scene. In this session she seems to feel that there are certain natural patterns of interrelationship, as in grammar, and that this included an intuitive awareness of parental intercourse. In the first dream that intercourse is attacked and derided. She had a prejudice against it, like a prejudice against Africans, and her associations to it suggested that she was aware how her thinking is dislocated by her attack on those natural patterns of relationships. She made an intuitive link between grammar and object relationships and she felt that there was a natural pattern in both.

Both the object-relations structures studied by us and the deep grammar of language have the same source in what Chomsky calls 'human functions'. Indeed, it seems likely that the development of language springs from the grammar of object relations rather than the other way round. An example might be the grammar which governs the relationship between subject, object and action.

29

How then is it that, despite such preconceptions which connect the subject with reality, there are so many distortions and misperceptions which tilt perception in the direction of the pleasure principle? I believe that this partly results from the fact that we have learned to recognize that perception is an active process in which phantasy and the perception of reality interact (Segal, 1964). Preconceptions or primitive phantasies are tested in perception, just as hypotheses are tested against reality. This matching of inner phantasies against external reality takes place throughout life, but is interfered with if the phantasy omnipotently distorts the object and interferes with reality testing. Reality testing then fails and the wish fulfilling phantasy is preferred to and dominates reality; but the dominance is always only partial.

Freud recognized this when he wrote as follows in the famous footnote to his 1911 paper on the 'Two principles of mental functioning':

It will rightly be objected that an object which was a slave to the pleasure principle and neglected the reality of the external world could not maintain itself alive for the shortest time, so that it could not have come into existence at all. The employment of a fiction like this is, however, justified when one considers that the infant – provided one includes with it the care it receives from its mother – does *almost* [my italics] realize a psychical system of this kind.

The battle between perception of reality and the omnipotent imposition of phantasy onto reality is a long battle which proceeds in small stages. In part, this battle is a constant attack on perception by the omnipotent self, and it is not only an attack on external perception but also an attack on perception of one's own inner states, and on the inborn phantasies such as those of parental intercourse, which interfere with omnipotence.

Money-Kyrle (1968) remarks that it is striking how children have every conceivable theory about parental intercourse except the right one. Both the perception of reality and the underlying preconception are attacked in order to produce such misperceptions. Clinically, what we see are objects which are based neither on pure perception of external reality, nor on the perseverance of primary internal phantasies, but are the result of the interaction between the inborn patterns and experience.

Perception is also distorted by the excessive use of projective identification, and here its effect is two-fold. First, the object is distorted because it is not seen as it really is but has properties attributed to it; and second, it has a concrete existence which is rigidly held onto so that it cannot function as a normal symbol (Segal, 1957; and Chapter 3). Infants under the sway of omnipotent phantasies create a world based on their projections in which objects in the external world are always perceived in the same way, since they reflect and embody the subjects' own primitive phantasies and parts of their projected self and internal objects. They are rigid and repetitive because they are not modulated by the interaction with reality, hence the repetition-compulsion described by Freud (1920).

I will illustrate such a rigid pattern in a repetitive dream from Mr B, a patient who suffered from gastric ulcer. He had had this dream which was close to a nightmare, on and off ever since he could remember, and as a very small child he remembered waking up in a panic from it. In the dream he is tied immovably to a chair in a half-lying position. He is threatened from all sides by several elongated animals with crocodile mouths.

The first occurrence of the dream in the course of his analysis was in the context of castration anxiety, the fear of having his penis bitten off or chopped off as a punishment for masturbating. It appeared again in the context of a phantasy of myself being pregnant, and anxiety about attacking the inside of my body and the babies there. The unformed, elongated shapes with crocodile mouths represented the vengeful, dangerous babies inside the mother. The dream kept recurring in various contexts.

In one session something struck me about his posture on the couch as he was telling me that the dream had recurred, and I asked him whether he had ever been swaddled as a baby. He said he had been, for four months, and he had also been told that he used to scream with pain almost constantly. The cause of the pain had been diagnosed as colic. I thought that the elongated body and the enormous, dangerous mouth was his experience of himself at that time projected outside into his object and colouring his perception. Since that session the dream stopped recurring, and eventually the psychosomatic symptom disappeared as well.

It seems to me that at the core of his personality this patient had a perception of an object endowed with his own characteristics as a swaddled infant, an immobilized body and a hungry, angry, enormous, biting mouth. The perception of this object is deeply repressed and split off from the rest of his personality. At the most primitive level it was contained in the psychosomatic symptom, his gastric ulcer. But it is also transferred onto other objects: women, children, men. The projections imbued the perception of those other objects with characteristics which were monotonously the same. He felt very persecuted by his wife, and sexual intercourse was disturbed by a phantasy of a *vagina dentata*. He perceived children as demanding and damaging and was persecuted by men, particularly in his professional life. There was a monotonous rigidity to his object relationships because of the constant projection into them of this basic persecutory object.

Such rigidity, however, is sometimes amenable to analysis, and to illustrate this I shall bring a session from another patient who does show a shift, to a more realistic view of the analyst as an internal object. Mr C swung between states of schizoid withdrawal and manic over-activity, very monotonously. Each of these states was accompanied by persecution, which drove him into the other state. The patient was not overtly psychotic and on a superficial level he functioned adequately, but his human relations were superficial and unsatisfactory. He first went into analysis in late adolescence because of a fear that he was schizophrenic. He came to me in middle age because of a general dissatisfaction with himself and his life. He came from Scotland and enormously idealized the land he owned there. For weeks before and after a holiday he would withdraw, in his mind, to Scotland.

The session I will report occurred a few weeks before a holiday which he was proposing to take in Scotland. For some time before, the patient had been concerned with his lapses of memory. He admitted something that I had noticed for a long time, but which he denied; namely, that if I made a reference to a previous session or past situations he often had no memory of them at all. The same was true within the session. I could refer to what he had said five or ten minutes before, and he would realize that it was a complete blank in his mind. He would cover up by over-talking, which he now admitted was often quite a conscious device to hide his lapses from me. Connected with this over-talking was his tendency to dispose of my interpretations by vague associations, abstractions and generalizations, stripping the experience of any emotional meaning, and often getting confused at the end. I sometimes experienced listening to him as like walking in a mist, unable to find one's way.

He started the session by telling me three dreams, the first of which he found very moving.

You were in Scotland and I was thrilled to see you. It was marvellous having you there. But it was not like the last occasion you were in Scotland. I had nothing to do with it. I did not even know what your lecture was to be about. It was a strange experience because I was so pleased to see you, and yet I felt so excluded. It was so awful not even knowing what you planned or what was on your mind.

This was in marked contrast to a previous occasion when I had actually gone to lecture in Scotland and the patient had been greatly pleased but had experienced it as though he had arranged the whole thing and could exhibit me, his marvellous analyst, to the Scottish audience.

In the second dream the analyst disappeared and the patient himself gave the lecture to a very big audience. However, he was given a theme that was much too vague and general, such as how to apply analysis to one's work and he was dissatisfied with it. The lecture itself did not appear in the dream, but afterwards there was a social gathering and a girl showed him a family watch which he had given her but which did not work and which he promised to fix. The watch was very big with transparent stripes

32

alternating with black, opaque ones. In the third dream he was trying to mend a crumbling wall.

His first associations were to my previous trip to Scotland, and how different it had been from the dream. On that occasion he had not felt excluded; he had felt enlarged. The painful exclusion in the dream was much closer to the way he often felt in England. But he found the dream very moving: it was so good to have me in Scotland, even though it was very painful. He thought he had the dream because of the relief he felt after the Friday session in which we discussed his lapses of memory and thought that the transparent and black opaque stripes were like lapses of memory: 'Now I remember; now I don't.' He also connected the watch with feeling very shocked when I ended the session on Friday. He usually withdrew and prepared for the end of the session, but this time it had taken him quite unawares. The crumbling wall he associated to a neighbour who built a wall on a crumbling cliff and made a much too heavy superstructure on something that did not have a proper foundation. He said he had had a very good weekend in Scotland and he put this down to the effect of the Friday session.

I kept an open mind. He always has a marvellous time in Scotland, and was invariably manic on holidays. We were a few weeks from the holiday. I wondered if the good weekend was because of clear patches in his head or because of the black patches, having got rid of the memory of the experience. However, it was significant that he did think a lot about the Friday session, and in contrast to the usual lack of memory he could immediately connect the dream with it. I took up his associations and linked them with the generalization and vagueness, which we had also discussed on Friday.

The first dream seemed to represent a shift. Keeping me in his mind as I really was meant he also had to admit the perception of me as a very separate object. He was not in control and not only was he not omnipotent and could not make me come to Scotland as he had felt on the previous occasion; he was also not omniscient and did not know what was on my mind. Hence, to accept me as this more realistic internal object was a situation of both gratification and pain. The next dream was an attack on this perception. I disappeared; he was me; he gave the lecture. In reality, he often behaved and felt as though he were me. But the lecture had no substance. The people in the audience were not real perceived objects but projected parts of his child-self. The tubular watch represented what he felt about his patchy memory. The wall with its too heavy superstructure which collapses because it has no foundation is exactly what happened when he gave his empty lecture. Somewhere in the background the crumbling foundations represented the analyst destroyed in his memory.

What I want to illustrate by this material is the shift in his perception of the object. The second and third dreams represent his more usual state of mind, with narcissistic object relationships achieved by projective identification by which the true perception of the object is annihilated. The first dream, however, represents a move to an internal object which is a combination of wishful phantasy: to have me in Scotland and also to have me as a part of himself in his mind, but it is also a perception – an object experienced as having given gratification, hence desired but not omnipotently possessed.

I want to emphasize the patient's recognition that *he does not know what is on my mind*. I have always been struck by the way some schizophrenics look into your eyes and say, 'I know what you are thinking'. This is not surprising if we realize that they believe this because the analyst's mind has been filled with thoughts they have projected there. In this way the objects are felt to be known through and through. In the schizophrenic this is a conscious delusion, while in the neurotic it is an unconscious phantasy which nevertheless colours the perception of external objects. By contrast, in his dream the patient does *not* know what is on my mind. One could say I am not a saturated object, therefore I am open to variation. When he re-projects such an object into the external world he can recognize what in the object does correspond to his internal phantasies, to aspects of his primary objects or of himself, and yet he recognizes too that he does not know everything about his object. It is therefore open to exploration and allows him to differentiate between external objects and his internal projected phantasy. In the re-internalization he also acquires a variety of objects with different characteristics. The move is from rigidity to flexibility in the perception of external and internal objects.

The nature of identifications also changed. In subsequent sessions the patient commented on the improvements in his memory. He also told me that in the past he did not bother to remember. He left it to me; it was my job. That was how analysis worked. Now he began to feel that he too could, and should, exercise this function.

But the ascendance of the reality principle does not mean that phantasy is abandoned. It continues in the unconscious and it is expressed symbolically. Even our most primitive desires find symbolic forms of expression. But how they express themselves is crucial. Freud has said that every man marries his mother; yet he expressed shock and horror at a colleague marrying a woman old enough, he said, to be his mother. Why is it that it is true that all men marry their mothers, and yet this universal phantasy can also be at the root of disastrous marriages and deep pathology? I have previously suggested (Segal, 1957) that it hinges on the nature of symbolism. I made a distinction between concrete symbolism, in which the symbol is equated with what is symbolized (the symbolic equation), and a more evolved form in which the symbol represents the object but is not confused and identified with it, and does not lose its own characteristics.

34

This view was later refined by others and developed in my later paper on the subject (Segal, 1978; and Chapter 3), in which the failure of the symbolic process was linked to failures in the containing function of the object. This is clearly seen in the case of pathological mourning. In normal mourning the lost object is retained in the mind in an alive way while the mourner is also aware of its real absence. But if the loss leads to the feeling of a concrete presence of a corpse inside one's body then the mourning processes cannot proceed. You cannot bring a real corpse to life, any more than you can change faeces back into milk. Such an object can only bring you down into melancholia or be expelled in mania, as described by Abraham (1924).

This is illustrated by a patient in the second year of her analysis. Mrs D came for difficulties in her relationships, but it soon became apparent that she was very severely obsessional. She was a painter, but because of endless procrastinations her work was always extremely slow, and for the last few years it had come to an almost complete halt. She spent hours collecting potentially useful objects, tidying, cleaning, attending to her clothes, make-up and so on and her days became completely consumed by these activities.

The material I want to present comes from a period about a month after a holiday when I had taken a fortnight off and she had responded by taking an extra week. In that extra week she had nightmares about ruined houses, explosions and the resulting rubble. Some time after the break, she eventually got her studio ready and was going to start work. She often worked from photographs, and during the holiday in Italy she had taken pictures of various interesting cemeteries, and had by now assembled sufficient pencils, paint, material and so forth so that she was ready to start.

One day, for the first time in a long time, she actually started drawing. She had told me that she planned a series of sketches and drawings of various cemeteries which could make a complete enough work for an exhibition. Her associations to the cemeteries were that she liked the ceremonial of burial and that her mother, who had lived in another country, had never had a burial in the way my patient would have wished. Her mother was buried like rubbish. That association was crucial, and enabled me to show her how her endless clearing of rubble and rubbish was connected with the thought that her mother was buried like rubbish, and that the endless task of clearing, organizing and tidying the rubbish was her way of trying to reverse the process. It was also possible to make connections with the extra week's holiday she had taken and her guilt at that point of turning her analytical house into rubble. In her drawing she seemed to have found another way of dealing with the situation, by giving her mother a proper burial, letting her die and keeping her alive in her mind. This had a parallel in the way she used to hang on to my words during my absences, when mostly they felt like meaningless fragments, but sometimes she was able to keep alive the meaning of what I had said.

She was very moved by the session, getting a glimpse of another kind of reparation possible to her but she showed a typical negative therapeutic reaction the next day. Having complained for years that her husband did not sufficiently care for her work and did not encourage her enough, she realized in the evening that she was furious because he had been so helpful in arranging her studio, and she felt that both he and I were too pleased at her having started to work. We just wanted to lock her up in the studio, so that she would not give us any trouble. It also meant that we did not want her to have a real child, and wanted her to be satisfied with work. She seemed to experience the session as an attack on her way of doing reparation, which had to be concrete, like having a child. In fact, it was not her husband and I who stopped her having a child, but her own procrastination, since she was then nearly 50.

This patient was consumed by repetitive, compulsive actions and her sessions were filled with endless repetitions of detail. She was the most over-talkative patient I ever had and often the barrage of words was like dead rubble, between us. The concreteness of her experience that her mother became rubbish inside her seemed to be connected with the compulsion to act as a means of projecting the rubbish outwards and in that way trying to clear it up. We can see how processes which interfere with perception have a decisive influence on the way we act.

Why is it that living in accordance with the pleasure-pain principle in a hallucinated world should lead to compulsive action? It is obvious that acting on delusion is irrational. But why does it compel action? I think this results from the fact that in the delusional world where perception is dominated by projective identification there is an irrevocable tie between the self and the object. The disowned parts of the self which have been evacuated by projective identification are concretized outside, and have to be dealt with by concrete action.

The compulsion to act is particularly devastating in those psychotic patients driven to violence, as in the case of a prisoner who described how he carried out the murder of two children.[3] He took the children to a wood to play with them because he thought they were lonely, and, feeling lonely too, he thought he would make them happy playing and he would be less lonely himself. However, as he kept them for a long time they were not amused any more, and as it was getting dark the little boy began to get frightened and started crying that he wanted to go home. The man took a stone and crushed his skull with it. He did not know why, and as the little girl was a witness he had to kill her too. That man, as a very small child, had been evacuated during the war. In his foster home he was ill-treated, terrified and lonely. He was so miserable that at the age of 3–4 he tried to kill himself by drinking cleaning fluid and eating shoe polish.

In his psychotherapy his material led the analyst to construe that the little boy was perceived by the man as though he was himself as a small child, and when he became frightened and lonely and started to cry it was as intolerable to the man as was the memory of himself in the same state of mind as a little boy. His suicidal impulse as a little boy became the compulsive murder of the little boy, seen as the child himself, who had to be killed. In my experience, a similar mechanism underlies the dreaded compulsion to kill the baby in severe post-puerperal depression. The baby may represent a hated sibling, but more powerfully it is the baby part of oneself.

Not only parts of the self but also internal objects may compel action when projected outward into objects, and such seems to be so in some cases where prostitutes are murdered. The compulsion to kill may come from a delusional source such as the voice of God, and the prostitutes are confused with a sexual mother and treated in the delusional state as if they *were* the sexual mother. Such hatred of a sexual mother is also linked with a delusional picture of the mother herself. All her other characteristics are split off and she is seen as nothing but a vehicle of obscene sexuality. We know from our clinical practice that in such a situation the child's own sexuality is also projected into the mother. Therefore, killing a prostitute would be killing both his sexual mother and his own projected sexuality.

These are gross examples, but this kind of concrete thinking also underlies the irrational behaviour of a neurotic, as was illustrated in the tidying up and procrastination of my obsessional patient discussed above. In the case of another borderline obsessional patient who used to deal with hunger by defecating, the underlying unconscious phantasy was that the perception of hunger was a bad thing inside him that he could get rid of by defecating. He had many conscious rationalizations of this behaviour and he dealt with mental pain in a similar way. When his mother, to whom he was extremely attached, died, he experienced no mourning, but had numerous dreams about her which he would write down in a notebook and then forget all about. This was a mental equivalent of defecation and he would evacuate his pain into the notebook and in that way get rid of it.

There are of course differences between psychotic and criminal acts and symptoms in neurosis, two major ones being that in the neurotic and the borderline patient ambivalence is more in evidence and the delusion does not invade the whole of the personality but is encapsulated in a symptom.

It is also important to recognize that phantasy exercises a lure which lures one into action (Wollheim, 1984). As a result of projective identification desire is vested in the object and the object which contains the desire exercises the lure. If the object is felt to be possessed by a part of the self, the self is then felt to be tied to the object and pulled by the object into compulsive actions.

Delusional actions also tend to be endlessly repeated and this compulsion to repeat has many sources. It is related to Bion's description of concrete Beta elements which are not suitable for thinking or experiencing in dreams or phantasy and can only be dealt with by expulsion through action (Bion, 1963). It also arises because the action never accomplishes its objectives. It is a delusion to think that we can get rid of impulses or parts of the self by projecting them into an object.

Thus, acting on misperception is both compulsive and repetitive, since it always misses its objective. But what about acting on desire?[4] How is this reconciled with the reality principle? Freud suggests that the reality principle is nothing more than the pleasure-pain principle tested in reality. Since a desire always gives rise to a phantasy of its fulfilment, the reality testing of a phantasy is like a wishful hypothesis which is constantly matched with reality (Segal, 1964, 1991a). If the phantasy is omnipotent the desire is replaced by a delusion, while in the more normal infant there is a capacity to perceive a reality which is differentiated from the wished-for phantasy, and in this way the phantasy is tested.

Reality testing also profoundly affects actions, since a realistic picture of the object can lead to the search for an appropriate action in order to obtain optimal satisfaction from the object. A rational action must be based on recognition of realities, including the reality of one's own phantasies.

Freud emphasizes the importance of the recognition of external reality, and we now recognize that external reality is inextricably linked with the recognition of the internal reality of one's own desires and phantasies. This recognition necessitates toleration of gaps in satisfaction, and therefore of one's own ambivalence towards the desired object. As I suggested earlier, Freud (1911a), speaks of two ways of dealing with this gap. One is through omnipotent hallucinatory phantasy according to the pleasure principle, while the other, under the influence of the reality principle, leads to the development of thought. He describes thought as 'experimental action' which, I believe, is already present in a primitive form in pre-verbal phantasy. Phantasies can be tested by perception, and through action; for example, crying when hungry, biting in anger, attracting attention and love with a smile, and so on. But there is also an experimental testing of the phantasy without an action. If phantasy is, as I suggest, a set of primitive hypotheses about the nature of the object and the world, one can experiment in phantasy by comparing different imagined outcomes. 'What would happen if . . .' is very different from the delusional phantasy which creates an 'as-if' world. A consideration of probabilities based on 'What would happen if . . .?' is a function of imagination as distinct from delusion and is the basis of flexible thought and rational action, since rational action takes into consideration the consequences of the action. Rationality necessitates imagination and the infant experimenting in pre-verbal phantasy which he tests in external reality is like a budding scientist, and a highly successful one at that, often amazing us with the speed with which he learns about the nature of the world.

In the course of development, and also in the course of a successful analysis, a shift must be achieved from an archaic phantasy organization, which distorts perception and leads to compulsive action, to one allowing a greater capacity for reality-testing. This shift is then reflected in the nature and function of the phantasies which reflect the shift from basically a paranoid–schizoid to a depressive-position organization. The gradual withdrawal of projective identifications, the lessening of compulsive and repetitive actions, and the change in the nature of symbolism are all conjoint phenomena characterizing evolution towards the depressive position.

In many of my papers, including those in this book, I contend that the basic internal conflict is between the life and the death instincts, and that development and maturation are linked with the gradual ascendance of the life instinct, and an integration of the death instinct under the aegis of the life instinct. In this chapter I argue that there is a basic conflict between the omnipotence of phantasy and the acceptance of reality, and that development and maturation reflect the gradual ascendance of the reality principle over the pleasure-pain principle. These views are linked to Freud's final theory of the conflict between life and death instincts by virtue of the fact that a major manifestation of the death instinct is the attack on reality.

This becomes abundantly clear in the depressive position, where it is the love for the object, and the love for one's life, as well as the love of life itself, which promotes the withdrawal of projections in order to preserve the object, and through the recognition of one's dependency to enable the self to survive in reality. The love of life leads to the preservation of one's object and oneself, which requires a respect for reality, while the death instinct includes the wish to disintegrate or annihilate the reality of life. Its ultimate aim is death.

Yet, paradoxically, the acceptance of reality includes also the acceptance of the inevitability not only of death but also of the existence of the death instinct within us. Denial and projection of this reality also leads to misperception and impulsive action. The life instinct, according to Freud, promotes integration, and that integration includes the recognition of the death instinct itself. What Freud called the fusion of the two I think is an integration, in which the death instinct is recognized and included into our mental lives without dominating and destroying them.

Notes

1 This chapter is based on the paper 'Phantasy and reality' (Segal, 1994a). It was originally written for the weekend Conference of the British Psycho-Analytical Society for English-speaking Members of European Societies, October 1992.
2 This is related to the point made by Wollheim (1984), who described how desire can become confused with belief. When this happens belief becomes incorrigible and irrational. It is not only distorted by desire but takes on a rigidity which makes it resistant to contradiction.
3 This man, who was in prison on another charge, was undergoing intensive psychoanalytic psychotherapy with an analyst, who consulted me about the case.
4 Wollheim's distinction between *acting on desire*, which is rational, and *acting on phantasy*, which is irrational, has many similarities to the link I am trying to demonstrate between phantasy and action (Wollheim, 1984). He also makes the point that acting on phantasy is compulsive, whilst desire, although a powerful incentive, does not lead to compulsive action. I agree with Wollheim's distinction, except in one respect. I think that acting on desire is also acting on phantasy. What he calls 'acting on phantasy' I would call 'acting on delusion'. Rational action also involves phantasy. But the difference is in the way phantasy functions. Or, to put in another way, the difference is in the level of phantasy. Acting on delusion is characterized by certain conjoint phenomena: a misperception of external reality, a misperception of internal reality, including the reality of one's desire, and a compulsion to act, rather than a choice of action.

3

On symbolism[1]

This communication falls into two parts. In the first part I give a short account of work which may be well known to some of you but not to all. In the second part I hope I am developing a little further the trend of thought started in 1957 in my paper, 'Notes on symbol formation'.

The concept of unconscious symbolism is basic and crucial in psychoanalytical theory and practice. The understanding of unconscious symbolism is the key not only to the understanding of dreams and symptoms, but to all unconscious communication. We come to know the unconscious by its symbolic expression. Most of the time, however, we use the unconscious symbolism rather like Monsieur Jourdain spoke prose, taking it for granted, and symbol formation, its inhibitions and pathology, are not subject to much detailed study.

In 1916, partly pressed by the necessity to differentiate the psycho-analytical view of symbolism from that of Jung, Jones (1916) wrote his major paper on symbolism. In it he defined what he called true unconscious symbolism in the following way:

1 A symbol represents what has been repressed from consciousness, and the whole process of symbolization is carried on unconsciously.
2 All symbols represent ideas of 'the self and of immediate blood relations and of the phenomena of birth, life and death'.
3 A symbol has a constant meaning. Many symbols can be used to represent the same repressed idea, but a given symbol has a constant meaning which is universal.
4 Symbolism arises as the result of intrapsychic conflict between the 'repressing tendencies and the repressed'. Further: 'Only what is repressed is symbolised; only what is repressed needs to be symbolised.'

He further distinguishes between sublimation and symbolization. 'Symbols', he says, 'arise when the affect investing the symbolised idea

41

has not, as far as the symbol is concerned, proved capable of that modification in quality which is denoted by the term sublimation.'

Summarizing Jones's points, one might say that when a desire has to be given up because of conflict and repressed, it may express itself in a symbolical way, and the object of the desire which had to be given up can be replaced by a symbol.

Of the points he states, some remain uncontroversial. For instance, that the whole process is carried out unconsciously and that symbols represent the self, the immediate objects of desire and their relationships, and also, that symbolism is the result of intrapsychic conflicts. Other points have since been opened to controversy. For instance, is it really so that a symbol symbolizes only one thing? Aren't symbols over-determined? Take, for instance, the snake. It symbolizes the penis, also often the faecal penis, the poisonous nipple, or even the baby's poisonous mouth. Sometimes it symbolizes all these things, and is over-determined. Defining symbols as an alternative to sublimation is also open to doubt. In fact, in practice, both Freud and Jones analysed the symbolism of works of art.

Melanie Klein, in contradistinction to Jones, considered that all sublimation depends on symbolism. She was drawn to a clinical study of symbol formation in her work with children, in which she studied the development of the speech, intellectual functions, interest in the world, as well as the pathology of this development. In her view, symbolism arises from the conflict that the child experiences in relation to his mother's body. His libidinal and aggressive interest in his mother's and later in both his parents' bodies, lead to anxiety and guilt which force him to displace his interest to the world around him, thus endowing it with symbolic meaning.

While Ferenczi and Jones considered that it is the libidinal link which allows the child to symbolize his own and the parents' bodies by objects in the external world, Melanie Klein added the role played by anxiety as a major spur in symbol formation. In the psychotic, symbol formation is at its most disturbed, and it is the analysis of a psychotic child, the first of its kind, that enabled her to describe and analyse a disturbance of symbol formation. I am referring here to her paper 'The importance of symbol formation in the development of the ego' (Klein, 1930). In that paper she describes the analysis of an autistic child. As it appeared in the analysis, Dick made in phantasy a very sadistic attack on his mother's body, projecting into her his excreta and parts of his body, which then became identified with parts of her. As a result of these attacks, his mother's body became an object of such intense anxiety that the whole process came to a stop. As, during the analysis, the unconscious anxiety diminished and became more manifest, the process of symbol formation was set again in motion, enabling the child to speak, play and establish relationships.

Melanie Klein came to the conclusion that anxiety spurs the development of symbolism, but excessive anxiety may paralyse it.

There is some lack of clarity in this paper between the idea that the child symbolizes parts of his body in mother, consistent with Ferenczi's ideas that symbolism comes out of projection, and with the idea that mother's body is the primary object to be symbolized. This became much clearer later on when Melanie Klein elaborated her concepts of the paranoid-schizoid position, projective identification and the depressive position. I have tried to put symbol formation and its vicissitudes in relation to these new concepts. I was particularly interested in trying to sort out the differentiation of symbolism in symptom formation and in sublimation. In my paper 'Notes on symbol formation' (Segal, 1957), I gave the following example.

A patient in mental hospital says he cannot play the violin because he won't masturbate in public. Another patient plays the violin and his material makes it clear that to him, too, the violin represents the penis.

What is the difference in the symbolism? In my paper I made the suggestion that symbol formation develops gradually from paranoid-schizoid to a depressive level of functioning. When symbols are formed by projective identification, the result is what I called a symbolic equation. A part of the ego becomes identified with the object and, as a consequence, the symbol is equated with the thing symbolized. The symbol does not represent the object, but is treated as though it was the object. Playing the violin is felt to be masturbation. In the depressive position the object is given up and mourned and the symbol is set up in the inner world – an internal object to begin with, representing the object, but not to be equated with it. The symbolic equation is used to deny the separateness between the subject and the object. The symbol is used to overcome an accepted loss. At moments of regression, symbolism may revert to a concrete form even in non-psychotic individuals.

I should like here to give an example. A neurotic young man is able much of the time to function on a depressive level. He can communicate in a symbolic way and has numerous sublimations. These achievements are, however, insecure, and at moments of stress he tends to use massive projective identification accompanied by a regression to concrete levels of functioning. Sometimes, for instance, he has near hallucinatory states of mind. He came to one session very perturbed because, on waking up, he had a hallucinatory experience. It differed from hallucination only in so far as he clung desperately to the belief that it must be the product of his own mind. When he woke up he felt his head was solid and he saw a motor cycle riding into his head. The rider had a kind of mask on, which made his head look like a finger. He felt terrified and thought his head would explode. Then he looked at his own index finger, and got frightened because his finger looked like a gorilla. He only emerged from a state of acute anxiety when he made himself remember the previous session in which he was disturbed by a very intrusive noise of motor cycles outside the consulting-room windows. He thought the motor cycles were connected with my son. He associated the gorilla to a psychotic boy who was described in a paper as looking like a gorilla. The finger was associated to anal masturbation, which he spoke of a few days previously. His anal masturbation was always associated with violent projective identification into the anus of the analyst/mother, as described by Meltzer (1966). We understood that the motor cycles outside the window represented his own intrusive self, identified with his finger and penis, projected into an external object, the motor cycle of my son identified with it, and intruding into him. It is important in this connection that there was an actual intrusive object in the world into which this projection fitted. It repeated a childhood situation in which there was, in fact, a very intrusive older brother interfering with his relation to the mother even when he was a tiny baby. His projections, thus, were concretized for him in the external world.

I emphasized this point, because I had come to see that it is an oversimplified view to think that projective identification *per se* leads to concretization. The nature of projective identification and its fate have also to be taken into account. A great deal of work has been done on projective identification since Melanie Klein formulated it, particularly by Bion in his work on the relation between the containing and the contained and Herbert Rosenfeld in his work on narcissism. The fate of the development in the depressive position is largely determined by the vicissitudes of projective identification.

Bion's (1957) model, which I find the most useful, is as follows. The child projects into the breast unbearable feelings. The mother elaborates them and if she gives an appropriate response, the child can introject the breast as a container capable of dealing with feelings. The introjection of such a container is the necessary precondition for the elaboration of the depressive position. But a great deal can go wrong in the projection. The relation between the container and the contained may be felt as mutually destructive or mutually emptying, as well as being mutually creative. If the relation between the container and the contained is of a positive nature, the depressive elaboration and the depressive symbol formation can proceed. If this relation is disturbed, it immediately affects the nature of symbol formation.

I have recently had the disturbances of symbol formation due to a bad relation between the container and the contained forced on to my attention by a patient who is not psychotic, but who has an extreme difficulty in communicating. She is a young woman of Russian extraction, but not brought up bilingually. Sometimes she blames her difficulties on her Russian heritage. She is also acutely aware of her own difficulty in communicating and symbolizing, and she tried to remedy it, not successfully, by taking up in turn the study of philosophy, philology and modern languages. In analysis the problem of communicating with me is paramount. Her verbal communications, particularly early in her analysis, were very difficult to understand. I often had difficulty in following the conscious meaning. She tends to misuse words, mix languages and so on. Often there is little connection between what she says, what she means to say and what she actually thinks. The unconscious meaning is often even more confused. In other patients, when verbal communications are so difficult, one often gets important non-verbal clues, but in her, the non-verbal clues are often lacking or misleading. For instance, the tone of her voice or her facial expression often bears no relation to her state of mind. Her symbolism is at times very concrete. She has states of bodily excitement, bizarre bodily sensations, psychosomatic, hypochondriacal, hysterical symptoms and often complains that she has no feelings, only concrete experiences. She often responds to interpretations by physical sensation. Words are experienced as concrete things, often felt as a lump inside her. This may be accompanied by fears of cancer. In those situations, one can often see that she feels she has invaded my speech and made it into a physical possession of hers. At the same time, there is an opposite phenomenon. Her speech can be called completely abstract. She speaks most of the time in metaphors, clichés, technical terms. She generalizes sometimes in a way which leaves no meaning. Sometimes she speaks for a long time and I realize she has said nothing concrete or real that I can get hold of. At the same time, I can observe how she empties my words of all meaning, like listening to an interpretation and immediately translating in into some philosophical or psychoanalytical abstract term, often distorting its meaning completely. The underlying phantasy is that she enters me and empties me of all contents and she feels equally emptied by me. Stealing is an ever-recurring theme. At other times, she may communicate dissociated fragments of bits of her experience that seem to function as Bion's (1957) bizarre objects.

In those modes of functioning, one can see a disturbance between the container and the contained. When she is over-concrete, the projected part is totally identified with the container. When she is empty of meaning, the container and the contained have a relation of mutually emptying each other. When she is fragmented and produces 'bizarre object' type of associations, her projection has split the container into fragments.

In her case, this mutually destructive relation between the part she projects and the container seems mostly to be related to envy and to narcissism.

45

Nothing is allowed to exist outside herself which could give rise to envy. I would like to give some material to illustrate this. She had several dreams characteristic of her, depicting her narcissism. For instance, she was in bed with a young man, glued and fused to him, but the young man was herself. Following several such dreams, she brought a different dream. She was in a house, the attic of which was disintegrating. She did not want to take any notice because she lived on the middle floor between the ground and top floor. She had a number of useful associations to the dream. She owns a flat in a house which has three flats. The owner of the house wants her to participate in costs for repairing the attic. She is furious about it because she feels it isn't fair. It's true she signed a contract that she would, but she was foolish to agree to it. Her own flat is not in danger from the damaged attic, being in the middle, but she feels bad about it because of her friends who live in the top flat. Then she said that the middle must be her tummy and started complaining of her physical symptoms. The attic must be her head which is in a terribly disintegrated state. She can't think, she can't work. She thinks her head should be entirely my concern. I have interpreted to her her repudiation of the analytical contract that we should both be concerned with her head, and related the friends who live in the top flat to internal objects, thoughts and feelings that she did not want to concern herself with. But somewhat later in the session I had noticed that, despite her complaints about the state of her head, there was something very superior in her attitude, particularly the fact that, though she complained in the session of how empty she felt and unable to communicate, she seemed to take quite a pride in her metaphors, which became more florid as the session progressed. When I interpreted that, she rather reluctantly said that, while she was speaking of the middle floor, she was in fact thinking of the first floor, an expression her family uses to denote 'upper class'. Thus it is her narcissism which prevents her relating to and taking care of internal objects and that in turn seems to prevent her symbolizing and communicating. The pain in her tummy – her middle floor – is where she keeps me as totally controlled by and identified with her gut. If she integrated me into her head, she would be aware of her own feeling of dependence, felt by her as great inferiority.

Verbalization can be looked at from the angle of the relation between the container and the contained. Unlike other forms of symbolism, speech has to be learned, though the baby begins by creating onomatopoeic sounds. Those sounds have to be taken up by the environment to be converted into speech, and later on words have to be learned from the environment. The infant has had an experience and mother provides the word or phrase which circumscribes this experience. It contains, encompasses and expresses the meaning. It provides a container for it. The infant can then internalize this word or phrase containing the meaning. My patient had the greatest difficulty in experiencing any interpretation, any phrase of mine as containing and giving expression to her meaning. Strange things happened to my interpretations. They could become a pain in her belly or a sexual excitement. They could be learned by heart and applied to others. They were frequently fed back to me as her own product, but usually a bit distorted, often deprived of emotional meaning, sometimes completely reversed. She had a dream, associations to which illustrated this difficulty. To understand them, I have to remind you of a beautiful passage in Helen Keller's autobiography. She describes there how she first rediscovered the concept of speech. For a long time her teacher tried to communicate with her by writing on her hand. Helen did not respond. After a long period of breaking and smashing and unconcern, one day she broke a doll and for the first time, cried. That afternoon when the teacher tried again to communicate with her and wrote a word on her palm, Helen Keller understood and responded. Thus a capacity to understand symbolic communication followed immediately and directly from her first experience of depressive feelings, an experience well familiar to those who analyse autistic children, first described by Emilio Rodrigue (1955).

Now my patient's dream. She dreamed of a little girl with long nails and ferocious teeth greedily attacking a table, scratching and biting. Her first associations were to my having given her my holiday date and, this probably stirring up her greed, she produced a kind of lament, without any genuine feeling, of how primitive she is, how the little girl in the dream represents her, and so on. But then she added she had another association. She recently read a book by, or about, a little girl who lost her sight and hearing and was like a little wild animal till the day she invented a sign language and taught it to her teacher. (The book was obviously Helen Keller's, as read by my patient.) I think Helen Keller's description and my patient's version of it exemplify different ways of symbol formation. Helen Keller with all her handicaps having achieved a complete communicating with her audience, and my poor patient still struggling with the problem of communicating in a way easily understandable to others. She still has not accepted that she learned to speak from her parents.

To summarize. I think that symbolism originates in projective identification, first of all in the relationship to the breast then to mother's whole body. When this projection results in mutual damage or an excessively omnipotent identification of a 'sticky' kind, symbols formed are excessively concrete, empty of meaning or bizarre. If the projection is not excessively envious or narcissistic and if the mother's response is not mutilating, the infant introjects a breast and mother capable of the symbolic function, in Bion's terms, capable of converting Alpha into Beta elements. When this happens symbol formation on the depressive level can proceed in the way I described in 1957.

Note

1 This chapter has previously been published (Segal, 1978). It was presented as part of a Colloquium on 'Symbols Formation' at the 30th International Psycho-Analytical Congress, Jerusalem, August 1977.

4

A delusional system as a defence against the re-emergence of a catastrophic situation[1]

The patient I wish to describe (Mr E) presents a rather unusual pathology, which leads to considerable technical difficulties. I have come to the conclusion that in infancy my patient underwent a psychic catastrophe and he has survived it psychically by building a delusional system. Any breach of this defence system threatens my patient with a repetition of the catastrophic situation. This situation of a delusional system as an attempt at recovery following a catastrophic situation up to a point bears out Freud's theory that a delusional system is an attempt at restitution of a destroyed world following a psychic catastrophe (Freud, 1911b, 1924a, 1924b). The nature of the catastrophic situation which I think is at the core of my patient's personality is, however, different from Freud's hypothesis of decathexis, and the dynamics of the delusional system have characteristics not covered by Freud's description.

In the first consultation the patient described himself as an obsessional neurotic.[2] He said he suffered from severe obsessional ceremonials and from an inability to make up his mind. (How serious the symptoms were I only found out in analysis. For instance, he could take nine or ten hours to get through his ceremonial before going to bed. In the early days of his analysis he once spent twelve hours making up his mind whether it was more efficient to take a bath before work or to do his work first and take his bath after.) He told me that he had spent the past eighteen months trying to decide on the choice of the type of analysis and of an analyst. This had been his full-time occupation during that time. He brought with him twelve or thirteen sheets of what he called a questionnaire, which he tried to put me through. And, *en passant*, practically leaving the room, he told me that he was a homosexual which did not worry him; in fact, he considers heterosexuality rather sissy; but it was very time-consuming and interfered with his efficiency.

The reason he sought treatment, he told me, was that he had a mission

49

in life to convert people to Christianity. He had undergone a conversion in which he became convinced that he was a very special chosen instrument of God. To perform his mission he must be perfectly efficient and his illness interferes with efficiency. He would need to be cured in under four years because otherwise he would be too old to enter a seminary and be ordained. His age was then 44.

Of the history I shall give only those elements which are directly relevant to my material. He told me he had a very happy childhood, a model childhood. In fact, he was breast-fed for about six weeks and he had an extremely traumatic weaning. It was 1917, and when his soldier father came on leave his mother weaned him in order not to spoil father's leave. There is a letter from his mother to his father saying, 'George cried for the breast but I didn't give it to him'. Not long after, his father was killed in the war. In the analysis we reconstructed that his mother must have been very depressed and also that some time after his father's death she left him and the family for several months – he thinks, in order to do nursing in France. Around the age of 1 year or 18 months he nearly died of pneumonia, but we do not quite know whether it was during his mother's absence or after her return. There is a photograph of him aged about 2, sitting in the pram with a completely vacuous expression. At that time an aunt was afraid that he was mentally deficient, because he would sit in his pram for hours without movement or expression.

His mother remarried and his brother was born when he was about 4. There is also a sister three years older. The whole family is very disturbed. Of his natural father we know little, as he is intensely idealized by the whole family as the romantic hero who perished in the war. There are, however, occasional hints of hypochondriacal and obsessional symptoms. The sister was either a severe obsessional or a simple schizophrenic. She was certainly quite incapable of independent existence and up to her death (while the patient was in analysis) lived at home. Like my patient, she had a religious obsession, but without his grandiosity. Her whole life was devoted to Moral Rearmament. His younger half-brother, certainly the sanest member of the family, was expelled from school for stealing boys' underwear; he is a homosexual who spent a number of years in the Foreign Legion in Vietnam following a legionnaire he was in love with. Unlike my patient, he is capable of work and had a spell in the Foreign Office; but for years now he has been acting as housekeeper/cook/nursemaid to his aged mother. The mother, intensely idealized by the whole family, was a beauty in her youth and at times appears as a monster of narcissism. She is completely oblivious of the illness of all her children and quite content to have them all at home adoring her. In recent years, following the death of her daughter, and faced with her own ageing, she has developed a senile psychosis which manifests itself, among other symptoms, in a quite overt inability to tolerate any situation in which she is not treated as the star. (This attitude I think was always characteristic of her, but her attractiveness, wealth and social position enabled her to maintain her narcissistic position without exposing her to any gross disappointment.) The whole family is excessively religious and exhibits a collusive megalomanic attitude to the rest of the world based on what they consider to be their superior social position. They live, behave, talk rather like a caricature of seventeenth- or eighteenth-century lords of the manor. This is unrealistic, even by their own standards, since in fact the family is one of relatively minor gentry, but the considerable wealth, mostly originating from the stepfather, enables them to maintain it. Nearly all relatives referred to by the patient – aunts, cousins, uncles – are homosexual or otherwise disturbed and eccentric. The stepfather, though obsessional and peculiar in many ways, appears as a very much healthier man than the patient's mother or father, and certainly gave my patient as a boy considerable care and devotion. This, however, did not do for the boy as much as it might have done because of the mother's idealization of her first husband and the general family collusion that the patient's father was in every way a superior being to his stepfather. The mother made no secret of the fact that she married the latter for his money.

As a small child, my patient never played, except for three so-called games: collecting apples and hoarding them; owning a bit of gravel-path on which he would not allow anyone to walk; and tearing paper. At the age of 8 he was sent to boarding school and there is an important memory of his first day there, the only experience ever of his having consciously felt depressed. In his preparatory school and public school he already exhibited secret grandiose delusions and marked obsessionality. It was in his preparatory school days that he developed the belief that he had a genius for strategy: one day he realized when doing Latin 'unseens' that if he did not know a word he could work it out from the context. He thought that he was the only one to have discovered it, and never shared his secret with anyone. From that thought developed the conscious conviction that he had a genius for strategy. The central theme of his life is his mission. As far back as he remembers, he had fantasies of being the President of the World, or the Pope. Finally he settled in a completely rigid way on the 'mission'. It very soon became apparent that the real Messiah in his mission was himself. His father's death, of course, contributed significantly to this system; he was the son of the Father in Heaven; an attitude in which his family to a large extent colluded, treating him as very special. All his life is a preparation for the fulfilment of his mission.

The content of the mission is generally vague, except on two points: (1) that it has to do with conversion; and (2) that because of his special strategic genius the mission is to be strategic, something like becoming the great strategist of the Church of England. The mission is linked with a quite indescribable arrogance and feeling of superiority which underlie all his activities and his very rare human relations. It is also a complete bulwark against guilt. When he started analysis it was clear that he had never in his life experienced a feeling of guilt. He lies, cheats and steals without compunction. He also finds it hard to visualize that other people may have different standards. He is always shocked and bewildered if someone refuses a bribe. At the beginning of his analysis he told me that it does not matter if he seduces a thousand boys if it does him good, since he might in the end be able to save a million souls.

The idea that he is a great strategist makes him lead his life as a series of what he calls 'operations'. In the first years of his analysis nearly all his life was consumed by the 'operations'. Some of them have a permanent status. To mention just a few: 'mentalism' is a way of thinking in very clear images; he once read a book about mentalism, which has become his great obsession and is felt as an extremely superior thing. In fact, it covers up defective thinking; very often he is quite unable to think, otherwise than in a most primitive, concrete language, but since his discovery of mentalism this is elevated into a great superiority. He can spend half a day on mentalism. Another operation, called 'recapitulation', often accompanies mentalism. He thinks he has got the power to recall in detail every conversation and event that he considers important. At the beginning of his analysis, every analytical hour was followed by what he called 'post-analysis', which usually took place in the lavatory and which consisted of a complete recapitulation of everything that was said in the session. This was much more important to him than the analytical session he had with me.

Another permanent type of operation is what he calls 'inspirationalism'. Inspirationalism consists of thinking about, and identifying with, very idealized figures. Usually they are very martial figures – Genghis Khan, Churchill, John Kennedy. Inspirationalism consists of a sort of long meditation about the hero and trying to 'introject' (his word!) him. For instance, on the radio there was a recording of Churchill's old speeches, and at that time he would miss as much as three days of analysis out of five because he would be either listening, recapitulating or mentalizing the speeches. Often he would miss listening to the speeches themselves, being too busy with his 'preparation'. (Preparations are, of course, also an operation.)

'Meditation' can have links either with mentalism or with recapitulation, but its closest links are with inspirationalism; meditation, at its purest, takes the form of curling himself up under a blanket in a completely foetal position and meditating.

Apart from these large operations, there is a host of minor ones, and it took years to elucidate them in analysis since they are so numerous and the patient treated them so much as a part of his everyday life. For instance, several times a day he retires into his permanently waiting taxi and has the heater switched on to produce an almost unbearable heat in order to 'bring blood' to his brain. He urinates every half-hour in order to relax his bladder, and so on.

Apart from the permanent ones, there is a host of occasional *ad hoc* operations. For instance, in the second year of his analysis, he decided that homosexuality disturbed him and he started an 'operation anti-homosexuality'. He found that usually when he had had a sexual contact with a young man he lost all interest in him. So the best way to cure homosexuality, he decided, would be to pick up all the potentially attractive young men in London to get them 'off his chest'. He had the grace often to make a slip of the tongue and call it 'operation homosexuality'.

Intermittent operations may be as autistic as the permanent ones, but they are more apt to involve people. 'Operation T' (for which he wanted to take a sabbatical year off the analysis) consists in manipulating and bribing people to get an introduction to a professor of history, T. In the meantime the patient has to read and memorize all his works to make a good impression on him; the aim is to have one conversation with the professor and get out of him ideas on how to reform the Church of England.

The smallest action or event can become the object of an operation, and it is always believed that analysis must take second place to the operation. It was a great breakthrough when he began to admit, after several years of analysis, that the common factor of all the operations was that they were 'operation anti-analysis' and that they were a gross interference not only in his analysis but also in his whole functioning and his life.

The operations were frequently interfered with by eruptions of sudden homosexual compulsions, leading to what he called 'nights on the tiles' or sometimes 'real marathons', during which he would spend up to thirty-six hours wandering in the street in search of homosexual adventure. On such occasions he would sometimes be in a completely dissociated state.

His relationship with his mother fitted in with the operations. Part of the time he would ignore and neglect her completely. But he idealized her, and for years denied all criticism and hostility. Several times a year he would turn to 'operation mama'. During the 'operation' they would live in a highly erotized state of mutual idealization; they would go on holidays which they called 'our honeymoon', drink and dance together till the morning (when she was over 80), and so on.

The 'operations' taken together formed a system in which the patient lived as almost completely omnipotent and controlling his environment, and almost totally shielded from contact with reality.

It is difficult to summarize the evolution of his analysis in the first five and a half years leading up to the more detailed material I wish to present. Broadly speaking, in the first part of his analysis one could see his attempt at recreating a complete inside-the-womb existence. The taxis, the meditation, the religion were all linked up with being entirely inside what seemed to be the womb; and, furthermore, inside this womb having an extremely exciting relation with a magic father's penis, all his objects – Christ, Churchill and so on – being mostly part-objects. His identifications shifted between himself being the omnipotent womb or the omnipotent penis, the emphasis being on omnipotent control. Any coming out of this situation was fraught with disaster. There was dream upon dream of coming out into the street to a terrible car accident or earthquake or other forms of death. He had a dream in which the other batsman's name, when he was batting, was Mortis, which I interpreted as 'timor mortis', a kind of linked partner that he was never without. I appeared in dreams frequently as a person waking him up; for example, I would be coming and opening the doors of the tent when he was sleeping or I would be coming in to wake him in the morning. This disturbance of his fantasy world by the analysis was felt as a terrible threat. If the fantasy of being omnipotent inside the womb was challenged, the womb would change into a behind. This was evidenced by such symptoms as sitting for hours in my lavatory, the terrific thrill of seducing a young man inside the back basement of the church, and a completely preoccupying faecal interest – all his sexuality was connected with faeces, giving enemas, getting enemas, listening to the sound of the enema in the other man's rectum, and so on. His name for it was 'shit-fun'.

The alternative to this situation of being in the womb or in the behind crystallized, during the last eighteen months before the period that I am going to discuss; it was building a 'faecal empire'. If he could not maintain the state of being inside the object, he turned to the idealization of his own behind and faeces. 'Post-analysis' was, of course, connected with it; he felt that the analytic session was just a kind of pabulum out of which he was making his own far superior analysis in the lavatory. There was always an insistence on my recognizing the superiority of all his products and there were endless dreams; for example, of eating faeces, making faecal babies or faecal penises. The collapse of that empire he felt unconsciously would face him with complete despair.

His relationship to me was characterized by the intensity of his dependence and its total denial. Every weekend and holiday would be marked by intense acting out; he spent hours in my lavatory and sometimes days in my street. The experience of dependence was, however, totally denied. He used a fleet of taximen to feed, fetch and carry him, and he was seldom without drugs, so he could always apparently easily replace me. And the objects replacing me were completely under his control. His own infantile experience was totally projected into me. He felt infinitely superior to me and he kept me waiting endlessly, being late, missing, withholding material and fees. The feelings totally missing in himself could be found in his fantasy of me. It was clear from his dreams and associations, even though consciously minimized, that as I was waiting I was supposed to be filled with desire, impatience, jealousy of his relationships, envy of his importance, anger and often despair. There were frequent dreams in which, represented by a thinly veiled substitute, I was supposed to commit suicide. It was clear that to be the one who is dependent and inferior is to be the one exposed to disaster. The projection into me of a desperate dependent infant resulted in a fantasy picture of me.

There were, however, other feelings which he projected into me quite successfully: he could fill me with anxious concern, hopelessness about the course of analysis, anxiety for him and his objects, and anger. He would say, for instance, coldly, 'Hitler knew how to deal with you people', in a way that would make me experience a momentary flood of hatred. Having dealt with all painful feelings by projective identification (Klein, 1946), he felt, of course, extremely persecuted; he felt threatened by my supposed possessiveness, greed, hostility and envy, which he felt were the motives of what he experienced as my attack on his system. He would announce, 'You are a saboteur – in wartime saboteurs are shot.' This persecution increased, of course, the need for control – every interpretation was at times felt as an attack to be warded off. If his control of the session was threatened, he would become very sadistic. He had endless ways of immobilizing me and torturing me mentally. The warded-off hostility would make its appearance. This hostility was not only sadistic, but murderous. I have already suggested that dependence or inferiority were felt by my patient as a threat of disaster. As his analysis progressed, it seemed to become increasingly clear that this disaster was associated with murderousness.

From the start, split-off murderousness played a large part in his material. Quite early on, he told me that he did not believe in free association: he explained that if one wants all the people to get on the bus one must form an orderly queue; if one leaves them to come as they wish a murderer running from justice would immediately jump the queue. When he was studying theology in town B, a prostitute was murdered and her breasts were cut off. My patient was so convinced that he would be accused of this murder that he purchased a false beard and departed from B. As he presented to me, he had plenty of rationalizations for his behaviour, but his identification with what he calls 'the town B murderer' was so convincing and his splitting so severe that I did occasionally wonder whether in fact he was the B murderer. His sadism and murderousness were often acted out in projection onto a homosexual partner. For instance, a paratrooper who boasted of machine-gunning civilians in Cyprus for fun became an object of intense admiration and desire. With this kind of partner he engaged in masochistic practices. (They differed from the 'shit-fun' objects who derived mainly from his nanny.)

The problem of his murderousness started coming into the analysis in a less split way in 'operation LSD', which lasted intermittently over two years. He wanted to leave analysis to have LSD treatment. The 'operation' was to find out the facts and make up his mind. LSD treatment fitted in well with his longing for an ideal magic penis, the penetration by which, and possession of which, would give him a magic cure and make him into a messiah. But it soon became clear that he was also longing for this ideal penis to be a murderous one. LSD unconsciously represented a licence to commit murder without guilt. A typical association: one day he said that he pleaded diminished responsibility for something he had done because he took drugs. When I asked him what he meant by 'diminished responsibility' he very promptly answered: 'If a doctor treats a patient by LSD and the patient then commits a murder – surely the patient is not responsible.' On reading in the paper about a murder committed under the influence of LSD, he said cheerfully, 'I don't mind the risk, if my chances of an LSD cure were 10 per cent and my chances of committing a murder were 90 per cent – I would still go ahead.' In a way, the LSD fantasy neatly summarized his life's alternatives: either he would succeed in becoming the Messiah, or he would murder and die.

The main problem of his analysis from the start, and to a lesser degree still now, was to establish analysis in the face of the 'operations' and to find links with his infantile self and the infantile transference, particularly the positive transference. There were some slender threads one could follow in that direction, from the start, but in the first years of his analysis his defences against recognition of his infantile needs were formidable.

In the fifth year of his analysis, however, we saw a beginning of the collapse of his belief in the omnipotence of the faecal empire, and some strengthening of the positive transference. He had a dream of standing on top of a mountain of sand which started crumbling under him, but somebody stretched out a hand to help him. Together with the beginning of the collapse of the faecal empire, there emerged in the analysis a part of him which he called 'baby Georgie'. He had several dreams of killing small animals. He told me that he was very kind-hearted and could never see an animal suffer without killing it. One day he chased a limping pigeon (which he believed to be a seagull) all down the road I live in to kill it with his stick. These little animals first appeared to be the injured breast (the seagull), which he could not bear facing. Soon, however, it became clear that it also represented his baby self. He had a dream in which a big black dog was chasing – with intent to kill – a tiny little dog. He himself kills the little dog to spare him the suffering. His own associations led us to interpret the dream in this way: the little dog was the normal baby George related to mother and her breast and identified with it (the seagull); the big black dog he called 'delusional Georgie' – omnipotent and faecal. I pointed out to him that what he considers his conscious, adult self also turns against the little dog and, though he does it out of pity, in effect he sides with the big dog. The role of what he feels to be himself in the dream is important here; at that time in his analysis he still mostly sided with the operations, and consciously deplored any insight which might interfere with them and what he called his 'efficiency'. The change in his attitude towards his illness came only very gradually. The struggle we always had to establish the analysis in the face of 'operations' became more clearly a struggle to rescue 'baby Georgie' from 'delusional Georgie' a struggle for the survival of what remained of a healthy infantile ego.

With the emergence of 'baby Georgie', he began to be more able to admit the importance of separation from me, although this would be quickly denied and reversed. For the first time, heterosexual interests made their appearance. First of all, as an 'operation' to help the analysis, he began frequenting prostitutes. In the transference for the first time a heterosexual father appeared as a helpful figure united with mother. He dreamed, for instance, that my husband came and told him to get out of the lavatory and go to the first floor, where his analyst had prepared a meal for him. He also began to appreciate me as a father in the transference, commenting on my firmness and perseverance. The emergence of a more positive and dependent relationship towards me as a parental couple mobilized a primitive Oedipal relationship combined with a dread of catastrophic weaning.

An important turning-point in the analysis was marked by a piece of dramatic and dangerous acting out. In the middle of October, I told him that I would be away for two days in November. Consciously he was very pleased, but his dreams showed a murderous reaction. The day after I told him, he dreamed that he was back at school, standing in the queue with other boys to kiss Mrs T good night. He jumped the queue. (As related above, it is the murderer who jumps the queue.) Mrs T was a very good figure in his preparatory school-days. The next night he had a dream in which the parents were seen in a murderously sadistic intercourse. Following that, the material seemed to be overtly cannibalistic. The next weekend he dreamed that a man was comforting a very ill little boy at school; the boy had lost both his parents. Nobody seemed sympathetic except the patient, who was explaining to a man that as the little boy's doctor was Jewish he must not be disturbed on a Sunday. He meant to offer his help to the boy but found himself eating two lunches and they were both of fresh meat; he felt there was something horrible about it. Then he went to the lavatory and tried to entice the little boy after him.

The little boy who has lost both parents and whose Jewish doctor is absent on Sunday obviously represents himself as a little boy, and he seems to have lost his parents through eating them (the two lunches of fresh meat). The latter part of the dream represents his usual narcissistic homosexual defence of turning for a solution to his own behind (enticing the little boy – himself – into the lavatory).

At the next session after that, I had occasion to point out to him that certain of his activities (like wearing two swimsuits when visiting a prostitute to avoid infection) seemed aimed at non-consummation. This excited him very much because he made a link between consummation and consumption, and described to me in great detail the fantastic rituals that have to be gone through before he can eat – he wondered if he equates all consummation with consumption. That night he had another cannibalistic dream: there was a period of famine at S (his country home). He was secretly and guiltily devouring meat. There was no one else about. At the same time he was on top of a mountain, having a very spiritual conversation with a bishop.

Getting in touch with his desire for the analytical meal seemed to confront him with fear, fear of starvation and secret, guilty cannibalism. The spiritual conversation with the bishop no longer satisfied.

Two days before my departure, he arrived pale and dishevelled, and announced, 'I might have been killed last night.' He described confusedly that he first went to Jackie (a favourite lesbian prostitute) and he played Dutch uncle to her and Betty her girl-friend. He drank a bottle of whisky but he was quite impotent. He talked a lot to them both about psychology and love-and-hate relationships. He went home to quieten down and thought he would get relief if he smashed a bottle in my window, but instead of that he rushed to Piccadilly and picked up a man. He talked to him about love–hate relationships but the man objected. The man said, 'When I get to a girl I only love her.' My patient talked to him about the B murderer enough to convince him. Then, at some point connected with a quarrel about money, the man went quite mad: he started dancing round and shouting, 'I am Jesus Christ! I am the King! You are the murderer of all these women! I know you, I am going to kill you!' To pacify him, my patient admitted to the B town murder and several others. Then the hotel-keeper, hearing the noise, intervened and my patient left the two of them fighting, while he fled to his waiting taxi – having a fit of maniacal laughter at the thought that the hotel-keeper would be landed with the murderer. He also thought that this would at last drag me into the law courts, and that too exhilarated him.

I had little opportunity to interpret in the session, but I did point out to the patient that the man seemed to be completely like a part of himself, thinking that he was a messiah, preoccupied with the murder of prostitutes and trying to project the guilt onto the patient. It was striking that, until I pointed it out to him, the patient was quite unaware of this resemblance. But he did remember in the next session that only a few days previously we analysed a dream in which he, the patient, was dressed in kings' attire. I also pointed out to him that the hotel-keeper was an aspect of myself and his wish for me to contain his agitated feelings in the session. In fact, he was unusually agitated for him.

It was only in the next session that we could sort out what had happened. Faced with the imminent loss of two days' analysis, he turned to substitute women, Jackie and Betty. He felt enormously attracted by Jackie's breasts and terribly humiliated by his impotence. He tried to reverse the situation of dependence and weakness by playing Dutch uncle to them and also by trying to project his love–hate feelings into them. They obviously did not take in this projection; it was at the moment when he experienced Jackie as very kind in a maternal way that his fury was aroused. She had stroked him, and said, 'Why don't you lie on your side, dear, you seemed to be doing better that way.' It was at that moment that he rushed out and had the thought about smashing a bottle in my windows for relief. Jackie obviously represented me. When the reversal of dependence did not succeed and she made him aware of his intense dependence and impotence – as in the analysis – he experienced a terrible humiliation and dread; it aroused murderous feelings that he could not contain. He needed relief. He had either to get rid of the feeling by acting on it ('getting it off his chest', his words) or to find a partner who would act it out for him. He rushed out in search of such a partner.

It became clear how precisely he can find a suitable object for projective identification, and really possess him with his projection. He later admitted that he must unconsciously have realized that the man was unstable mentally: his eyes were peculiar, and also when the patient started talking about psychiatric treatment he was surprised how much this uneducated bum-boy knew about electric shock, insulin treatment, and so on. He then had a passing thought that the man must have been in hospital. Having got hold in that way of a suitable object for projections, he obviously started to work on him with constant talk about ambivalence and the murder of women, until he got this unstable man completely maddened.

The role of the hotel-keeper is very important. The patient wondered later what he would have done if the hotel-keeper had been a woman, and he came to the conclusion that he would have acted in the same way because he has to save himself for the mission. The hotel-keeper obviously represents an aspect of the analyst who is always left holding his murderous self. In relation to this aspect of me he feels he always wins. If, as the hotel-keeper did in reality, I manage to contain and control his projections, he experiences great relief. If, however, I were to succumb and either become identified with his projections as his keeper might have been if killed by the maniac, his omnipotence would triumph unbridled.

My view of the events following my announcement of a two-day absence is as follows: The analysis thus far brought about a certain mobilization of 'baby Georgie' feelings in relation to the breast-mother in the transference. The expected two-day deprivation re-awakened oral deprivation, jealousy and envy-feelings which led to murderous and cannibalistic impulses which he could not contain or control. He dealt with them by massive projective identification onto his sexual partner, converting the situation of murder into one of self-destruction. This, too, he managed to avoid by subsequently projecting the role of the victim onto the hotel-keeper.

I think that this sequence of events throws some light on his psychopathology. His megalomanic delusion and the complex obsessional system needed to maintain it defend him against a recurrence of an early catastrophic situation, the abrupt weaning and the subsequent loss of both his parents. Usually these two events, as appearing in the transference, are telescoped into one. These events must have given rise to murderous and cannibalistic fantasies and a conviction that he had murdered both his parents. Sometime after the session I have reported he dreamed that he was clinging to a white cupboard; it disintegrated and he was falling. The white cupboard was a remembered cupboard from his nursery. He obviously feels that if he clings to the breast it will disintegrate and he will disintegrate with it. For him, getting in touch with any human feelings of love or dependence is linked with the expectation of a catastrophic ending. I do not wish to imply that the abrupt weaning and separation from his parents were the unique cause of his pathology – there were features in his early breast relation which made him particularly unable to cope with the trauma – but the catastrophe and the fear of its repetition became the nodal point of his psychopathology.

To defend against this catastrophe, he had to wipe out 'baby Georgie' and his real object relationships – the parents – and to develop the megalomanic delusion in which he was self-sufficient and omnipotent and all objects were objects created in his fantasy, predominantly from his own faeces.

In his delusional system he had to restitute not only lost objects but also lost functions of his ego. For instance, 'inspirationalism', in which he 'introjects' his objects, acts as a substitute for the normal functioning of introjection, which is severely impaired in him and which he tries to recreate by his own effort. He fantasizes a figure which he thinks would satisfy his needs and then by conscious manipulation tries to introject that figure and make it a part of himself. Mentalism is a substitute for the capacity to think and particularly to reflect. He tries to teach himself rules of thinking and to overcome the handicap of the concreteness of his thoughts by making out of this concreteness a virtue and trying to learn how to manipulate his visual thoughts. Recapitulation is an attempt to substitute for spontaneous memory, a memory which is interfered with both by the blocking of his introjective processes and by severe splitting. All these functions, like his objects, have to be restituted and omnipotently controlled.

However, this megalomanic obsessional system itself becomes in fact a chronic catastrophe. It is the existence of the system that prevented him from making contact with such aspects of his mother as were available to him and from renewing any real contact with her after her return. It prevented him from benefiting sufficiently from the paternal kindness of his stepfather or the devotion that both his siblings had for him. Baby Georgie and his potential for growth were stunted not by the 'catastrophe' but by the delusional system developed to prevent the recurrence of the catastrophe.

Furthermore, since his dependence is increased because of this lack of growth, and yet he is unable to acknowledge any dependence, maintenance of the system depends on a ceaseless exploitation of his real external objects and the ceaseless projection of painful feelings, denied in himself, onto them. Hence, of course, the megalomanic system is accompanied by constant persecution. The whole system is based on hatred, envy and fear – love and dependence being denied.

Seeing through this is terrifying to him. A few years ago he had a dream: he was facing an enormous and completely empty room. In his associations it emerged that, if he gave up his mission and the operations, he would find that his life was entirely empty. 'Fifty years', he said, 'of nothingness', and equally empty is his internal world. The delusion plays two roles here: it is to fill the emptiness that he creates in wiping out 'baby Georgie', but of course it also creates the emptiness in that it prevents baby Georgie from living, as in the 'little dog and big dog' dream.

Soon after the acting out reported in this paper, he had a dream in which he spilt some corrosive fluid on to a couch and then used a fire extinguisher – he does not know whether to mend the damage or to cover it up. The whole room got full and messed with extinguisher fluid and his host came into the room and was very angry. He felt terribly anxious and ashamed in the dream. He commented that the dream was his first nightmare, which in a way surprised me since the Marquis de Sade is mild compared with the patient's dreams, but he explained that this was the first dream in which he actually felt the anxiety. He associated the burning stuff to his hostility to me, related to an event in the transference, and the extinguisher to the defences he uses against experiencing it – the extinguishing of all feelings. He felt that the dream made it clear how much more damaging were those defences than the original feeling. This dream

61

shows a considerable re-orientation in his attitude to his delusional system; and indicates some movement in his analysis. Having held me over the years as a container for his projected feelings, he is now a little more able to introject me and identify me with a part of himself that is beginning to contain his own impulses and fantasies. Also, his repeated and relentless attacks both on his analysis and on myself personally are beginning to give him some confidence in the survival of his good object, which enables him to integrate some of his aggression. The changes in him so far have been quantitative, not yet amounting to any appreciable qualitative change. Thus his absences and latenesses are now very unusual. His heterosexuality is beginning to be better established (though still very primitive), his homosexuality less destructive and compulsive. He has also cut down on drugs and drink, which at times made the analysis well-nigh impossible; and there is less dangerous acting out. The 'operations' – though by no means abandoned – are clearly felt by him now as a symptom and have been very much curtailed in time and in intensity. In his relationships he seems much more human. He sometimes expresses affection for me now, and gratitude that I did not let him destroy the analysis.

Discussion

This case raises a number of technical and theoretical problems. From the technical point of view, there is the question of indication for psychoanalytic treatment. Should this man have had psychoanalysis at all? And does the analytical treatment present a danger of infringing his defences and therefore bringing about a catastrophic situation, as had nearly happened in the acting out I have described? This is a difficult question to answer: the danger was certainly there. On the other hand, I am convinced that psychoanalysis is the only method that has any chance of making inroads into his psychopathology. He has in the past had any number of physical and psychotherapeutic treatments which left no appreciable mark on him. The psychoanalytic treatment, on the other hand, is slowly affecting his structure. I think the dread of the catastrophic situation has very much lessened, and the danger of murder or suicide has in fact appreciably diminished. His delusional defence system has lost some of its rigidity and, in the patient's words, he feels that he is 'getting humanized'.

From the point of view of research, I think the psychoanalytic treatment of this case very worthwhile. For me it threw a great deal of light on one possible type of delusion-formation. I think the psychopathological constellation that I have described here has not been described in the past, and I think that it may apply to a number of cases, particularly those with a mono-delusion.

Similar cases have been described by Bychowski in his paper on the obsessive-compulsive 'façade' of schizophrenia, but he does not elucidate their dynamic structure (Bychowski, 1966). In Freud's writings (1911b, 1924a, 1924b) he does describe delusion as a restitution and a defence system in a situation in which a 'catastrophe' has happened. His description of the nature of the catastrophe, however, is in the nature of a psychological speculation, based on the hypothesis of a decathexis of the external world.

In the case I describe the catastrophe is the infantile situation in which the ego is flooded by destructive and self-destructive impulses threatening annihilation. The defensive role of the 'operation' is to restitute omnipotently a fantasy world in which dependence on objects is excluded. Destructive and libidinal impulses and fantasies are contained in the defence system: on the one hand, the sadistic control; on the other, the 'saviour' elements. The destructive elements, however, predominate, and the whole system is an aggressive attack on reality. I have come back to using Freud's term 'restitution' and have avoided speaking of 'reparation', in that this restitution is not a reparation in terms of the depressive position. The aim of the restitution is narcissistic and elements of love and concern for the object, which are predominant in depressive reparation, here play a very minor role, though they are not entirely absent. From the diagnostic point of view, I would class this patient as a borderline case. Though his delusion is frankly psychotic, the obsessional system which he has developed is preventing an overt psychosis. The basic psychotic structure derives from an infantile psychosis on the borderline between childhood autism and childhood schizophrenia.

Notes

1 This chapter has been published previously (Segal, 1972). For professional reasons it has not appeared in previous collections of Hanna Segal's papers.
2 In this he resembles the patient described by Bychowski (1966).

5

Early infantile development as reflected in the psychoanalytical process: steps in integration[1]

I have given a sub-title to my paper because I found I couldn't tackle the subject indicated in the main title in its entirety. To present one's ideas about infant and child development and the manifold ways it is reflected in the psychoanalytical process is truly a theme for a book rather than for a paper. I say 'manifold ways' because the psychoanalytical process does not repeat in any simple linear way infant and child development. Patients come to us with their internal world structured in a particular way. As the transference develops they project their internal objects and parts of themselves onto us in a way which reveals the object relationships, anxieties and defences underlying the structure of their personality; the situation becomes dynamic again, and we discover the early infantile conflicts and object relationships which led to the creation of those particular structures. Transference is not a simple repetition of childhood. When certain internal figures and parts of the selves are projected onto the analyst, the psychoanalytical process modifies the nature of internal figures and relationships. Thus, in analysis we are dealing not only with the historical past but also, dynamically, mostly with an ahistorical past which keeps changing and altering in the psychoanalytical process. Such historical past as is relived, at times in a very feeling way, is relived of course not in a chronological order, but in terms of evolving internal dynamics of the transference relationship. It is mostly after the session, or after long stretches of analysis, or maybe towards the end, or even after the end, of the treatment that we can reconstruct in our mind more exactly the genetic development of the patient. This can best be presented in a fairly full case history. I have done, for instance, something approaching such a reconstruction in an earlier paper (Segal, 1972).[2]

The patient in that case had been abruptly weaned at three months and soon after that his father was killed in the war and his mother left for about one year. This factual external history was unearthed slowly and painfully, the patient having told me originally that he had a very happy and uneventful childhood, and strongly clinging to that belief. From the point of view of his internal development, it slowly emerged that this early situation gave rise to overwhelming aggressive and cannibalistic impulses which were then felt by him to be the cause of all the disasters, leading to a total internal disintegration. In this context he developed a narcissistic delusional system. In his analysis it became clear that he went through a short clinically autistic phase between the ages of 1 and 2. The narcissistic delusional system he developed almost precluded his making an object relationship with his mother when she returned, and later with his step-father and step-brother. In latency he organized defences which defended him against an overt psychotic breakdown and bolstered up the delusional system. In analysis he quickly developed a delusional narcissistic transference, and only very gradually, and at that, partially, could we bring to light the traumatized infant confronted with catastrophic anxieties.

But presenting a case history is not the theme of the Congress. The theme is early infantile development. By early infant development, I understand the first two years of life or so. These early months and years are of course of fundamental importance in the development of the personality. At that time the basis of the personality is laid down and certain vital functions of the ego, crucial to its development, must be established – such as: thinking, symbol formation, playing, talking, walking, and so on. It is my contention, not original of course, though still controversial, that these functions evolve in the context of object relationships. The failure in these object relationships affects them in a very fundamental way. Some integration of the ego and its relationship to objects has to be achieved for these functions to develop satisfactorily.

Freud has shown us that we have on the couch not only an adult, but a child within the adult, and that it is the child that develops the transference relationship. With the development of psychoanalysis we have become increasingly aware not only of the child, but of the infant within the patient, and with the basic infantile transference. The infantile part of the patient can manifest itself in verbal or non-verbal ways, but even when it is non-verbal it can eventually be at least partly verbalized, the analyst providing the words for still unverbalized feelings – the way in which in infancy the environment largely provides the vocabulary for the infant's experience when the child is learning to speak. This infantile, pre-verbal part of the patient may be integrated well enough in the rest of the personality and not need to be interpreted at a given moment. We can, for instance, deal with later material and take for granted the basic capacity for communication, but when the early infantile situation mobilized in the analysis gives rise to disturbance it makes itself felt immediately.

To give a very simple example: I can think of two patients with very characteristic head movements. One of them turns his head slowly from side to side. The other one has a way of sticking out his jaw, clamping his teeth. Both these movements look extraordinarily like the head movements of babies turning away from the nipple or the bottle. (The patient who stuck out his jaw was a bottle-fed baby. The one who turned his head from side to side was a breast-fed baby.) Whatever the apparent response to the interpretation, when I notice these head movements, I know that resistance at a deeper level is operating. But what goes on in this infantile part at those moments has to be found out from the context and from more explicit material. For instance, in one situation when I drew my patient's attention to his movement he reported that he dreamed about a poisoned stream. His turning away from the analytical feed was due to a phantasy of a poisonous breast and was linked with a deeply suspicious attitude towards me of which, at that point, he wasn't conscious. In another case, the patient dreamed that he was on a fast roller-coaster, feeding his baby with orange juice, turning his back on a woman selling cartons of milk, and trying to hide her from his son lest he ask for the milk. His turning away from the analytical situation followed a session which he particularly valued. In that case, the turning away was linked with envious competitive feelings. The baby son represented the baby himself, the orange juice urine, and the roller-coaster masturbatory excitement. He wanted to hide from himself his infantile need for the breast, represented by the satisfactory session, and to feed himself on his own urine – the unconscious content of his masturbatory phantasy.

These infantile manifestations are discreet in the not very disturbed patient, and the analyst has to be well attuned to this level of communication to pick them up. The disturbed infant appears more grossly and concretely in the psychotic patient like an adolescent hebephrenic I treated who actually chewed my books when she felt greedy and envious about the knowledge she thought I possessed; or tore threads out of the cover of the couch, chewed them and spat them out as an expression of oral and anal attacks on a feeding object.

But infantile development, even of the first two years only, is also too large a subject for a paper, so I will confine myself to discussing only some aspects of steps towards integration.

In my experience, early infantile development is reflected in the psychoanalytical process in the fluctuating moves towards integration. We can gradually observe splitting, fragmentation, projective identification, giving way to withdrawal of projections, bringing together of splits and bringing about a more integrated self and relationship to the object. This brings with it an increased capacity for symbolization and verbalization.

I should like to bring here a dream in which the patient shows a movement from non-verbal to verbal communication. This patient had been greatly disturbed in her infancy by her mother's pregnancy. The next sibling was born only thirteen months after her. A fortnight before the dream an accidental meeting with me outside the consulting room was experienced by her very violently as a repetition of her mother's pregnancy. For about two weeks she felt very paranoid about myself or anyone who could represent either me or a sibling. The material she brought was fragmented, incoherent, sometimes nonsensical and thrown at me in a hostile, provocative, disruptive way, making it extremely difficult for me to think, reflect or bring anything together. One could say that she was communicating verbally, since she was talking, but it was the underlying non-verbal experience of her bombarding me thus that was the more striking. Words were used as missiles.

At the same time I was aware that she was withholding other thoughts, 'sitting' on other material. She seemed inaccessible to interpretation (though I suspected she wasn't totally inaccessible – I had been through such phases with her before). Two interpretations seemed to make better contact. One was when I pointed out to her that the way she nursed her grievances was very similar to her relation to faeces in childhood as she had described it to me before. The other interpretation was one I gave her in the last session preceding the dream. In her anger and disorganization she made certain arrangements which made it possible that she would have to miss a session, and I pointed out to her that despite her hostility she gave some indication that she was worried about this possibility.

The next day she came in quite a different mood and told me a dream. She said that she dreamed about being in a session, and that she brought me a complaint. 'I mean I didn't talk about it, I actually brought it to the session. The complaint was I was shedding from inside my body all sorts of bits and pieces, little animals, maybe rabbits, bizarre fragments that could be more faecal. I thought (in the dream session) that the rabbits could be babies, but no, they were too bizarre. I was terribly anxious and I felt I was falling to pieces. You started explaining what was going on, but you conveyed that it could not be put into words. You painted for me a background and some figures. I wondered which was more important, the background or the figures. The figures became my parents. When that became clear I threw the bits at them and they – the bits – became dots. I wondered if it is an attack and I thought, yes, it probably is. Then you say: but the dots are also tears. I feel tremendously moved and not anxious any more and this is the first clear communication in words in the dream.' Her associations were to rabbits as her wish to have hundreds of babies in competition with me, but also to an infestation by ring-worm which she had a month previously, and which made her very anxious about infecting me and was associated with many dreams about creepy crawlies. She also associated to the previous weeks when she was biting her fingers, an intermittent symptom, and felt she could really chew me to bits; also to her nursing grievances which she then threw at me like faeces, referring to my previous interpretation.

My view of the dream (which does not mean that this is what I interpreted at length to the patient) is the following. I think that in the dream she is showing a pre-verbal paranoid-schizoid experience. She has fragmented herself and dreads disintegration. She has also in phantasy bitten me to pieces, which then became the faecal bits (grievances), or were idealized into competitive faecal pseudo-babies (rabbits out of a hat). These fragments and bits were thrown at me with hatred (aggressive projective identification), resulting in a state of persecution and confusion which characterized the two weeks preceding the dream. My painting of the background and of the two figures represents the experience of my understanding her, even though she appeared to reject all the interpretations. Through the process of being understood she becomes less broken up and more aware of her own aggression against me as the parental figures, and then the tears come; the fact that I interpreted that she was concerned about missing the session was very moving to her. I had indicated to her that despite her barrage, I didn't lose touch with her other feelings about me as she had herself.

In the past this patient had spoken movingly of the older child of a friend. When the friend became pregnant, that child wasn't quite as young as she herself had been when her mother became pregnant but she still couldn't talk much and my patient was very concerned about that. This was linked with an awareness, of the particular distress of being herself overwhelmed with painful feelings at the time of her mother's pregnancy when she had no means of expressing them. She couldn't talk, she couldn't walk, all she could do was the kind of bombardment, screaming, urinating, defaecating, linked with omnipotent projective phantasies.

The patient's dream shows a simultaneous integration of the parental figures which appear clearly, the integration of love and hatred, and the integration and verbalization of earlier primitive non-verbal experiences. This is facilitated by her experience that her non-verbal communication has been contained and understood by the analyst – at least to a sufficient extent – the frame and background of the picture in the dream. It is out of that background that parental figures slowly emerge. To put it in the theoretical framework which I use, I would say that the dream shows a confluence of a simultaneous move from the paranoid-schizoid to the depressive position, and from Beta to Alpha elements, as described by Bion. When a depressive integration is achieved, then, as is shown in the dream, the earlier experiences can be integrated and symbolized in a dream and eventually verbalized. If the integration fails, speech may not be achieved, as happens in autistic cases. In this patient some integration was achieved:

the relation to her parents, one could say, was patched up, and she identified with a typical English upper-class father, academically successful and highly verbal. But the earlier experiences remain split off.

This is shown in another dream sequence where I failed to get in touch with her archaic material. The patient reported that she had two dreams. The first one was a nightmare which she couldn't remember, or maybe she couldn't put into words. There was no story in it, probably no people, just a feeling of disintegration and attacks. But the second dream she could remember clearly. She was passing an exam and felt anxious, not knowing what to write about, but someone said, 'Doesn't really matter what you write about, or whether you know what you say, or whether it's true, so long as it makes a good coherent story'. So she decided to write about corn. She knew very little about corn, but she can always write a good plausible story, and so she started writing quite happily. The dream referred, I thought, to the previous sessions in which both the patient and I felt we were dealing with some very coherent material in a way that seemed to both of us reasonably satisfying. But I had ignored some fleeting hypochondriacal symptoms and some slight incongruence in the material. I think the corn is the sessions she felt to be corny because they did not touch on the nightmare feelings that manifested themselves subsequently in the unremembered nightmare. She was reliving an experience with an object lacking in understanding of her primitive anxieties and colluding with her defences – the verbal facility being part of those defences. She had successfully projected this object into me and I must have at least partly acted it out for her – falling into interpreting at the wrong level which was too easy, too corny. This sequence I think reproduces what largely happened in her childhood. In fact she became a glib talker, a chatterbox in childhood, later a clever girl at school. But she remained cut off from her deeper experiences, which remained in her psyche like a focus of infection, and from the earliest childhood she had periods of paranoid and depressed silent withdrawals. (I am aware of another possible interpretation of that dream. Corn is good basic food and she is rubbishing it as an envious attack. However, the whole context and my counter-transference experience made me take it up the way I did, though envy is an important factor in the patient's personality.)

The material I have presented so far deals, I think, with problems of integrating very primitive levels of experience. In my next example I want to present a different problem – a move towards the completion of weaning, which had not been psychologically achieved in infancy.

This young man comes from a family of impoverished Scottish gentry who lost their land. They have some foreign aristocratic connections. There is a family feeling of undefined superiority, including moral superiority, coupled with a sense of deprivation and persecution since the family had indeed known hard times. This family culture has influenced and played into his own pathology. He is newly married to an English girl of a more bourgeois background. An important aspect of his pathology was a narcissistic attachment to the breast. The position he always sought was that of an infant inside the breast, controlling it and identifying with it. Any breach in this situation brought about violence, which was contained in, and controlled by, obsessional and psychosexual symptoms. He showed little aggression in his life, but had a streak of silent but very effective cruelty. The narcissistic and sadistic aspect of him was in conflict with another part of his personality, always struggling to achieve a different kind of relationship with his object. Achieving a warm and loving relationship, however, was hampered by the intensity of persecutory guilt due to complex factors which preoccupied much of his analysis. This interplay led to vicious circles, since the narcissistic posture and the associated cruelty increased his persecutory guilt, and the difficulty of bearing intense guilt would in turn throw him back onto narcissistic positions.

Preceding the session I am going to report, having made considerable progress, he was beginning to contemplate the termination of his analysis. This brought about a violent protest from the narcissistic part of himself and he became demanding and quarrelsome in relation to everybody around him, and full of endless resentments. He reverted to what he called his 'high horse' attitudes, which were characteristic of him when he started his analysis but which he had largely superseded. All this, however, was accompanied by painful insight about his character and behaviour, and great longing to be different. He associated one day that his resentments themselves were like a protective coat. It was like still being inside the object. It wasn't ideal, but both he and his objects were entirely taken up with his complaints, so he still didn't have to let go of the object. As we were working through this problem one day he brought a dream.

At the beginning of the session, I pointed out to him that he felt a certain situation to be an insurmountable obstacle. (I thought: he makes mountains out of mole-hills, but didn't say it in order not to impose my own imagery.) He laughed and said 'You almost interpreted a bit of the dream I have not told you yet. I dreamed that I was on a mountain, looking at another mountain which seemed huge. I said that's Mount Everest. But Joe Mann, who was with me, said no, it is Mont Blanc. Of course Mont Blanc is pretty high, but it is not Everest. I looked again and I saw indeed it must be Mont Blanc. It was less rugged and I saw people skiing down the slopes. It could be done. There was some question whether Mann and I had skis but I suppose in the end we must have had some because there is another part of the dream. I skied down and was about to board a bus to return me to the village from which I started.'

Here he interrupted the dream for the following association. 'You know

70

what I have in mind, not just going up and coming down the same way. In some lovely Austrian resorts you can go up one way, then there are many different pistes, not just always the same one, and you come down in a different place and take a bus back to your base. The place must have been in Austria because the name of the village was something like Johann and the only association I have to Johann is that it is an Austrian name.'

Then he went back to the dream. 'At some point I took the wrong bus and had to go back and change. There was a choice of buses at some point. There was a lovely English solid red bus, but I think I took another one which was a rather shabby Paris bus by mistake and I had to change.' He associated his wife's solid English virtues with the solid bus; he was currently quarrelling with her. He thought he too often dismisses her good aspects. He thought skiing down Mont Blanc must have something to do with his coming down off his high horse, which might not be as difficult as he thought. Mont Blanc he associated to the breast, and thought maybe it is not so difficult to come off his high horse in relation to me. He was puzzled about Mann, whom he likes but has no particular associations to. I suggest that the significance of Mann was in his name (a man) and related it to his uncertainty whether he had skis – was he a potent man? He then started talking about wanting and dreading to end his analysis and about weaning: how do babies ever accept weaning, why should they?

I shall not describe the interplay of association and interpretation because many elements of the dream were related to work done before. But briefly, I think that the skiing down from Mont Blanc represents weaning; going back always the same way is not accepting the weaning; in fact, all the perverse side of his sexual phantasy was linked with wanting to get back to the possession of the breast in an infantile, narcissistic way. Getting on the French bus, which he also described as shabby, is full of meaning. 'French' for my patient always associates with me, so taking the wrong French bus is like taking the same piste again (not giving up his phantasy of some sexual possession of the analyst mother). He also associated 'shabby' and 'French' to a semi-pornographic French film with lots of hints about various aspects of oral sex. He thought soixante-neuf and French kissing particularly French. He found it stimulating because of the tongue penetrating and the complete equality in the couple. All these French activities represent to him the regaining of the narcissistic possession of the breast. The baby's tongue penetrating and controlling the breast and the mouth-tongue being a mirror image of the breast and the nipple. Contrasted with that is the opposite; going down Mont Blanc and not insisting on always taking the same piste is accepting weaning and finding a different meaning to sex, represented by the English red bus.

One could summarize it thus: to become a man he has to accept weaning and not insist on always going back the same way; for instance, not to use sex to regain a particular narcissistic position in relation to the breast. There are also many – different – pistes in the attractive Austrian resort.

He had been complaining recently of the narrowness of analysis and analytic interpretations. I interpreted the narrowness as the one piste he is always taking and the many different pistes as a broadening of interests, particularly to include the whole family: his family at work, where he tends to ignore co-workers in his lab; his present family and his family in the past; in particular, to include in his picture of the family, his father and siblings – the same, of course, applying also to the transference. The coming down from Mont Blanc is felt by him to be dangerous because of the overwhelming rage, the frustration it gives rise to in him. Every frustration also a dethronement, coming down from a great height. And, indeed, in the next session he was directly furious with me, as a chronic, grumbling resentment gave way to a more open rage. A theme that preoccupied him also at that time was his fear of a phoney reconciliation leading to phoney relationships and making his new marriage false. We have often seen in the past that he feels so dependent, whether it is on me, his wife or his parents, that if he quarrels he has to make it up quickly to regain, in reality or in his phantasy, his position of the favourite. His general lack of aggression with me or his wish quickly to make up was due to his wish to regain a phoney marriage with me, a phantasy that he wasn't a patient and in a part of him a dependent child, but he was with me in a phoney marriage, the baby as the lover and dictator of the breast. He was now aware of his anger with me on many counts, and was seeking some way of reconciling which would be different from the phoney marriage. In the dream he returns to base, the Austrian village, obviously linked to analysis, but by a different route, a different kind of reconciliation, based on the acceptance of the weaning, his own rage and more genuinely reparative feelings that go with it, and that in this situation he experienced increasingly both to his wife and to me.

There were more ramifications of the dream: for instance, his facing the Oedipal situation – the other man in the dream – in a way less narcissistic and more direct than in the past. The man in later sessions appears both as a rival and a guide (the analyst as father). What I hope to show is an important point of integration in which he faces and struggles to overcome his narcissistic object relationship and to accept weaning. That experience of weaning has to be resolved and integrated to allow growth and true genitality.

It is interesting that in both examples the patients are concerned with issues of falseness and truth – in the first case with corn; in the second with phoniness. Moments of integration are also moments of truth, however primitive the experience. I have brought two clinical vignettes to show the manifestation of what I call the analytical infant on the couch. In the first case I try to show how verbalization is connected with a movement to the depressive position; in the second, the problem of weaning (also an aspect of the depressive position). The question is, what is the correlation of the psychoanalytical infant with the historical infant? The psychoanalytical infant, we assume, repeats some of its history, but also he evolves differently. I would like to think that in the case of the woman patient an integration of previously split-off autistic areas is gradually achieved; in the second case, that a weaning which had never been achieved psychologically is gradually achieved. But what conviction can we have about the correspondence of the psychoanalytical infant with the historical infant? In the case of later childhood we get some confirmation from recovered memories and also from direct observation of children in analysis. It is not surprising that it is the early infant development that remains most controversial, lacking direct confirmation, since we cannot psychoanalyse infants. Yet psychoanalysis has the ambition not only of dealing with an ahistorical past, but also of providing a theory of development. How sure can we be of the correlation between the analytical infant and the actual infant of the past? We have some confirmation from infant observation, but that is only partial. We can observe behaviour, but cannot observe internal mental states. We get, of course, some confirmations from patients often while in analysis finding out more about their own infantile history. Such confirmations sometimes are very dramatic. For instance, once, interpreting a dream, I suggested that the patient as an infant experienced hunger in a particular way because he also felt immobilized, and I asked him if he had been swaddled. He then found out that indeed he had been swaddled till about four months of age.

But mostly we base our growing conviction on the accumulated analytical experience, its correspondence with life historics and infant and child observations, which enable us to form an idea of infantile development and its vicissitudes.

Summary

The contention of this paper is that early infantile development is reflected in the infantile part of the transference. When it is well integrated it gives rise to an underlying non-verbal communication which gives a depth to other communications. When not integrated it gives rise to acting-in as a primitive mode of communication. When this is understood the primitive experience can be integrated, symbolized and partly at least verbalized.

The development of the infantile part can be followed in the fluctuating moves towards integration. Two examples are given. In one case I show how analytical understanding leads to the integration of a split-off, primitive, pre-verbal experience and the connection of such integration with the development of speech. I also show how a failure of understanding on the analyst's part, repeating a developmental failure, can affect this process adversely. In the second case I show integrative processes connected with weaning and the integration of the weaning process with genital sexuality.

Notes

1 This chapter has been published previously (Segal, 1982). It was presented at the 32nd International Congress, Helsinki, July 1981.
2 This paper entitled 'A delusional system as a defence against the re-emergence of a catastrophic situation', appears in the present volume as Chapter 4.

6

Some clinical implications of Melanie Klein's work: emergence from narcissism[1]

Looking at Melanie Klein's work some sixty years later, it is difficult to grasp the magnitude of the revolution she brought about in analytical thinking. Her discoveries of the early infantile object relationships and anxieties added a new dimension to psychoanalytical work. They brought to life the infant in us. The new perspective she brought to bear on infantile development not only gave rise to new work among those known as Kleinians, but also influenced deeply the whole approach to psychoanalytical work, I think, even among those who have hardly heard of her and those who oppose some of her findings.

In her paper 'The origins of transference' (Klein, 1952), she says:

> For many years – and this is up to a point still true today – transference was understood in terms of direct references to the analyst in the patient's material. My conception of transference as rooted in the earliest stages of development and in deep layers of the unconscious is much wider and entails a technique by which from the whole material presented the unconscious elements of the transference are deduced. . . . For the patient is bound to deal with conflicts and anxieties re-experienced towards the analyst by the same methods he used in the past. That is to say, he turns away from the analyst as he attempted to turn away from his primal objects; he tries to split the relations to him, keeping him either as a good or as a bad figure: he deflects some of the feelings and attitudes experienced towards the analyst on to other people in his current life, and this is part of 'acting-out'.

I think few would quarrel with this formulation today, but equally few, I think, appreciate that it was still considered novel in 1952; and that such an understanding of transference necessitated a study of splitting mechanisms and projective identification which she had described as originating in earliest infancy.

75

It is well known that Melanie Klein contended that primitive object relationships exist from birth. This view today is gaining increasing acceptance. Early object relationships are rooted in the interplay of reality and phantasy. The concept of phantasy is of course crucial to understanding Melanie Klein's views. She describes how, prompted by desires and anxieties, infants in phantasy organize their object relationships in both a wish fulfilling and defensive way. Phantasy is the meeting ground and outcome of desires, anxieties and defences. It is the understanding of the functioning of primitive phantasy that is the basis on which her understanding of the transference and its unconscious roots is based.

Melanie Klein introduced the concept of positions to conceptualize her idea of early development. I shall not restate her formulations, since I think this audience will be familiar with the concepts of the paranoid-schizoid and the depressive positions. I shall only remind you that the paranoid-schizoid position is dominated by fears of annihilation and fragmentation. The object relations are to part-objects, and defences are predominantly fragmentation, splitting, projective identification and idealization. The depressive position is characterized by an ambivalent relation to whole loved objects, a budding sense of psychic reality, with the accompanying anxieties about guilt and loss. The move from the one to the other is a move from predominantly psychotic to neurotic functioning. Omnipotence lessens and the ego grows in strength.

The concept of position is not the same as that of a phase of development, though the paranoid-schizoid is organized earlier. 'Position' describes the state of the ego, typical anxieties, object relations and defences which persist at every level. The Oedipus complex itself can be organized predominantly in the paranoid-schizoid or the depressive way. The persistence of the paranoid-schizoid position in varying degrees interferes with the working through of the depressive position and underlies pathology.

From the clinical point of view careful and detailed following in the transference of the shifts and fluctuations between the two positions bring the richest rewards. The analysis of the early infantile paranoid-schizoid anxieties and defences and of the defences against the depressive position diminishes splitting, persecution and idealization and eventually allows the patient to relate to and to internalize a good object. This mitigates the destructiveness of the early superego, helps the integration of the ego and increases its strength.

I shall confine myself here to discussing the implications of early object relationships for the analysis of narcissism. We see now increasing numbers of narcissistic and borderline patients and much work is done nowadays on this problem, and much of that work (for instance Kohut's) seems to leave aside Klein's discoveries and the light they throw on narcissism. Melanie

Klein made only two direct statements about narcissism. In her paper on 'The origins of transference' (1952), she says:

> The hypothesis that a stage extending over several months precedes object-relations implies that – except for the libido attached to the infant's own body – impulses, phantasies, anxieties and defences either are not present in him, or are not related to an object, that is to say, they would operate *in vacuo*. The analysis of very young children has taught me that there is no instinctual urge, no anxiety situation, no mental process which does not involve objects, external or internal. . . . Furthermore, love and hatred, phantasies, anxieties, and defences are also operative from the beginning and are *ab initio* indivisibly linked with object-relations.

In the same paper she states:

> For many years I have held the view that auto-erotism and narcissism are in the young infant contemporaneous with the first relation to objects external and internalised. I shall briefly restate my hypothesis: auto-erotism and narcissism include the love for and relation with the internalised good object which in phantasy forms part of the loved body and self. It is to this internalised object that in auto-erotic gratification and narcissistic states a withdrawal takes place.

This hypothesis contradicts Freud's concept of auto-erotic and narcissistic stages which preclude an object relation. Freud's view, however, is not unequivocal; some of his statements are contradictory.

Her second extended reference to narcissism is in her paper 'Notes on some schizoid mechanisms' (Klein, 1946). In this paper she differentiates between narcissistic states and the narcissistic object relations and structure. The narcissistic states she relates to the withdrawal to an idealized internal object (as described above). The narcissistic object relations and structure she relates to projective identification. Her view of narcissistic object relations continues Freud's work on narcissistic object choice, but emphasizes also the elements of control of an object implicit in the concept of projective identification. It also links with internal structure in that the re-internalization of the protectively possessed object affects the structure of the ego and the superego.

In *Envy and Gratitude* (Klein, 1957) she describes fully the deployment of projective identification as an implementation of envious aims and also as a defence against envy – for instance, getting into an object and taking over the object's qualities. She does not in that connection refer to narcissism. Yet in this work it is implicit that there must be an intimate relation between narcissism and envy.

Freud's description of primary narcissism is that the infant feels himself to be the source of all satisfaction. The discovery of the object gives rise to hate. One could describe envy in a very similar way. The way primary envy is described by Melanie Klein is as a spoiling hostility at the realization that the source of life and goodness lies outside. To me, envy and narcissism are like two sides of a coin. Narcissism defends us against envy (as was described by Rosenfeld and others). The difference would lie in this. If one believes in a prolonged narcissistic stage, envy would be secondary to disillusionment. If, with Melanie Klein, one contends that awareness of an object relation and, therefore, envy exist from the beginning, narcissism could be seen as a defence against envy and therefore to be more related to the operation of the death instinct and envy than to libidinal forces.

The self-destructive as well as destructive nature of narcissism was borne in on me in the analysis of a particularly narcissistic patient (Mr M). His pathology is complex. One could describe him as a homosexual, since homosexual difficulties brought him first into analysis, or as a manic depressive, since he had psychotic manic breakdowns in the course of his illness. Megalomania is an important feature; so is promiscuity verging on erotomania. Omnipotence and narcissism are at the centre of his pathology. M's relation to women illustrates best the nature of his object relationship. He is prone to phantasying himself as superman. But at some point in his analysis he realized that his idea of being a superman was that he would be so admired and adored that women would look after him totally and he would never have to do anything; and he laughed wryly at himself, realizing what an infant he was. So, apparently, he was in search of an ideal or caring mother. But it wasn't so simple. He also needed to project into a woman a needy, greedy, aggressive and envious infant part of himself. He had a phantasy that in ejaculating, he was putting into women little homunculi that would possess them and he was implanting a need for M that would torture them forever. His eyes played a similar role. He was quite successful in implementing those phantasies and his life was largely consumed by getting women and/or running away from their demands. There was a similar relation to an internal object. One phantasy underlying his relationship to women is that he had removed a nipple from the breast; his penis has become the nipple; the woman's breast with the hole gets filled with his projected hunger and desires and becomes a vagina. When this object is re-introjected, his ego is like a shell containing an excited and destructive breast with a hole.

The whole system in him hinges on denial of dependence and envy. This became particularly clear in a serious negative therapeutic reaction. Following intense psychoanalytic work before a holiday he had managed to improve his relationship to the one steady girl-friend he had and, more significantly, managed to complete a piece of work (inhibition of working capacities being one of his important symptoms). During the break he got involved in a seduction of a particularly destructive kind and very nearly had a psychotic breakdown again. This was contained in the analysis. After a few weeks he had the following dream: There was a blind and deaf man. M, or a shadowy figure, were ineffectually trying to help him. But it didn't work and the man got hold of some earth-moving equipment; probably he went mad.

He associated first to what we had been talking about recently: how he was trying to block all insight and make himself blind and deaf, and to his fear of going mad again. He thought the blind and deaf man was himself and the earth-moving equipment associated to his mania. He also mentioned that the previous night he had watched *The Third Man*, and in the film there was some reference to meningitis. In this film, as most of you probably know, Harry Lime steals penicillin from the hospital and children ill with meningitis become deformed monsters or die through being given diluted penicillin. His mention of *The Third Man* gave me the clue to the shadowy figure who, he said, could be himself. In the film the first glimpse of Harry Lime is as a shadowy figure in a doorway. I suggested that Harry Lime, who steals penicillin and gives it out in diluted form, must be himself. He was first shocked that he didn't see it himself, as it is always a shock to him if he hadn't thought of an interpretation himself, and then associated that the diluted penicillin must be what he gives to women when he seduces them. (In the past we analysed how he uses psychoanalytic insight itself to provoke transferences in women by giving them interpretations.)

In the next session he was preoccupied with the thought, why does diluted penicillin do harm? Is it only because it prevents the children from having the right penicillin, or is it also poisonous by itself? He wondered why his 'diluted love' does harm. The 'diluted love', in this case the narcissistic love, is poisonous because it separates one from real love. But what struck me most and what I drew his attention to, is that the blind and deaf person in the dream is also himself, and that it is himself he is feeding the diluted penicillin which destroys his senses, his sanity and ultimately his life, and it is himself that he deprives of love. And, indeed, one may say that this man who apparently devotes his life to adoring himself and getting himself adored in fact is deficient not only in loving, but also in feeling loved and in constructively loving himself, caring for himself.

Herbert Rosenfeld, in his papers 'On the psychopathology of narcissism' (1964) and on 'The life and death instincts' (1971), described in detail what he calls destructive narcissism, narcissism which is an expression of envy and self-destructiveness, and he described the use of projective identification and narcissistic object relationships, both as a defence against and an expression of the death instinct. I think I differ from him at one point. He differentiates libidinal from destructive narcissism. I think that at base all persistent narcissism is based on the death instinct and envy, although libidinal elements enter of course as well in the fusion of instinct. But it is always under the domination of the death instinct. In the case of M, for instance, the libidinization itself is at the service of destruction and self-destruction.

I think that Freud's concept of the life and death instincts could resolve the problem of the usefulness, or otherwise, of an assumption of primary narcissism. The idea of the life instinct is the love of life which includes love of self and life-giving objects. Self love and object love are not in conflict. They are complementary components of the same instinct. The relation to the ideal object, the first expression of the life instinct, does not give rise to persistent narcissism. Klein intuitively called it a narcissistic state – that is, temporary: it evolves into the relationship to a good rather than ideal internal object and is the basis of self-respect, self-preservation, as well as of love, respect and preservation of loved objects, external and internal. On the other hand, the death instinct and envy give rise to narcissistic object relations and internal structures which are destructive and self-destructive.

Emerging from such narcissistic structures necessitates a withdrawal of projective identifications, a working through of envy and defences against it, and a gradual shift from the paranoid-schizoid to the depressive position, with a concomitant diminishing of omnipotence. I shall describe the fluctuating shifts and the emergence from narcissism in a much less ill patient.[2]

Mr F was stably married and had several children. His wife was largely the container of better parts of himself. He managed his work as an architect, but in a very inhibited way, and was happier with the business side or the engineering side of his profession than with its artistic aspects. He also had difficulties in dealing with clients or colleagues, being secretly both controlling and paranoid, though this was fairly well disguised. At the beginning of his analysis he was enormously passive. It soon became apparent that he lived largely in an omnipotent phantasy of living inside me and having complete possession. In his dreams he was often in buildings, fortresses, desert islands and so on. He was apparently quite unaware of my existence other than as a medium he lived in. At the same time he was secretly taking over my very idealized characteristics.

Over weekends and breaks he never thought of me or missed me, but he reacted very strongly. He would either go into a dreamy, withdrawn state or act out in a manic way. For instance, he would spend hours exercising to pile up muscles on his chest and shoulders – representing to him breasts. Or he would become very anal, phantasying getting inside women's bottoms, or ideally, his own. These states were invariably accompanied by persecution, and he was forever fighting with intruders at his work and home. In his dreams, fortresses were under siege and in one, a desert island he lived on was surrounded by cannibals in boats who were going to land. He was narcissistically inside of and identified with me, his depressed, intrusive, cannibalistic self projected outside. His awareness of his own destructiveness was minimal, and persecution was mainly dealt with by denial.

A typical dream: he dreamed of a girl mime of his acquaintance. He saw her in the dream miming a very gaudy figure. She was in a room with a funny ceiling, round, concave and also gaudy. The ceiling he associated both to a womb because of its colour and gaudiness and to the breast. He immediately recognized that the mime girl was himself since in the previous session he spoke of his imitating me. So he was both inside a womb/breast and being it.

Recently, this structure had begun to give way by gradual steps. Against great resistance he moved to a better job in a bigger firm. This move was resisted because it meant to him relinquishing in part the phantasy that he lived inside my house, owned it and did my work: so it didn't matter what he did at work or provided for his family and his own home.

Simultaneously a new figure appeared in his dreams and associations which he called 'the little man'. The little man controlled everyone, especially his mother.

He used to believe that in father's absence he was mother's little man, omnipotently owning and controlling her. Now it dawned on him that as a child he was little and open to experiences of deprivation, jealousy and, particularly, envy of the big ones. His narcissistic structure and belief in the little man's omnipotence were protecting him from experiencing that. The patient was very shaken by this discovery.

A couple of weeks before the material that I shall present came up, he saw in a book shop a copy of my new book, and he wiped this perception out of his mind for days. Only his dream material alerted me to that possibility. Soon after admitting it he started a Monday session by saying that he smelt his farts and he liked the smell, which rather upset him, but he had good dreams. In his first dream he wrote a book. Five chapters were fine, but the following two were wordy, confused, grandiose, too voluminous, windy. In the second dream his sister-in-law was there and he thought – 'there will be trouble because he will want her to shut up, not to wake Bobby, his son. She doesn't like being shut up.' In the third dream a friend, D, knew the name of a good restaurant. He himself didn't know any names of good restaurants, so he had to believe D.

He was pleased with the dream about the book with the first five chapters and the next two. This surprised me because he invariably associated five with the five sessions. It seems to me that the first five chapters are the chapters we wrote together the previous week and the two chapters are the chapters he wrote by himself over the weekend. Through denying my role in the process and pretending he wrote the five chapters himself, he left himself full of hot wind over the weekend. The significance of the second dream about his sister-in-law goes back several years to the evening of this woman's childbirth. When I had hinted at his envy of her and anxiety about her, he had contended that there was nothing more to childbirth than to having a stool in the lavatory, and that there was nothing either to be envious of or anxious about; and he was very upset when the woman nearly died in childbirth the next day. She also represents me waking up Bobby, the child himself, to the realization of his envy of a pregnant mother and his anxiety about her.

The further dream about his friend knowing the name of the restaurant which he doesn't know relates to his not knowing the source of his food – myself, or his mother – and not knowing the difference between food, babies and faeces. D is also in analysis.

The next day he said, 'We talked about food yesterday, and I had a dream about a restaurant. There was a party going to a restaurant on top of a hill or mountain.' It could be Sardinia or Sicily, or in his own country. He very much wanted to go too but didn't know if he was invited, if he at all belonged or deserved to go. But someone said, 'Well, he also made a contribution; he can come too.' He was enormously pleased and relieved. The restaurant was very pleasant and rather modest, and there were few people.

The dream struck him as very unlike any of his other dreams. His isolation, feeling that he didn't belong either to his original family or to his profession was always a very important feature in his character. He was surprised that in this dream he really wanted to belong and was allowed to. The hill and the actual building of the restaurant had many associations to his childhood, and the number of people he said was like a family. In this dream he seems to recover a family. He also related the dream to his increasing feeling that maybe after all I had been kind to him (my actual house is also on a hill).

In this dream he has emerged from the narcissistic position of the previous day and has begun to face the depressive position. The following weeks were marked by repeated fluctuations between taking refuge in a narcissistic structure and emerging from it and getting in touch with good objects and good feelings – but also with the intensity of the envy that this aroused. For instance, one day he started by saying that the session wouldn't be much good because he had no dream and not many thoughts. Then, half-way through the session he realized, to his surprise, that a lot that was new had come out. It occurred to him that, without realizing it, he always thought *he* makes the session and ignores completely any possibility of my contribution making any difference. The other day, he said, he thought his dream wasn't interesting and was amazed how important it turned out to be. He said he now realized that he had always considered his analysis important, but it didn't seem to have anything to do with me. He had thought of me as a kind of *hausfrau* who happened to be there as well. At the end of the session he cried – unusual for him. The crying was mobilized by remembering that he thought in the waiting room that one day it will be time to stop coming here. He dreaded the loss, felt grateful and guilty at his past ignoring of me.

Next day, however, he was withdrawn and rather hostile. He dreamed that a little girl was constantly present and interrupting his intercourse with his wife. He interrupted me when I spoke in the session, and completely forgot his own feelings in the previous session. Thus, the little girl represented his envious attack on our good intercourse. After my comment on the dream, he remembered that the day before, after the session, he had thought that it was intolerable to think of me as so important to him and to cry.

In the last dream I shall report his envious spoiling of good objects, and the recovery of them is, I think, clear. He dreamed that he was by a beautiful pool with a nice family. In the background there was a snow white mountain; possibly there was a tunnel under it. A dog shat into the pool. The father of the family removed the shit and he thought, 'How disgusting'. But nobody else seemed upset. The dog did it again and this time when father removed the shit, he splashed the patient, who was very indignant. The beautiful pool and family he associated to his wife's family, who were particularly kind to him and his wife that weekend. He said he found it hard to bear. This was partly jealousy. Her family was better than his. But also he said he found it difficult to tolerate that they had such a beautiful house and pool in the country and were so generous. (At the time he owed me some money.)

It was easy to relate this also to what he felt were good experiences increasingly felt by him in his analysis, and to his envy of the analysis, seen as beautiful and rich. The dog shitting into the pool is the spoiling part of himself. There had been a lot of material about soiling and spoiling recently. The analyst is the father who removes the shit, but also splashes him; doesn't let him, in the patient's words, 'get away with it'. There is an envious attitude as well as hidden admiration of this paternal role of mine, because he added that he did feel contempt and disgust for the father in the dream doing such a filthy job, clearing up after a dirty dog.

Towards the end of the session he told me that he had asked a greengrocer for some Cape Delicious apples. The greengrocer said they hadn't come and the patient felt overwhelmed with fury; he felt the man wanted him to believe that Cape Delicious didn't exist. It took him some time to realize that the man meant only that they hadn't come in yet. The previous sessions again contained a lot of wiping out of insight and what he experienced as the goodness of the analysis, and he admitted that it had immediately followed his despising of the very help he experienced from my work (the father cleaning the pool). I therefore interpreted to him that the man who wanted to make him believe that a good, desirable and therefore also enviable object never existed and still doesn't exist, is himself, and it was this that made the prospect of forthcoming weekend (it was a Friday) so desperate. For him the weekend is not a matter of waiting two days, but of a possible total loss if he is dominated by the part of himself that makes him believe good things don't exist. But the greengrocer representing that part of him wants to make him believe that, but he isn't completely successful any more. The 'little man' is not omnipotent.

The patient's upset and anger are an indication that he has an increasing belief that good objects can exist; the restaurant on the hill in the first dream reported; the good family by the beautiful pool; the Cape Delicious; and he is increasingly struggling against the part of himself that has the power to wipe it out at the service of his envy and narcissism.

This is not a technical paper. I have made no attempt to show the acting out and in, the interplay of transference, counter-transference and so on. I have also left out the patients' history and the account of external factors which contributed to their difficulties. What I attempted is to illustrate with some clinical material the following points.

The narcissistic structure originates in the paranoid-schizoid position under the dominance of envy and the defences against envy. It depends on the operation of splitting, denial and projective identification. The emergence from a narcissistic structure necessitates the analysis in the transference of this primitive type of object relationship: this enables the patient to experience his envy and explore its roots, and to begin to face the depressive position which allows him to recover his good human objects and his own capacity to love.

Klein's work on early object relationships and her concept of positions brought a new understanding to the complex relationships which underlie narcissism.

Summary

The thesis of this paper is that Klein's work on early object relationships throws significant light on narcissism. In the author's view, narcissistic structure is an expression of, and a defence against, the death instinct and envy. The life instinct includes love of the self, but that love is not in opposition to a loving relationship to an object. Loving life means loving oneself and the life-giving object. In narcissism, life-giving relationships and healthy self-love are equally attacked.

Two examples are given. The patient with strong psychotic features, M, illustrates the self-destructive nature of narcissism. In patient F, who has a narcissistic character structure, the author describes the emergence from a narcissistic state. In this state the patient lives in a phantasy of being inside of, controlling and identifying protectively with an object which is both idealized and degraded. All negative feelings are projected outside, giving rise to persecution, which is frequently dealt with by denial. This structure depends on denial, splitting, idealization and projective identification. The analysis of the underlying object relationships and anxieties leads to an emergence from that state. This confronts him with his dependence on a good object and mobilizes his envy. The persistent analysis of the fluctuations between his flight to a narcissistic structure and his confrontation with love and envy gradually enables him to face more fully his depressive position and to regain his confidence in a good object and his own capacity to love.

Notes

1 This chapter has been published previously (Segal, 1983). It was read at the London Weekend Conference for English Speaking Members of European Psychoanalytical Societies, 3 October 1982.
2 Rosenfeld (1971) describes libidinal narcissism as a self-idealization achieved by introjective and projective identification with the ideal breast, corresponding to Klein's description of the narcissistic state, but having become structuralized. He shows that on analysing the structure one immediately mobilizes envy. Therefore, what he calls libidinal narcissism is also based on, and a defence against, envy. The difference between that and what he calls destructive narcissism may be one of the degree of domination of the death instinct over the life instinct. There is such a difference in degree between my patients M and F.

7

The Oedipus complex today[1]

It is implicit in Klein's description of the depressive position (Klein, 1935) that the Oedipus complex is unavoidably part and parcel of working through the depressive position. Klein characterizes the depressive position as that phase of development in which the infant begins to relate to mother as a whole person. That means he perceives her more as she is in reality; that is, not split into a good and a bad one, not a part-object, like the breast, in the infant's possession, not saturated by projective identification, but as a separate person, having a personality and a life of her own. That 'life of her own' principally includes the father as a sexual partner.

In the depressive position, the infant increasingly relates to an external reality and differentiates it from his internal reality, the reality of his impulses and phantasies. Coming to terms with this reality, inner and outer, involves coming to terms with the Oedipus complex.

Klein assumed that because of these developments one could say that the Oedipus complex starts in the depressive position. Nevertheless, triangular relationships exist before the depressive position and some of them could be seen as pre-Oedipal or else as the primitive roots of the Oedipus complex.

The triangular situation sets in as a result of splitting processes. There is an early split between the good or idealized aspect of the breast and the bad one, so that the infant is confronted with two objects: the object of desire and that of hatred and fear.

In my Introduction to Melanie Klein's work (Segal, 1964), in the chapter on the paranoid-schizoid position, I described what I called the 'third area'. I described two patients, one borderline schizoid and one psychotic, who could relate to me only by splitting off hateful aspects of both themselves and me into a third area, described by one of the patients as 'bloody mish-mash', repeating the situation in which an infant can only relate to, and feed from, the breast provided he can split off hatred and persecution and locate it in this third area. Such a third area, or third object, which contains the unwanted aspects of the self and object, is inherent in the paranoid-schizoid position. This triangular situation is the background of a pre-depressive Oedipal constellation because it gives rise to a readiness for a perception of a third object. The father's penis is a ready recipient of such split-off projections.

A patient, whom I will call Mr R, and refer to again, had a hallucination that a motor cycle was riding into his head. The rider had a kind of mask on, which made his head look like a gorilla. He felt terrified and thought his head would explode. Then he looked at his own index finger, and got frightened because his finger looked like a gorilla. He had a number of associations to this event, but the two central ones were to the gorilla, which reminded him of a psychotic boy; and to the finger, which was connected to anal masturbation, which we had spoken of previously. His anal masturbation was for him always associated with unconscious phantasies of violent intrusion into the anus of the analyst-mother. We understood that the motor cycle represented his own intrusive self, identified with his finger and penis, and projected into an external object, the motor cycle which he had heard outside my window the previous day.

Cases in which this early splitting and projection is maintained in later development often give rise to a situation which appears to be Oedipal: one parent idealized and desired; the other one hated and persecuting. But if one looks closely at the material it is not a true Oedipal situation but a continuation of a part-object relationship with excessive splitting into ideal and persecutory objects.

This kind of part-object relationship may also characterize the early perception of the mother as a whole person with a whole body. Anatomically, so to speak, she is seen as a whole object, but the emotional relation can continue very much on a part-object level. The mother's body is seen as containing both riches and horrors, and among them the father's penis is seen as a part-object and a possession of mother's, sometimes idealized and desired and sometimes very persecutory.

Some patients, mainly women but sometimes also men, come to analysis in the hope that the analyst will help them to find a penis or the knowledge of how to acquire a penis. For the woman this can be a husband or a lover, while for a man it is usually potency they are searching for. Frequently these patients have no idea of a man who would be a person. So, again, what appears as an Oedipal situation – that is, rivalling mother for father – is in fact a very primitive situation, more to do with envy of mother than with Oedipal jealousy, and a wish to rob mother of her possessions.

Recognizing father, or to begin with, often on the part-object level, a penis, as not being a split-off good or bad aspect of the breast and not being saturated by the infant's own projections, but as an object in its own right, with its own characteristics and its own functions different from those of the infant or the mother, is an important step in development. The father can then be seen as protecting the mother and the child from a stream of mutual projective identifications, in phantasy and in reality. It is an important factor in establishing the mother's right to separateness. He can also be perceived as a provider of goodness for mother, of the kind that the infant cannot provide. It establishes early on the differentiation between both generations and sexes, essential for healthy development.

I shall illustrate this by some material from a later phase of the analysis of my patient Mr R. One day he told me that, as he was going past my consulting-room door to the waiting room, he became very anxious because the thought occurred to him that there was no guard at the door and nothing to stop him from getting into the consulting room and interfering with the session of my other patient. Then he added, 'Come to think of it, there is nothing to stop me doing what I want on the couch. For instance, if I wanted to, I could lie upside down.' Then he giggled, and became embarrassed as he realized that upside down in the bed is the position he was in during some love play with his girl-friend the night before. So, apparently the situation was as follows: There is no guard at the door, no husband. He could have intercourse with me as his girl-friend and have our positions upside down; that is, with him dominating me – apparently, a plain Oedipal situation. He went on to tell me a dream. He said: 'I had a dream in which I was explaining to M [the girlfriend] about my hallucinations. I was telling her, 'Look, I dream up a car and there it is.' And the car appeared.' He got into the front seat. But there was no partition between front and back – no pole to lean against. He started falling backwards, feeling an utmost panic. And he woke up with severe anxiety.

My understanding of his associations preceding the telling of the dream, and the dream, was as follows. The pole is a phallic symbol. But also, I am of Polish origin, and he knew that my husband's name is Paul. In the absence of the pole, the father, or the penis in the vagina, there is nothing to stop him not just from having intercourse with his mother on a genital level, there is nothing to stop him from unrestrained projective identification with her, leading to the loss of boundaries, confusion and panic. What he seems to explain to his girl-friend in the dream is that when he projects himself into his mother, what used to be his thoughts, 'what he dreamed up', is felt by him as a reality in the external world. But the whole process, instead of hallucination, at that point gave rise to a dream. Sometime later in his analysis, it became apparent that his hallucinations disappeared from the time this dream had been analysed.

Several years later, after considerable change and improvement, the patient was getting married. Before his wedding, for which he was missing a few days of his analysis, he showed considerable ambivalence to myself representing the father. When he came back from his honeymoon he said that he had never been so moved in his life as he was at the actual wedding ceremony. He decided to marry in church in deference to his dead father, though he himself was not religious. He asked for his father's favourite hymn – 'The Lord is My Shepherd' – to be sung at the wedding ceremony. He said that he had never in his life been so happy and so unhappy at one and the same time. He did not know if at that moment he was regaining his father or losing him. He was so aware of his father's presence in his thoughts, and so acutely aware of his real absence from the wedding. He then told me a dream he had had the night before in which a fisherman was to take him out to teach him to fish. The fisherman's hands were bandaged because they had cuts on them. But the fisherman assured him that he could still keep his promise.

In the last session before the break I had occasion to point out to him that he was very cutting to me. I was the fisherman/father with the bandaged hand, but one who was not so resentful as to withdraw his help.

One can see that the first dream is what I would call *pseudo*-Oedipal. On the face of it his first associations to that dream are of an Oedipal nature, wanting to make love to the mother/analyst. But what the dream reveals is something quite different. What he wants is to project himself into the analyst in a way which results in confusion and panic. In the second dream, on the contrary, the father is seen as a separate person with a truly Oedipal ambivalence, the experience of loss and guilt. This can lead to an introjection and a positive identification with his father's masculine qualities.

There is also a difference in his mental functioning. The first dream explains his propensity to hallucinate, a failure of adequate symbolization – what he thinks *is*. In the second dream the external and the internal situations are clearly distinguished. He is aware of his father's real absence, since he is dead, and at the same time his presence in his (the patient's) mind. His thought is not a hallucination but a memory of experience.

In recent years, we have been paying increasing attention to the relationship between the early Oedipal situation and processes of symbolization and thinking. I have contended that adequate symbolization can only be established with the working-through of the depressive position and the differentiation between external and internal realities. I have become increasingly convinced that accepting the reality of the father and the Oedipal couple is essential in this process. Attacks on the parental couple, and the links between the parents, unavoidably disrupt processes of thinking. Hatred of the parental coupling becomes a hatred of thinking. Britton (1989) describes a patient who, whenever she thought he was thoughtful, would scream at him 'Stop this fucking thinking!'

A session of a patient of mine, Mrs C, illustrates such a disturbance. She started the session by telling me that she had two very tiny fragments of a dream. In one, she saw me surrounded by middle-aged, stupid, altogether despicable men. Of the second fragment she could remember only that it had something to do with African land and African people. The first dream seemed to both of us pretty obvious, with an impending long weekend. But the hardly remembered fragment dream brought surprisingly rich associations. To begin with, she expressed again her horror of racial prejudices she cannot free herself from, and which she detests in herself. That seemed to provide a link between the dream of men I may spend my weekend with and the other one about the Africans. But her other associations were more unexpected and illuminating. The patient is a form teacher and she started speaking about a child's difficulty in learning any grammar, particularly foreign grammar. She thought Africa may represent what this girl feels about foreign grammar as totally exotic and incomprehensible. This child, she said, is quite clever, but very disjointed. She seems unable to make certain connections, and this seems particularly obvious in her total inability to grasp the rules of grammar. After all, grammar, with the sort of patterns it describes, should come more naturally. Then she laughed, and said, 'Maybe to her grammar is so foreign and exotic – just like parents in intercourse must appear to the child – beyond reach, incomprehensible, exotic, foreign.' This patient is often preoccupied and disturbed by very primitive fantasies of the primal scene. In the first dream that intercourse is attacked and derided. She has a prejudice against it, like a prejudice against Africans. And her associations to it suggest that she is aware how her thinking is dislocated by her attack on those natural patterns of relationships. It is interesting that this patient, who had no acquaintance with Chomsky's work, assumes, as he does, that we have an inborn sense of grammar.

This takes me to another aspect of the problem, which is the connection between the Oedipus complex and Bion's ideas of the relationship between the container and the contained as the basis of the mental apparatus and the capacity to symbolize and think. To remind you very briefly. Klein (1946) contends that the infant deals with disturbing feelings and experiences by projecting them outside, a projection which gives rise to the phantasies of a bad breast, and attaches itself to the realities of bad experiences. Bion (1962, 1963) introduced the idea that such primitive projections are also the infant's first means of communication. The mother receives the infant's projections and modifies them by her reactions, like taking away his hunger, fear or pain. To deal with his pain the infant gets rid of what Bion calls 'Beta elements', inchoate, concrete – feelings experienced as things which can be pushed out. If the mother's response alleviates these experiences the baby can take them back inside, modified by understanding, and they become elements which he calls 'Alpha'. But the infant also introjects the breast that can contain and modify the projections, and it becomes that part of himself that can transform Beta into alpha elements available for symbolizing and thought.

Bion speaks of the relationship between the container and the contained and the introjection of the container. I do not know if he ever refers to it as 'mental space'. I see it as also providing mental space, in which feelings and thoughts can be contained and worked on.

Bion's 'container and contained' is basically a two–body relationship. But he does say that when the relation between the two is good it produces a third, which is benevolent to all three; and when it is bad, produces a third which is disruptive. Britton (1989) has suggested that a mental space at the beginning of the Oedipus complex becomes a triangular space, with three apexes: father, mother and child. In that space there is an elasticity of relationships: there is a relationship like that between the three lines linking the vertices; there is a relation between the mother and the child; one between the father and the child; and one between the father and the mother, of which the child is the observer. The third excluded can be hostile or disruptive, whether it is the child or one of the parents, or the child's phantasy of one of the parents, as was the case with my patient with the motor-cycle intrusion. But if the third excluded is benevolent it is an important part of the mental apparatus because it becomes the reflective part in the patient's mind, that can observe himself and his phantasies about the parents. And it is also the part capable of benevolent, or neutral, curiosity about the external world.

When the parental relationship is unbearable to the child there is an attack on the link between the parents, and the self and the parents, and the destruction of the triangular mental space. This is illustrated by my patient, Mrs D, who was tormented by recurring panics. Though intelligent, when in a state of panic, whether conscious or unconscious, she loses her concentration and all ability to think. In one of the sessions she described acute anxieties about a hole in a wall. Some building work had to be done in her house; she could not imagine it being done without a big hole in the wall. She thought her children could fall through the hole, or she herself, and anyway the thought of this big black hole put her in a panic. It was fairly clear in the session that she had no idea in her mind that the builder might know what he was doing. (The transference implications were obvious.) When this was interpreted, she told me that she had another panic which had assailed her on the way to the ses sion: she had lost her diary which had confidential information about herself and the work in her office, involving other people, and the loss of the diary could be catastrophic. It slowly emerged that the loss of the diary had to do with her having read a poster of a lecture I was giving, jointly with a man. She did not intend to attend this event, but she also wanted to forget the date, not to be troubled by it. The indiscretion referred to what she felt was the indecency of my exhibiting myself on a platform with the man.

The next session was very difficult, and analytic work was hardly possible because of the patient's determination to break any links. Two themes seem to have emerged: one of an internal tormentor. It eventually led to a phantasy of a hand cruelly squeezing out a breast that was filled with a boil. The second theme referred to sexuality. She felt that I and others were trying to impose on her a view of sexual intercourse as something pleasurable and non-destructive, which was a denial, and idealization, since 'I thought everybody knew that sex was always sado-masochistic'. Another view she had of sex was as of two people coming together in intercourse in cruelty to the third person in front of whom they were exhibiting, so as to inflict on this third person unbearable feelings of exclusion, inferiority and jealousy. Some links could be established; for instance, the parents-myself cruelly exhibiting to the child and the resulting destruction of her relationship to the breast; but the patient remained on the whole disconnected from me, angry and very anxious.

In the third session, as she was speaking of the hole, some music from the neighbouring flat could just be heard in the consulting room. She drew my attention to it, and said it made her think of people dancing. She did not feel disturbed or persecuted by it. Eventually we could establish that the terrible hole in her mind was the missing space in which she could perceive the parents, represented by me, dancing together. Later in the session, she started speaking about her difficulties in writing a report she had to do at work, but in a much quieter and more understanding way.

This patient had an idealizing relationship to the breast, but this relationship was very fragile, only to be maintained by a splitting-off of ambivalence. The appearance of a third object turns everything into torment. Not only is she tormented by phantasies of sexuality infused with cruelty, but the original relation to the breast is destroyed by this intrusion and also turns into torment. When this intrusion happens, her mind becomes itself disjointed and fragmented, and she becomes filled with intense paranoid and hypochondriacal phantasies. At those points her capacity for understanding and symbolization gets lost. My talking to others is experienced as my forcing her to witness an actual sexual intercourse. The bad feelings about me become a tormented and tormenting poisonous breast inside her, experienced in her physical symptoms. She can get rid of the resulting persecution by making a hole in her mind instead of a space accommodating the dancing parents. However, later in the third session she shows how the containment and understanding provided by the analytic situation led to a transformation of Beta into Alpha elements.

The importance of the role of the observing part of the parental intercourse is shown in the following material.

Two dreams of a patient (Mrs K), in an advanced stage of her analysis, illustrate some features of this triangular space. The first dream follows an event in the transference. I asked Mrs K if she could come ten minutes earlier for her session. She gave me apparently good reasons for not being able to change her time. As I had unavoidably to leave my consulting room at the earlier time, I had to tell her that I was sorry, but I would have to cut her session ten minutes short. It soon transpired that in such a case she could think of ways of coming ten minutes early. The next day she had the following dream. She was walking down a lovely road bordered by leafy trees. But she came to the end of the road. There was no way to go on. She retraced her steps, and on the way she saw a clearing, and in that clearing a couple were having a very vigorous sexual intercourse. The intercourse was not only physical. The man seemed to have been telling the woman how passionately he loved her. She observed this scene with great interest. Her first association was to tell me that there was nothing voyeuristic or exhibitionistic about the scene. The couple were making love in a clearing in a forest. They were concerned with one another, not exhibiting. She had no voyeuristic excitement. She did not seek to see them, unlike in some other dreams, and she was just interested, not excited. She associated the end of the road to my firmly telling her that I wished to end the session ten minutes early.

I think that the leafy road which she enjoyed so much represents her phantasy of being inside me controlling me, a very common psychic stance in her. The frustration about the end of the session shows her that this has come to an end. She sometimes uses the expression 'No way!'. 'No way' can she maintain the phantasy of being inside and controlling me. When she gives up that phantasy she is confronted by another space which opens a clearing in which the parental intercourse happens. And in the dream it is unspoilt by voyeuristic projections.

Further work of course led to the recognition of repressed feelings of jealousy and rage, and she had to make room in her mind for those feelings as well. But it is important that she could be also an objective and appreciative observer.

Some time later she had a similar dream, bringing another aspect of the new space and a new way of relating. In the dream she was in the kitchen with me, washing up. We were talking about marriage, and I was telling her that I married a Pole because Poles are so passionate. In that dream her relation to me in terms of feeding and washing up is not spoilt, and is even enriched, by her knowledge of me as part of the couple. Similarly, her relation to me as mother does not disturb her own appreciation of the man. It is important that her relationship with her own husband had improved recently.

The primitive Oedipus complex is a part-object relationship dominated by splits and projection. The mature genital Oedipus complex necessitates the recognition of parents as separate, complete persons in a relationship with each other, including a sexual relationship. The acceptance of this configuration is very painful. Unlike the relationship between the container and the container as a two-body relationship wholly beneficial to the child, this is a situation in which the child is the third, excluded, with all that implies of jealousy, envy, rage and depression. Patient K, whose two nice dreams about the parental intercourse I have reported, had another dream, later on, after a successful holiday. She called to me to mend a light in her room. I came in, but accompanied by my husband. She was in an absolute rage. All weekend she was surprised at her rage, and rather ashamed of it, since we did mend her light. But the point was she did not really like the light being mended, since it showed me as a couple and brought the awareness that I depended on him for help, not on her. The working-through of the Oedipal ambivalence, and the mobilization of reparative impulses, results in the establishment of an inner world with a creative sexual couple at its centre. The Oedipal scenario is always with us in one form or another but it evolves from primitive forms to more mature perceptions.

Note

1 This paper has been given in several versions at different meetings. It has not previously been published.

8

Paranoid anxiety and paranoia[1]

Paranoid anxiety, like the poor, is always with us. Indeed it is difficult to find a patient who would not to some degree have paranoid anxieties. We are all apt to defend against guilt, loss or even uncertainty, by looking for somebody to blame. Some potential for paranoia is also necessary as a basis for discrimination. Like Freud's statement about the infant's original relation to objects, 'This I shall take in; this I shall spit out', we must 'taste' experience, keeping in mind the potential that it might be bad as well as the potential that it might be good (Freud, 1911a). And underlying the 'potential for bad' are not only our past reality experiences but also our repressed paranoid phantasies, which have to be tested by experience. Indeed, if we meet someone apparently free of paranoid anxieties or suspicions we suspect that he suffers from 'anti-paranoia' and is using idealization and denial to keep his mind free, possibly from paranoid anxieties too real and frightening to bear. Of course some individuals are more prone to paranoid suspicions or anxieties than others, and it may be built into the character, and some degree of paranoid distortion invariably accompanies neurotic conditions, without amounting to what we clinically call 'a paranoia'.

This proclivity to paranoid fears has unconscious roots in infantile development. In the earliest phases of development, called by Klein 'the paranoid-schizoid position', the infant deals with the chaotic impact of external and internal stimuli by splitting the object and the self into an ideal and a bad one, and in this way trying to create some order in their world. A crucial role in this splitting is played by projective identification, in which the infant also gets rid of whatever is a painful or bad experience by trying to project it outside into the object, thereby increasing the badness of the object. And similarly, parts of the self felt as good and constructive may be projected into a good object, making it more ideal but stripping the ego of its potential. But in normal development, such projections are gradually

95

withdrawn and the infant is able to tolerate more the knowledge of real objects and their good and bad characteristics, and the infant's own ambivalence, which also leads to guilt and dread of loss. The child gradually comes out of a more hallucinatory or distorted world into a world of reality, including the reality of their own desires and conflicts – psychic reality.

Defences against this very painful situation, such as manic defences, always include some regression to the prior position, some re-splitting, though the splitting may take slightly different forms from that between the good and the bad. It may be between the triumphant and the destroyed, and so on.

This propensity accounts for our tendency to relapse into states of mind accompanied by paranoid anxieties and suspicions due to a regression to the paranoid-schizoid position, as I have described, but which are still subject to reality testing. The projective identification is at the root of it but it is more flexible and more easily withdrawn. It allows the existence of doubt, in contrast to the absolute conviction characteristic of the psychotic delusion. Somewhere at the core there is usually a more psychotic situation which can at times be mobilized and, partly at least, modified in analysis, but it exists in a deeply repressed state in an otherwise non-psychotic though disturbed personality.

The kind of patient I have in mind is illustrated by Mr X who was a rather paranoid personality. He was suspicious and quarrelsome with men, particularly those in authority, and got on badly with his wife, towards whom he was rather paranoid. Although devoted to his children, and on the whole a very good father, he felt readily persecuted by their demands. At one point in his analysis he reported a recurring dream, which he had had since ever he could remember. In the dream he is in a half-lying position, tied to a chair, surrounded by elongated animals with huge, toothy jaws. He identified the animals as resembling the jaws of crocodiles. This dream kept recurring in the analysis in various contexts. At times it was associated with fears of castration; at other times with fear of unborn babies inside his mother, containing a projection of himself. The last version of the dream, after which it stopped repeating, we could understand as the truly psychotic relation to a devouring part-object, actually located in the gastric symptoms from which he suffered.

One day I was struck by his own half-lying position as if being tied to a chair, and it occurred to me to ask him if he has ever been swaddled. It turned out that he had been swaddled till the age of four months and had had a great deal of colic. He was a screaming baby. It seemed to me that, swaddled and deprived of movement and of any possibility of motor discharge, he was particularly prone to violent projections, vested maybe in his scream, making him live in a world in which he was surrounded by projections of his bodily experience of immobility, maybe some visual experience of his bound-up lower part of his body (the elongated shape) and his mouth – hungry, screaming, wide open, biting – which must have felt to him enormous. After that session the dream disappeared, and in so far as I remember, it was then that the gastric symptoms began to subside.

By contrast, let us look at an adolescent hebephrenic patient I had in treatment. One day, following a phase of considerable improvement, she came into the room dancing, twirling, muttering incomprehensibly, and making gestures of throwing something round the room. And the gayer she was, the more depressed I found myself feeling. Noting that in her better phases she was a great reader of Shakespeare, it struck me how much she resembled Ophelia strewing flowers. When I suggested that, she immediately calmed down, after saying sadly, 'But Ophelia was mad, wasn't she?' Getting in touch with thoughts about the death of her father was felt by her as a terrible persecuting dead body inside her. In her fragmenting and dispersing of the flowers, my patient was minutely fragmenting a dead object and her perceiving self, and projecting confusion and depression into me.

Both patients reacted to the approach of depressive feelings by a re-awakening of paranoia. But both the symptomatology of the patient and the nature of the transference were very different. The way of understanding the first patient was through his dream and associations; while with the hebephrenic it was through her actions and my counter-transference. Both patients reacted to situations of stress, and particularly guilt, by a regression to a paranoid-schizoid position. I think the difference was basically in the nature of the paranoid-schizoid position to which they regressed.

Since Klein's (1946) first formulations about the paranoid-schizoid position, many of us, particularly those working with psychotics – Bion (1957), Rosenfeld (1971), Sohn (1985) – have begun to discriminate between various aspects of projective identification, in particular, between more or less disturbed forms of projective identification. Bion distinguished between projecting whole parts of oneself into the object, more easily re-integrated; and what he called pathological paranoid anxiety, in which the infant attacks and fragments his ego with great violence, and those fragments are projected into the object, fragmenting it so that it becomes what he calls bizarre objects, fragments of objects containing fragments of ego imbued with extreme hostility, like the fragmentation of the self into the scattered flowers by my Ophelia patient.

A similar scatter was shown by another patient of mine, who had a hallucination of being attacked by thousands of little computers possessing his brain. The thousands of computers invading his brain we identified first as my interpretations, but those computers were also returning fragments of the results of an omnipotent fantasy he had which ran for weeks, having to do with installing computers in all the schools through which he would be able to control all the education in England. Fragments of himself were supposed to be lodged in every school in the country. Bion describes the bizarre object as a fragment of the object containing a fragment of the projected ego imbued with great hostility. That is what the patient's computers were – a bit of him inside a bit of me invading his mind with the utmost hostility.

But this fragmentation is only one possibility of a bad relation between what Bion called the container and the contained (Bion 1963). I think that clinically one can detect the move from paranoid anxiety to paranoia partly by the degree to which not only impulses and fantasies, but also the judging parts of the ego, are projected into the object, robbing the subject of his mind. My patient vested his intelligence and judgement in the computers, which then came back to judge him.

I think it also depends on the degree of completeness of identification; that is, the degree of omnipotence. When the infant projects into the parental figure he may retain an experience of being contained even if he attributes to the container some of their own characteristics, like dangerous greed, hostility or possessiveness. The projections may nevertheless be modified by the mother's understanding, and as a result loosened and re-internalized. But if the degree of identification is such that the experience of containment is totally lost and the object just becomes completely identical with the self, modification short of understanding that process is not possible. And this makes it extremely important technically to interpret it at the right level – and certainly not to attempt to reverse the projection by a simple interpretation of projection.

This is shown very neatly by an interpretation made by a supervisee of mine. A patient who had been for a long time on the waiting list of the clinic, having originally come with the anxiety of being a homosexual, had, unknown to my candidate, become psychotic during the waiting period. When, after a short preliminary interview, he came to his first session, he glared at the couch, and said, 'I will not lie down for you. I lay down and submitted to men often enough.' His looks and his demeanour, as well as the communication, clearly conveyed that he was in a completely deluded state. The candidate responded by saying, 'You are afraid that I shall not be able to distinguish between psychoanalytic treatment and buggery.' This communication made the patient relax almost immediately, and the psychoanalytic process had started.

The candidate picked up immediately not only that the patient himself made a concrete identification between lying on the couch and analysis and his homosexual experience; he also understood that the confusion was projected by the patient into him, and not only was the homosexuality projected into him, but also the psychotic functioning itself. Later in the treatment it appeared that in the waiting period, unable to tolerate the waiting, the patient did have his first homosexual experience and became psychotic after it. He obviously equated the first session of analysis with his homosexual experience.

Obviously, the experience of this patient was very concrete, in keeping with my description of concrete symbolism and Bion's description of Alpha and Beta elements. According to Bion, the infant's first experience is largely what Bion calls Beta elements – inchoate, fragmentary and concrete elements of experience. The only thing the infant can do with them is to project them outwards into the maternal breast. If the mother responds adequately to this experience of anxiety projected into her, the infant can re-introject those Beta elements, converting them by mother's under-standing into Alpha elements of thought and feeling. The infant can also introject the maternal container, the mental space and the mother's Alpha function, which is the ability to convert Beta into Alpha. Operating on Beta elements is the hallmark of psychotic thinking.

I want to illustrate how this process of conversion of Alpha into Beta can also be reversed. The patient who had the computer episode has now been twelve years in analysis with me. He has had two severe psychotic breakdowns, one right at the beginning of the treatment, necessitating hospitalization for several weeks, and one, later, for only a couple of days. Since that time he had a few psychotic episodes: the one about the computers some years ago, and a more recent one two years ago. All these were contained in the analysis, and he shows considerable improvement in his personality and the quality of his life in general, with great improvement in his professional life and considerable changes in his sexuality.

The last episode, which happened during his wife's pregnancy, was connected with bad and fraudulent building work on his attic, which he had undertaken in a very manic way. It led to the collapse of the roof, and the patient had a short and violent manic episode followed by deep psychotic depression. Both mania and depression were accompanied by violent paranoia and delusions about his builders, and enormous murderousness towards them.

Since then, his fear of madness has often been contained in dreams about flooded houses, collapsing roofs and attics, and so on. There is a reference to that in the material I want to present. It is also important to know that ever since he entered analysis this patient, who is a scientist, has been planning to write a book which would revolutionize physics and which would put in their place all the great theories that he admires. Even though his intellectual functioning has improved, and he in fact has written many interesting articles during his analysis, the book is still the great aim.

On Friday two weeks ago he had a dream. In the dream there was a dinner party and he was sitting opposite me. R was also there, sitting on a potty and looking self-important. Sometime during the party a small child started screaming and I was trying to deal with him in a very competent and professional manner. In fact R has just published a book which is the object of great envy for the patient; and the patient, together with some other friends, are organizing a party for R. He had also heard in the past from friends about a dinner party in my house, at which R was a guest. Sitting on the potty is very much linked with the patient's past, in which his omnipotent attitude was often depicted in dreams as sitting on a pot like a king on a throne and producing marvellous, huge stools.

I will not go into the details of that session, but the dream is clearly a reversal of both the party for R's book and the party many years ago which R attended in my house. The party is for my patient and the excluded-child part of the patient (the weekend) is split and projected. His real feelings are put into the screaming child, and his omnipotent 'king-on-the-pot' into R.

The patient was quite able to follow my interpretations and much of the dream was understandable to him, and the emotions were quite vivid. At some point he shouted, 'It's my party, so I can do what I please with it!' – and then felt abashed as I pointed out to him that the actual party was supposed to be for R, with his, the patient's, help.

I shall give you the Monday session in fair detail, to show why this patient, who on Friday functioned on a very neurotic level, was, and may be still, threatened by a return of psychosis.

He was a few minutes late, which always worries him, and said he was late because he was browsing in a book shop. (This is still connected with the book; he is planning to apply for a grant to give himself time to get on with it, but has gradually begun to think in the sessions that his research project is still very vague and grandiose, and that even if he did get the grant he would feel very fraudulent about it.) He was also delayed by a deaf man asking him for directions in the street as he left the Tube.

He then said that the weekend was quite good, but he felt worried because his dreams, which seemed to him good to begin with, became very troubling later. The first dream was that there was some flooding into the house. A small pipe was leaking in the attic, but he found some simple wooden gadget with which he could hinge the pipe and then direct it to a big pipe outside. Later on in the dream he was looking at a model. He was on the way to sitting an examination, and looking at the model he wondered whether that model was really good enough to sustain his research plan.

He then had a few associations, first about the relief that the pipe stopped leaking; and to the Friday session, in which he thought that the links I had made about his dream of the party brought him great relief. That must have been the wooden gadget. He then had some associations, which sounded to me perfunctory and bookish, about the pipes being maybe small and big penises. (He is very given to such bookish associations, and yet at the end of the session I realize that they also have a deeper significance.) The gist of our understanding of these two dreams was that after feeling unhinged he felt hinged again, and this enabled him to take a saner look, not only at the model of his book but also at the model of his mind, and he was more willing to examine it more critically.

But the next dream he said was very much on the old lines. And then it became very fragmented and he woke up very worried. He was sitting beside Susan. They were joking about cunts. He did not know what the joke was. But when he woke up he felt very uneasy about it. Susan is married to C, one of the great intellectual heroes of my patient. My patient knew her before and he associated that he felt he had some power over her because of the things he knew. She told him that her first boyfriend left her because he was put off by her screaming at the point of orgasm. He also held it against her that she was Jewish and hid the fact from his friends. The patient also felt guilty towards her because he made a nasty anti-Semitic joke about her: when she borrowed a book from him he told friends that she gets her books the Jewish way. He himself got several books recently the same way. He does not like Susan. She is very envious of her brother, but uses the fact that her brother wrote a book to bugger him, the patient, with. He is also very jealous of Susan being married to such a man as C. He immediately recognized that Susan's screaming at orgasm must have something to do with the screaming child (himself in the Friday session and over the weekend). And he is again confronted with a most enviable couple: R as my dinner guest and Susan married to C. The woman screaming at orgasm is very significant because the patient used to be very promiscuous in a very cruel way, projecting the screaming into women by his sexuality.

After some talk about this dream, he returned to the weekend. His neice, Susie, who was staying in their house, was not very well and he got up several times to look after her. He had the usual worry of being either too brutal or too seductive. He then had very fragmented and troubled dreams. His first dream was about Susie. She was horribly mutilated by someone having raped her vaginally and buggered her with some wooden peg. Then he was looking into the mirror and found some horrible growth in his ear. He associated the rape and buggery of Susie with his usual anxiety about his relation to his neices, and then looking into the mirror he connected with his habit as a child and as an adolescent of trying to see his anus in the mirror, a very complicated gymnastic procedure, and also to the fact that he often masturbated anally with a wooden brush. He had not noticed two significant features: first, that Susan and Susie have the same name; and, second, the re-appearance of the wooden peg – a link to the first dream of the very helpful wooden gadget.

101

He was again, as on Friday, faced with the enviable couple, particularly in this case envy of me as the woman who makes helpful interpretations, and he deals with it in phantasy by a violent intrusion, raping and buggering me, converting the grown-up Susan into the dependent child Susie. He also chooses a woman, Susan, into whom he can project his screams by raping and buggering her, and filling her with envy. This is accomplished by the wooden gadget. I think this in a way is the crux of the dream.

The Friday session was felt by him as my making links which were emotional and mental. This brought him a great relief, and he was able to subject his own state of mind to an examination. But the same wooden gadget which plays this helpful role in the first dream becomes his possession and becomes completely concretized: it becomes a wooden gadget with which he can bugger me up and explains how he tried to bugger the session up by the profuse and disconnected associations to penises mentioned earlier. The Alpha element has been transformed back into a Beta element. The mental link became the concrete object, both his possession and an element that can only be used for projection.

One could argue that I chose a very insignificant element of the dream to which to attach so much importance, but it seems to me very much the crux of the matter. The patient can be helped to function in a less concrete way, but there is still a core of Beta functioning and, under the stimulus of deprivation and increase of jealousy and envy, he reverts to it and transforms the Alpha elements back into Beta.

Like the patient I described with the gastric ulcer, this patient still communicates with me through dreams and associations. Nevertheless, he himself is very aware that his dreams are 'blueprints for acting out'. They define how he is going to function during the day. The acting out in this session was minimal: being delayed by the books and the deaf man. But he still spends a large part of his time living in an imaginary world, and recently he spoke of living in a world of duplicates, the duplicates being a combined him and me, a sort of hybrid figure which he projects everywhere.

But to return to the paranoia, the dream of Susie reveals what he does to me in his phantasy where I am turned into this buggered-up child; but the dream about his ear is a paranoid dream. The growth in his ear is the same as the computers. It is my words that become a cancer in his ear. But he does not let those words in. He forms in his ear a sort of Beta-element screen that prevents my words from penetrating any deeper. It is truly a deaf man that has made him late for the session in which he will have to listen to my words.

Note

1 This chapter has been published previously (Segal, 1994b).

9

Termination: sweating it out[1]

I have entitled my paper 'Sweating it out' because this patient had had as one of his symptoms profuse and offensively smelling sweating – really smelling of fear – and the last few months of the analysis he again sweated a few times on the couch. And those last months one could say he was really 'sweating it out'. Freud once observed that at the end of the analysis patients sometimes revert temporarily to the early symptoms. This has not been frequently my experience. More often – and this was markedly the case with that patient – old themes are taken up. Anxieties are reawakened, defences of the past remobilized in sessions, but not necessarily resulting in the re-appearance of symptoms; as in this patient, termination was a time of working-through, sweating it out, at times with a great deal of pain. What he had to work through was the final facing of separateness and separation with all the attendant anxieties and depression. The patient had always been exceedingly sensitive to separation. In the early years of his analysis he was regularly physically ill before or during holidays.

He was virtually symptom-free over several years. When he started, his sexual life was in a mess. He was very perverse, mostly in fantasy, but also in acting out. He was, in turn, grandiose and feeling disintegrated by anxiety, occasionally transitorily hallucinating. In previously describing this patient (Mr R. in chapter 7), I emphasized his pathological and excessive use of projective identification and identified the moment when he came out of it, which was one of the turning points of his analysis. He is now very happily married with a family of two children, very successful in his profession, a very gifted and respected physicist.

He remained a fairly anxious person and is still inhibited in reading and writing, though in the last few years he started writing papers. (As a child he was so inhibited intellectually that he was discouraged from taking A levels – willing but not intelligent enough, was the school's verdict.) In fact, he is very bright and once out of his difficulties, he achieved good

103

academic status. But throughout his childhood and adolescence he was lost in a permanent day-dream.

His reasons for staying in analysis were mainly his realization of remaining character weaknesses – for instance, a tendency to placation, and insufficient courage in standing up for his ideas and his fear of regressing, should he stop. He was very worried, for instance, about occasional recrudescence of nasty pornographic fantasies when thwarted or anxious. But underlying that was a fantasy that analysis was, or would end in, a marriage between us – a marriage in which he would fuse with me and eventually would become me. The only way of separating from me which would not expose him to jealousy or envy would be by becoming me. For instance, sometime before Easter (his analysis was to finish at the end of July) he had read Melanie Klein's *Narrative of a Child Analysis* (1961) which he referred to as 'Richard'. He dreamed that he was writing 'Richard' and felt embarrassed telling me the dream. Not being able to maintain that he was Mrs Klein/me exposed him to recognizing violent feelings he found hard to bear. The day after the Richard dream he was worried because he bought boots with sheepskin linings. They were very expensive, and he felt guilty towards his family. But he also felt very guilty about the sheep – killing them to get into their skin. On the way to the session, mixed with thinking about the sheepskins, he realized he was also thinking about my funeral – how would it be? He thought he dreamed of metal coffins. He also noticed that, passing a funeral, he again started to salivate as he always had in the past.

This cannibalistic fantasy (he had many others of that kind) was at the service of projective identification – biting his way into me to get into my skin. This was a defence against loss, but also, and predominantly, against envy. He recognized with a lot of pain that he just could not stand the thought of me being better known as an analyst than he was in his field and his own feeling that his papers were not up to mine, Klein's or Freud's; he did not write Richard!

The patient had resorted again to the projective identification so prominent at the beginning (becoming Mrs Klein, getting into my skin). This led to the experience that the working-through of his projective and cannibalistic wishes was felt by him as my expelling him from inside me. For several days he had been surly, feeling, as he told me, that all he wanted to do was to stay on the couch and to sulk. Then he brought the following dream.

He was late for a student who, he felt, was very rejecting of him. He was giving him a tutorial in a dreary basement. Then he drove out and it was, as he said, like a dream within a dream. He thought, 'I know these crossroads. That's where I had a terrible fight with an obstetrician. I saw my head covered with blood. As I told you, it was like a dream within a dream.' He associated to the student in the dream that he was also about to terminate his course. The student represented himself rejecting me, and his being late for the student represented his unwillingness to face that aspect of himself. Curiously, though at this stage he was very perceptive about his dreams, he had no associations to the crossroads with which he was familiar and his head being bloodied in his fight with the obstetrician. I suggested that the familiar crossroads were his fantasies of birth. He then realized that he was not sure if the blood was his own; in fact, his bloodied head reminded him of the birth of his first son – a forceps birth which was very traumatic. For a time brain damage was suspected. Following that he remembered another bit of the dream. The choice he had at the crossroads was one road leading to the downs full of rabbit holes. The other, probably the right one, led through a territory unknown to him. He associated to the end of the treatment and his choice of being born and facing the unknown future or trying to hide again inside the analysis like a womb or a rabbit hole – 'To be or not to be.' He often felt bitter about his cowardice, looking for holes to hide in.

For several days he struggled with this problem. He realized again something familiar from the past – that in my building he was all eyes, ears and nose, and had a fantasy that he knew everything that was going on in me and my house. He had a dream of being in bed with his mother, legitimately he said, as his father was out. There was some return of violent and cannibalistic fantasies. He once started the session by complaining of the district he lived in, which was a bit slummy, saying there was too much violence – 'I can't afford to live there' – with a determination to move to Hampstead where I live. It was clear he felt he could not afford to separate off from me because of the violence which it stimulated in him. He talked to a friend who terminated analysis a year before and complained that R, her analyst, pushed her out, but kept her blue-eyed boys (two members of his professional team).

That night he dreamed that he was in analysis with R, but the session paradoxically lasted only twenty-five minutes. Then he was in a session with me. He was silent, and I said, 'It seems you don't want to be helped by me.' He then experienced a wave of absolute fury and hatred and had a determination not to tell me anything. But then he did tell me in the dream, whatever it was, and the atmosphere in the session changed and he was full of affection. He obviously found it hard to give up his fantasy of his being my blue-eyed boy whom I would keep forever and, to begin with, was full of fury. He did not want to be helped, because to be helped meant to be helped to finish his analysis and face both separation and his envy of being helped. In the dream, however, when he could get in touch with the feeling, he overcame the fury and love came back. The next night he dreamed that there was a house on the hill which looked very nice and of which he was very fond, but it was quite clear to him that the house wasn't his.

105

When he could face his separateness from me, the Oedipal themes returned. For instance, just before Easter he dreamed of M working in the British Museum Library and he hated him for working in his library. He has heard someone referring to M and myself in the same breath. After Easter he had a dream of being a Polish insurgent who attacked violently someone whom he thought was a Polish oppressor on a railway track. He knew I was Polish. He associated the railway track with his return to analysis. But he also said that the Polish oppressor wasn't nearly as terrible as it was made out to be. The oppressive Polish government did not compare, for instance, with Chile or South Africa. The oppressive, hated father he linked with his stepfather, whom he considered a tyrant. Soon thereafter, having been quite difficult, he became very affectionate and smiling. I had become his real father, but one felt to be easily homosexually seducible. His father had died when the boy was 12, and his mother remarried. He dreamed that when he was 16, his father returned. It turned out that his father hadn't died but merely left mother for another woman. He felt enormous love and relief. From various associations and his seductive smiles at me, it was clear that the other woman was himself. He was very upset at recognizing that at work he found himself again placating and seductive to dominant male figures. There had always been a difficulty with this patient to maintain a good father figure without homosexualizing it. There was a split between his stepfather and his father. He hated his stepfather who, he felt, was a tyrant. The father, on the other hand, was often felt (I think without very realistic grounds) as being open to homosexual seduction and alliance against women. This became crystal clear in those last months of treatment. He recognized that there was a great deal of strength, masculinity, and positive guidance that he received from his stepfather despite some of his rigidity and severity. On the other hand, his own father was less soft than in the patient's fantasy. The problem was of tolerating the jealousy or envy of a father who could be potent, good and not homosexual.

He had a dream about a watch given to him by a much admired uncle. In the dream, he had in the past paid an enormous repair bill to get it repaired. Now the bill was much smaller, but he realized that he was very reluctant to pay it. He boasted to somebody that he had a wonderful watch repairer, but that person told him, 'Ah, but he's an alcoholic, he is no good.' The analysis of the split between the father and the stepfather mobilized the envy of the potent analyst/father who could give him a watch (reality sense) and was a wonderful repairer. The watch and the repairer were both devalued. He was too mean to acknowledge the debt and repay it, though he acknowledged that the cost was not great. Meanness of a pathological nature was a marked feature of his character, which greatly altered in his analysis.

He recalled that there was another part of the dream, very vague, 'having to do with loops on railway lines and going round the bend'. He said he had messed up some appointments at work and didn't work very well. No wonder he thought he was going round the bend – becoming loopy – if he could not look after his analysis 'watch'.

In June I had to take a week off. The most primitive phantasies and defences reappeared. He remembered dreams of two nights during the break. The first lot he thought was more positive, but the second one was a terrible nightmare. In the first dream he was in a desolate landscape in exile. He was aware that his analyst had gone, but in the dream it meant that everything else was gone too – for instance, his place of work and his home. He felt desolate and anxious, but he also felt that somehow he could manage on what he had within himself.

In the second dream that same night his little boy lost a milk tooth, but the new one was already there; so there was no gap, no pain. The little milk tooth was also like a drop of curdled milk. He thought those dreams meant that he could manage the weaning and the loss, even if it felt as if he had lost everything. I thought, however, that the end of the second dream contained a denial. There was no gap, no pain. But his dream later in the week, the patient said, was a terrible nightmare. In the first part he was conferring with a child oncologist, discussing a child who may have been mentally deficient or may have had a brain cancer. That reminded him of how he had always been convinced that he was mentally deficient and that his fear had left him in the last few years. But the second part of the dream was terrible. He was holding his baby son who was horribly mutilated. He was only a mouth. The patient could not feed him because he had no inside. He had no senses – no sight, no hearing, not even a sense of touch. The only way to save him and re-unite him with himself was to give him to his mother. So it seemed that when I, the mother, went, all went with me, including most of himself. In this dream he came back to the most violent and primitive projective identification in which he put into me his sense organs, his insides, and left himself mentally deficient and unable to introject – he could not be fed. This dream recalled again severe mutilations to his mental apparatus which were prominent in the early years of his analysis and made him dread that he was mentally deficient or mad. The analysis of this was followed by a great deal of relief and improvement.

In a later session he said that the paper which he thought he would never finish, to his surprise was nearly done. He related a number of positive developments, including the fact that a mess he had made quarrelling with the head of his department – one that made him anxious for several days and that he thought was irreparable – he quite easily cleared up as soon as he could admit his own mistake.

He had a dream, in which he was in a kind of mess, maybe a reference to the mess he made in his head. He went to the home of his friend, David. All the family was there. He was acutely aware that he was not a member of the family, but he was welcome. After a time he left David's home and felt very different – confident that he could clear up any difficulties. He associated that David was a very good leader, and it was as though he himself, through staying in David's house, had acquired this characteristic. He commented on how different this dream was from many other dreams or fantasies in which he was invading David's house and ending by getting off, with him, either excluding the wife or the wife excluding him. His dream was reminiscent of the one of the house on the hill which did not belong to him, but it included the whole family. It also emphasized that when he was not intrusive and possessive, then he felt welcome and free to choose what he wished to identify with. It signified a renewed withdrawal of intrusive projective identifications with sexual parents which underlay his perverse sexuality. But it also linked with his growing recognition that, though I represented his parents, I was not even family. He was a visitor in my house. The analysis of that dream and associated thoughts eventually centred on a renewed mourning in relation to his father. Until he came to analysis he had not mourned his father at all after his death. He just became ill and even more withdrawn than he had been previously. In analysis he was able to mourn his father. But he told me now that he could never mourn his father completely so long as I was there because he had a father in me. It was only at the end of analysis that he could face that he really had no father.

In the last two weeks of analysis he was preoccupied with death. He always had a terror of death to the point of thinking that if there was death, then life was not worth living. Part of his avoidance of separateness was that separateness is the first intimation of death. He started a session saying, 'I have two dreams about my death. In the first one I learned that in 2017 the world will disappear. It wasn't through a catastrophe of nuclear explosions like in my previous dreams. It was just that the world will run out of fuel or life. The earth will get exhausted – or just entropy.' He associated to the conversations with his father, whom he often asked, 'What will I be like in such and such a year?' And the father would tell him, 'You will be grown up, or married, or old.' But they never reached a point at which the father would say, 'By then you will be dead.' Neither had the courage to face it. His father died when he was 70. He himself will be 76 in 2017. Maybe, he said, he allowed himself the benefit of a new average life expectancy. But he seemed somewhat uneasy.

In the second dream he was in bed and his wife with a child went upstairs. He was left quite alone and resigned. He had let them go. There was an evolution in his thoughts about death. As he noted in his

108

associations, he used to think of death as the result of destructiveness – atomic explosions. When we originally agreed on the date of termination, he had numerous dreams of war, atomic explosions and so on.

In these dreams, death was a natural event; there was also an evolution as between the first and second dream. In the first dream he took the world with him. But in the second dream he was resigned to dying alone and allowing the others to live. The acceptance of the end of his analysis, birth, separateness, weaning, Oedipal renunciation – all these were experiences allowing him to live as a separate individual, but they were also a preparation for death. I was also a representative of death to him. This was clear in the next session. He felt frightened of me and did not know why. Then it turned out that he was frightened because the date 2017 in the dream was a cheat and he knew it should have been 2010 and he did not tell me. (It had to do with a mistaken date in his driving licence.) So he was still trying to cheat death, and cheating death and cheating me were the same thing.

What am I trying to say in this paper? Some may think that a patient who has such primitive fantasies and defences and resists the ending so much is not ready to stop. That was what my patient often tried to make me think. I had few doubts that this decision was right. What are my criteria? Very broadly, I could say that my criterion would be a sufficient move from the paranoid-schizoid position, with a predominance of splitting, projective identification and fragmentation, to the depressive position, with a better capacity to relate to internal and external objects. In the depressive position the patient has to face separateness, conflict, as in the dream of the session in which he hated me, and an integration of hatred. He has to bear loss and anxiety, as in the dream of the exile, and has to be able to internalize a good experience and learn from experience, as in his dream of the visit to David's house. Part of this working-through is also an eventual acceptance of death – particularly at his age – just past mid-life.

The complete resolution of the depressive position is never achieved. It was the patient's fantasy that one day he would be free of fluctuations. In his mind that meant becoming like me – perfect. In fact, fluctuations remain throughout life. The assessment has to be about the severity and persistence of bad states of mind. In this patient the fact of ending re-awakened the most primitive phantasies and defences. But the situation was very different from that at the beginning of his analysis. The symptoms were minimal and the regressions were mostly contained in dreams, fantasies and the sessions. He was not getting stuck at any point. He was very quick to perceive what was going on in him and could tolerate a lot of pain and anxiety. He would say, for instance, with great pain, 'The moment your back is turned, I am up to my old tricks.' Whereas in the past he had acted out in relationships and symptoms, he now could tolerate the knowledge of disturbing parts of himself. He had internalized a good analytic experience enough to re-establish good internal objects and to internalize the psychoanalytic function of self-awareness. This is illustrated by one of his last dreams.

He dreamed of a gadget which had five U tubes. His association was to 'you', meaning me – five being five sessions. It also reminded him of a piece of equipment, a manometer that went wrong at Chernobyl. But it also reminded him of a gadget associated with his work as a very young man. A friend who was a hospital consultant was looking for ways to measure directly the blood pressure of the vena cava in cases of suspected internal haemorrhage. He had an idea how it could be done and entrusted my patient with working out a suitable instrument, which he did very successfully; the very next day after the gadget was delivered by the workshop, it probably saved the life of a young man. Neither he nor the consultant ever published this result.

This last association was surprising. We were familiar with a pattern in which (before his analysis) he would become someone's blue-eyed boy and invariably failed to live up to his promise, abandoning or messing up any piece of research he was entrusted with. He never before had told me of this success. He had never made this result public to me or even to himself until now. I think that this U-tube gadget is a manometer to warn him of possible disasters (Chernobyl) and is the analytic function he had internalized. And this is associated also with a rediscovery and re-owning of constructive successful parts of himself. He is the young man whose life has been saved – something he can now allow himself and me to know. It is published between us.

Note

1 This chapter has been published previously (Segal, 1988).

10

The uses and abuses of counter-transference[1]

The concept of counter-transference may be used in many different ways. Freud (1910b) considered that the analyst should take an objective view of the patient and that the feelings that are aroused in him are due to the counter-transference; that is, the transference onto patients of feelings about some objects in the past. I think nowadays it is recognized that the analyst does have feelings about the patient and that indeed those feelings may often be a useful clue about the way the patient is relating to him. It does not of course exclude the kind of counter-transference described by Freud; that is, an interference in the psychoanalytic process by the analyst's own unrecognized problems.

Most analysts use the term 'counter-transference' broadly to cover all feelings or phantasies aroused in the analyst in relation to the patient, whatever their origin. I think the way we approach counter-transference now has partly to do with the change in our views on transference, and first of all on how transference affects the analyst. We do not quite believe in the objective, totally detached observer. Up to a point analysts do have a transference onto the patient in that we do transfer aspects of earlier object relationships onto any new significant object, and there is no doubt that patients are significant objects in the analysts' lives. The question is more about the nature of the feelings; to what extent the infantile aspects of our own selves are contained and modified and do not distort perception and objective assessment. We also view differently the transference that the patient has on the analyst; while in the past we spoke of the patient projecting *onto* the analyst, more commonly we – or at least some of us – think now in terms of the patient projecting *into* the analyst. When we think of a patient projecting onto the analyst we think in terms of misperceptions of the analyst due to the patient's phantasies. We do not think of it as in any way affecting the analyst. When we think of projecting into an analyst we think of the patient aiming at affecting the mind of the analyst, in an attempt to actualize (to use Sandler's term) or act in his phantasies (Sandler, 1976). When this attempt succeeds, our counter-transference is affected to some extent, sometimes to a considerable extent.

This view of transference and counter-transference, which I share, is based on the idea of projective identification, particularly as elaborated by Bion (1962, 1963). In his view, projective identification is not only an omnipotent phantasy in the infant's mind but also a most primitive method of communication, in that the infant has a great capacity to evoke feelings in parental objects, to begin with by completely non-verbal means. This kind of non-verbal communication is always involved in discourse. We do not communicate with one another like computers. There is always a plethora of non-verbal communication which adds depth and meaning to our interchanges, not only in analysis. But sometimes, and in analysis in particular, this non-verbal acting-in (and I include in this, speech used for acting-in) is predominant and is not a background to and accompaniment of other communication; on the contrary, it can be a disruption to more symbolic forms of communication. It is useful to distinguish between what is pre- or non-verbal and what is anti-verbal. Non-verbal is often communicative. Anti-verbal is an attack on verbal communication and thought, to avoid contact, communication and insight. One must not assume that all non-verbal is acting-in and all verbal is communication. Speech itself can be used as an action; for instance, flooding the analyst with confused profuse material. Acting-in is usually motivated by the wish to get rid of unwanted parts of oneself and by the wish to affect the analyst's mind.

I will give a very gross example of this, one that stayed in my mind for many years and happened, I think, before the subject of counter-transference was in the forefront of our attention. When my patient, Mrs P, was a child, her mother was killed in a car accident, her father being the driver. One of her symptoms was an inability to learn to drive. After a few years' analysis, she learned to drive, both cars and motor cycles, and she was commuting to analysis from a nearby university town. She had always had a tendency to negative therapeutic reactions, but this particular improvement mobilized it strongly, and she became quite manic. In those days I was probably not very skilful at detecting her very skilful projective identifications.

One day she gave me a rather frightening account of how recklessly she drove her motor bike. The next day, she missed the session without letting me know – which had never happened before. I was exceedingly anxious, and also guilty, wondering what I could have done wrong to induce her to have an accident. The next day, she turned up, cool as a cucumber, and I was furious. I recognized, however, that she had inflicted on me an experience of her own, of waiting for her parents to return home, and

112

being told of the accident. But that recognition came to me only after her return. In between I had been dominated by her projections.

This is a very gross example, and the projection easily recognizable. It refers to a very traumatic experience in childhood, rather than in infancy, but the power of the projection, which affected my state of mind, derived from its being rooted in a more primitive infantile state of mind and mode of operation. We do know how often patients seek to stir our anxiety, curiosity, jealousy, anger and so on. Most of the time we can recognize these patterns, and not be unduly affected – maybe just enough to alert us to what is going on. But in some situations the patient can significantly affect the analyst's peace of mind. The degree to which we are affected is, I think, related to how primitive and disturbed the projective experience is. The nearer patients are to psychosis the more they operate by primitive projective identification, and the more we have to rely on our counter-transference; but also the harder it is to experience it and understand it. Mrs P was not psychotic, and though she regressed to using a very primitive way of communicating, the experience projected was not psychotic, and was relatively easy to recognize, as at that point it was not fragmented.

This was not the case with a borderline patient, Miss X. Her major complaint on coming to analysis was her unpopularity. I should not have been surprised, but I was, at the degree to which I came to dislike her myself – and this despite feeling sorry for her and understanding how much she suffered through her parents' illnesses. The experience of closeness with her was an experience of almost unceasing discomfort or pain. She evoked anxiety, confusion, guilt, anger, irritation; occasions on which I felt more relaxed were dangerous. I was immediately and unexpectedly assaulted in some way or other. Her stream of accusations was almost incessant.

This patient was the child of parents who had hated one another at the time of her birth. So far as I can reconstruct, from infancy she was flooded with extreme anxiety by her mother, an anxiety neurotic, and with hatred derivative of her mother's hatred for her father. The father, on the other hand, a near psychotic, flooded her with either aggressive accusations or gross sexuality. She described how, after she was older and her parents divorced, her father would pour accusations and complaints about her mother at her and how, when she was with her mother, the mother on a few occasions pinned her to the armchair and made her listen to violent attacks on the father. This latter situation probably reproduced what was originally a non-verbal but violent experience of projection from both parents.

In the counter-transference, it was this experience that she tried to inflict on me, often with success. I frequently felt with her that I was pinned into my armchair and forced to listen to violent outpourings of accusation against some third person. I felt attacked; I did not want to hear them and could not defend myself against them. The experience is not that of a parent bombarded by infantile projections, but of an infant bombarded by overpowering projections, often beyond its understanding. This lends to the counter-transference feelings of a particular kind of helplessness, and there is always a danger of reacting by withdrawal, omnipotence, hatred of the patient and so on – in other words, of mobilizing our own infantile defences against helplessness. We are all familiar, of course, with patients reversing roles and putting us in the position of a helpless child. But here I think there was an added dimension; that of projecting into the analyst the experience of a child being projected into, which gives to the counter-transference a particular kind of helplessness, which Grinberg calls 'projective counter-transference' (Grinberg, 1962). Miss X was a border-line case, and her method of projecting infantile experiences into the analyst may be what protected her from psychosis.

In the psychotic, counter-transference is the most striking feature, and is often very hard to understand. In my paper 'Depression in the schizophrenic' (Segal, 1956), I described a hebephrenic girl who had not spoken for weeks. She was obviously dominated by hallucinations of a very violent kind, and kept grimacing, jerking, pulling threads out of the couch and breaking them up. There was a feeling of great violence and fear in the sessions. All I could catch in her mutterings, or occasional screams, were some references to God and the Devil, and I could interpret something about her splitting. After weeks of this behaviour, gradually her movements became more harmonious and less violent. She became remote and smiling in a very cut-off way. And I was gradually invaded by extreme depression. The more her movements became like a kind of dance, the more desperate I became; till one day, while dancing around the room, she seemed to be picking up imaginary things from the carpet and making movement as though she was scattering something round the room. And it struck me that she must have been imagining that she was dancing in a meadow, picking flowers and scattering them. And it occurred to me that she was behaving exactly like an actress playing Ophelia. As the patient in the past had identified with characters in books or plays, I felt on fairly secure ground in saying to her, 'It seems to me that you are being Ophelia'. She immediately stopped and said 'Oh yes, of course.' And then she added sadly, 'Ophelia was mad, wasn't she?' It was the first time she admitted that she knew about her own madness. For the rest of the session she spoke to me in a saner way than ever before. I could interpret to her that she felt she contained a dead father-lover in her, and that the experience was so unbearable she was breaking it up into little fragments which she was throwing into me so that I should become depressed and fragmented. Instead of being a single individual I became a scattered audience. The next

114

day she was very persecuted, dreading that I was going to push the fragments back into her. But again she became sane for a while when this was interpreted.

In these examples one could see that the patients projected into me their own experiences. But this of course is not always the case. Sometimes the deciphering of the nature of the experience is quite difficult and we do not know who we are in the transference. Sometimes it is internal objects that are projected, and the analyst is induced, often in very subtle ways not easy to recognize, to act out for the patient some object in the past. In the case of Miss X, it was very difficult to disentangle whom I represented in the transference. Sometimes it was a part of herself; sometimes her father persecuting or seducing; sometimes her cut-off and accusatory mother. But those objects were also infused by her own projections. For instance, the sexual father was also clearly seduced by her sexual bombardments. I could see in the counter-transference how easy it was to become persecuting under the sway of her provocations.

I find it easiest to think of the transference/counter-transference in terms of Bion's model of the container and the contained. The patient projects into the analyst unassimilated, un-worked-through parts of their inner world, as in Bion's description of the infant projecting Beta elements into mother. The analyst has a feeling response to them, but also an understanding of them, and containment is this understanding. Then, if this can be conveyed back to the patient, at an appropriate moment, the Beta elements are modified by the analyst's capacity to contain the feelings and understand them, and transformed into Alpha elements capable of being used by the patient. I would emphasize that the essential element of containment is the analyst's understanding. It is true that the psycho-analytical setting is a condition *sine qua non* of containment and the patient's attacks on the containing function are often expressed as attacks on the setting. Similarly, the analyst's failure to contain often takes the form of altering the setting, sometimes with apparently good motives: wishing to accommodate the patient, for example. But the setting itself is not sufficient for a psychoanalytic containing; it is only an essential condition of it.

Silence alone is sometimes considered to be containing, but although often necessary to allow the patient time to express himself, it does not by itself provide a dynamic containment. In my *Introduction to the Work of Melanie Klein* (1964), I spoke of a borderline patient who, after many sessions with a silent analyst, started to hallucinate. Her experience of the silence was a total lack of containment during which thoughts became pictures which terrified her. That patient was in fact, herself a silent patient for a long time, but when her silences were understood and interpreted, gradually a meaningful dialogue emerged and she never hallucinated.

115

I think that the counter-transference experiences which are produced in us by the patient can only be understood and modified if the analyst has what I would call a good counter-transference disposition. It is a basic disposition which allows us to be receptive to projections without becoming identified with them.

How is such a disposition achieved by the analyst? It must include the analyst's capacity to be in contact with their own infantile experience, which resonates with those of the patient; and to be in touch with it without being overwhelmed by it. This necessitates being identified with a maternal container capable of containing both the patient's and the analyst's infantile selves. But there is also a part of the analyst which enables them to look at the interplay between the patient's feelings and their own. The analyst looks at the container–contained interaction from a neutral point of view. So I am in fact describing a triangular situation, a feeling interaction between the patient and that part of the analyst which is receptive and responsive to the patient's feelings, and an observer and interpreter of this interaction.

The way I visualize it is that when our counter-transference is in a good functional state we have a double relation to the patient: one is receptive, feeling, containing; the other is observing the process, and understanding the patient's communication and the interaction between their and our feelings. It is also active, producing or giving understanding and structure by interpretation. Both maternal and paternal functions are involved, and a good counter-transference disposition depends on an internalized good couple in the analyst's mind. This constellation of their own internal objects is what gives the analyst a capacity for understanding, strength and peace of mind, but this state of mind is often disrupted.

The triangular situation itself, the basis of the analyst's containment, comes under attack by a destructive part of the patient. It is true that projective identification is often used to communicate. But it is not only or always so, and often only partly so. It is also used for opposite reasons, to confuse the analyst and prevent understanding, and to attack the analyst's peace of mind, particularly in the context of the triangular situation.

I described how Miss X projected into me her experience of quarrelling parents who had projected into her. But at the same time she herself could not tolerate any two objects coming together otherwise than in mutual destructiveness. For instance, a recurring picture in her mind, symbolizing parental intercourse, were two wasps urinating and defecating into each other. I came to understand why I found it so intolerable when she pinned me into my armchair and poured a stream of hatred, contempt and abuse at some other object. I found it so intolerable because she was always attacking an imagined good internal object of mine. She particularly attacked the analytic method and what she suspected to be 'Kleinian' interpretations. In other patients this attack sometimes takes the form of the patient feeling a liking for the analyst as a person, but hatred of analysis and the analytical function. In this the patient also hates the analytic object to which his analyst is internally related. As a patient of mine put it, 'I hate this Freud in your mind.' Sometimes the analytic thinking or interpretation is felt as a hated third object interfering with the patient's wish for a dyad in which the patient's projections would take over and dominate the analyst, a point emphasized by Britton (1989,1991).

Some projections are intended to communicate the patient's state of mind. Others are meant to interfere with the analytical understanding. The patient attacks the analyst's functioning, good internal objects and peace of mind. And not being perfect, we are disturbed by this kind of projection. But if we understand our own disturbance, and its origin in the patient's functioning, then those projections too are converted into communications. They give us understanding, even though the patient may not want us to understand.

In the analyst's mind, too, there are elements hostile to this configuration, and this has also to be watched for, because Freud was not wrong in seeing the potential for interference in the analytical process by the analyst's unconscious and inappropriate feelings. I think what is involved is not only particular feelings about the patient, but an unconscious attack on the internal analytical object, similar to the attacks that arise from the patient.

We do know now that transference is mainly unconscious, and that the conscious feelings in the patient are derivatives of unconscious ones. But we often tend to forget that the same applies to the counter-transference And I think we must be very aware of the dangers of trusting our counter-transference too much. I think the idea of the counter-transference has become a bit too easy. For instance, it is used as an excuse for acting-in. An analyst will say, 'The patient projected it into me,' or 'He made me do it.' I remember a comment of Mrs Klein in a supervision, when the candidate said the patient projected his confusion into him; Mrs Klein commented, 'No, my dear, you just were confused.' The over-trust in our counter-transference, without sufficient objective backing, can often be misleading. Our conscious feelings are not always as trustworthy as we would wish them to be.

I would like to give an example which a candidate in supervision kindly allowed me to use. He had a very difficult patient, a severely withdrawn young woman, who missed sessions and was very silent. When she did speak she was usually very rejecting and castrating to him. The counter-transference was very hard to bear. On a Monday, at the beginning of the session, she said that she never had any strong feelings about her analysis, and did not see much point in it. Towards the end of the session, on very good evidence, the analyst interpreted how effectively she conveyed to him that she perceived him as quite ineffectual and useless. It was not a new interpretation – he had made it on other occasions. But on this occasion she had a most powerful emotional reaction. She burst into tears and said she felt horrible; that she did not want to make him feel like that at all; that it was not his fault at all, quite the contrary; and she was sobbing in an inarticulate way. The analyst mentioned that in contrast to what she had said at the beginning of the session she did seem to be deeply affected by what he had said. She tried to compose herself, and then tried to dismiss it, saying that it was not an unusual reaction for her – it could happen if she was reading a book or watching a film. She missed the next session, and in the session after that she was very scornful when the analyst tried to make a link with her reaction on Monday. For the rest of the week the sessions were very difficult; and the analyst, though making some reference to her strong emotional reaction on Monday, mainly concentrated on her reaction to the weekend and the impending holiday. On the Friday she was completely silent. The candidate told me that despite this behaviour all week he felt she was more in touch; and that in the Friday session, in which she was completely silent, he still felt it was not the hostile silence of the past, and that the patient was more in touch. He felt at ease.

It seemed to me that the use of his counter-transference – simply deducing her state of mind from his being more at ease – was very misleading. I knew that towards the end of that week he was in a very good mood for personal reasons. But also I felt, partly supported by a few bits of material the patient did produce in that week, that his counter-transference was not what he felt it was, in other words, that he felt in better contact. I very seldom comment to candidates about their counter-transference, but this candidate was so conscientious about describing his counter-transference, and to me this was so striking, that I told him what *I* thought his counter-transference was. I thought that not only was the patient absolutely overwhelmed by her emotional experience; but that he himself could not tolerate the violence and depth of her emotions, particularly guilt, and was very thankful that it was not repeated.

In fact, analyst and patient colluded in choosing a schizoid withdrawal rather than facing an intolerable sense of loss and guilt in either of them. The candidate took my comment very well, and took up this theme in the following week, which gave ample confirmation that the patient had been massively projecting into him intolerable guilt, and he had dealt with it by withdrawal. Looking at it retrospectively, we could see that the analyst's complacency was partly a function of the patient's projections, the intolerability of which induced his withdrawal. And in her other relationships that pattern sometimes appeared. People were often surprisingly tolerant of her aggressive and unpleasant or withdrawn

118

behaviour. But, as she complained, they were never really involved with her, and did not understand her at all. So, correctly understood, the analyst's counter-transference was informative about her relationships. But of course the analyst's counter-transference was unconscious. He did not know that he was frightened and colluding with her withdrawal. He mistook his complacency for an improvement in the patient. Here too a triangular situation was involved, and the supervisor was the one observing the interaction.

In a more experienced analyst that observer would be more internalized, and it would make him more suspicious of his too comfortable state of mind. We must both be aware of our counter-transference, and wary of it. We must never become so preoccupied with our own reaction that we lose sight of the patient's actual material and feelings. Generally, I think it is unwise to interpret on counter-transference alone, when not supported by observation of the patient's material. The counter-transference is only a clue; the material still has to be understood. We must always remember that counter-transference is the best of servants, but it must remain a servant because it is absolutely the worst of masters.

Note

1 This paper has been given in several versions at different meetings. It has not previously been published.

PART TWO

Literature and politics

— 11 —

Joseph Conrad and the mid-life crisis[1]

In 1895, when he was 37 years old, Joseph Conrad published his first book, *Almayer's Folly*. One could say that he made a meteoric appearance in English literary life. There were no prior publications (except possibly a short story sent to a competition) – no juvenilia. He was immediately recognized as a major writer by such people as Wells, Henry James, Galsworthy and Edward Garnett, who recognized a master. That is not to say that there was no further development and change in Joseph Conrad's literary achievement. New themes emerged, and his style – a bit over-flowery in his early books – became terser and more self-contained. Nevertheless, there is no doubt that his first books, *Almayer's Folly* and *An Outcast of the Islands* (1896), were books of a fully mature writer.

Conrad started writing in 1889 and took five years to complete his first book. What strange metamorphosis occurred? He himself could not account for it. In his *Personal Record* he says:

> The conception of a planned book was entirely outside my mental range when I sat down to write; the ambition of being an author had never turned up among these gracious imaginary existences one creates for oneself in the stillness and immobility of a day dream.

What prompted him to write 'was a hidden obscureness, a completely masked and unaccountable phenomenon'. Unlike such writers as Proust, who analysed and could illuminate the springs of their own creativity, Conrad apparently remained unaware of the forces that made him into an artist.

Can psychoanalytical understanding throw any light on this strange transformation of a professional sailor into a major writer? The two years preceding his setting pen to paper and the five years of writing *Almayer's Folly* were marked by restlessness and depression. He had just achieved his Master's Ticket but couldn't find a command. He spent months in

123

Amsterdam waiting for a berth. The way he describes in his letters the gloom of Amsterdam is not unlike the way he describes Brussels as the Sepulchral City in which Marlowe waits for his trip to the Congo in *The Heart of Darkness*. He was repeatedly ill, having to give up a berth on a good ship through illness. He gave up another good berth as a first mate out of sheer ennui, as he says in one of the letters.

Finally, in 1889 in Bangkok he got his first command, on a ship called *Otago*. It is on that ship of his first command that he started writing. After a little over a year, however, he threw up the command because he got bored with the route, and the shipowners wouldn't agree to a change of itinerary. He became obsessed with the idea of going to Africa. When he was a little boy he pointed out the Congo, at that time still a dark, unknown spot on the map, and said, 'When I grow up I shall go there'. In his mid-thirties the determination to go there surfaced with full strength. While waiting to find an opportunity to go there he returned to Poland to visit his uncle/ guardian, Bobrowski. At that time he also wrote feverishly. When he finally started for the Congo to take command of a small river steamship, he took with him the first six chapters of *Almayer's Folly*. The experience for Conrad, like that for André Gide, was shattering. The brutality, the naked exploitation, the horror, affected him deeply. Personally, he was racked by depression and illness. He went on writing but it was touch and go, and he nearly lost his manuscript. Uncharacteristically for him, he didn't even fulfil his contract and returned to Europe ill and shattered.

He was ill, depressed and disgusted with himself and his body. As he was swollen by arthritis, he described himself as a ridiculous Punch figure, such as he had seen in childhood. Getting a good berth as first mate of the *Torrens* by the end of 1891 seemed to lift his depression somewhat, and for the first time he showed his manuscript to an educated Canadian who encouraged him to write. But the better conditions didn't last. He had to return to Poland to visit his uncle who was terminally ill, and again nearly lost the manuscript. He then had to take a disappointing and humiliating berth as a second mate. By then, however, the writing was beginning to play a major part in his life. He wrote of those days:

> I had given myself up to the idleness of a haunted man who looks for nothing but words wherein to capture his visions, and for many years Almayer and the world of his story had been the companions of my imagination without, I believe, impairing my abilities to cope with the realities of the sea life.

In 1894 his uncle died, 'taking my soul with him' (*Il a emporté mon âme avec lui*). Within three months of his uncle's death Conrad completed his book, gave it to a publisher, and started writing *An Outcast*. He also met his future wife, Jessie, and became engaged. Though for a few years he would still look for employment on the sea, 1894 and 1895 are the years in which he finally assumed the responsibility of being a writer.

I have gone into some detail of Conrad's life because it is on the experience of those years that are based the three stories which I think illuminate the emotional constellation which was the source of his creativity. 'The Secret Sharer' and 'The Shadow-Line' are stories of young men taking their first command – the time of life when Conrad himself first started writing. The third story, *The Heart of Darkness*, embodies his experience in the Congo. In those stories, and in particular in the last one of the three to be written and the most mature, 'The Shadow-Line', Conrad depicts, I think, his mid-life crisis and the emotional constellation which mobilized his creativity.

Elliott Jaques, in his paper 'Death and the mid-life crisis' (1965), gives a vivid description of the passage between early youth and late youth and maturity:

Around the age of 37 we reach the point of mid-life half of our allotted life span, three score and ten. It is like reaching the crest of a hill. Up till that time one goes up. Suddenly at the peak we realise that we are over the top and have begun the descent towards death.

Jaques quotes the opening stanza of the *Divine Comedy*, begun by Dante at the age of 37:

In the middle of the journey of our life I came to myself within a dark wood where the straight way was lost. Ah, how hard it is to tell of that wood savage and harsh and dense, the thought of which renews my fear. So bitter is it that death is hardly more.

At mid-life we have to enter that dark wood. At that point we usually have to face the death of our parents (in the case of Conrad, of his uncle/ guardian), to assume fully the parental place ourselves – in the case of Conrad, the first command – being master of his ship. And we also have to face the prospect of personal death. 'The paradox is that of entering the prime of life; the stage of fulfilment, but at the same time, the prime and fulfilment are dated, Death lies beyond.' How we face this paradox depends on the state of our internal world and the extent to which we have been able to work through the persecutory and depressive anxieties. If they are not sufficiently worked through, death is imbued with paranoid–schizoid terrors of fragmentation and persecution, and the prospect of death cannot be faced. The mid-life mobilizes again such problems which have not been sufficiently resolved. According to Jaques, the mid-life crisis is particularly important in the life of artists. He lists a large number of them who stop creating or die around the age of 37. Others, who overcome the crisis, seem to mature. Their method of work and style change. They go into their second or third manner of work and frequently live to a very ripe old age. Today one could quote as examples Picasso and Henry Moore.

Why is the mid-life crisis so particularly significant in the life of the artist? Jaques' observations and his analysis of them is consistent with my view that artistic creativity is a way of expressing and overcoming the anxieties of the depressive position. I also suggested that it depends on the acceptance of one's personal mortality (Segal, 1952).

In the mid-life crisis this is goodbye to childhood and youth, depressive anxieties have to be worked through again and the prospect of one's personal death has to be faced realistically. Some artists don't start producing until after the mid-life crisis. The necessity to resolve their internal conflicts forces them to create. Freud started writing *The Interpretation of Dreams* around that age and Melanie Klein became an analyst.

Conrad's 'The Shadow-Line' is the most marvellous description of the mid-life crisis. It was written in 1916 when his son was in Flanders, and is dedicated 'To Boris and all others who, like himself, have crossed in early youth the shadow line of their generation'. But it is based on his own experiences of the time of his own crossing of the shadow line when he took, in Bangkok, his first command at the age of 32. The opening sentences of this story are:

> Only the young have such moments. I don't mean the very young. No, the very young have, properly speaking, no moments; it is the privilege of early youth to live in advance of its days, in all the continuity of hope, which means no pauses and no introspection.

And later in this passage he says: 'Yes, one goes on and time too goes on – till one perceives ahead a shadow line, warning one that the region of early youth, too, must be left behind.'

> This is the period of life in which such moments of which I have spoken are likely to come. What moments? Why, moments of boredom, weariness, of dissatisfaction – rash moments. I mean moments when the still young are inclined to commit rash actions, such as getting married suddenly, or else throw up a job for no reason.

He speaks of later youth: 'The green sickness of late youth descended on me and carried me off.' The narrator, like Conrad himself, throws up his berth for no good reason, out of sheer envy. This green sickness is not really a depression. It is characterized by boredom, futility, irritability; the young man has no idea yet of the underlying depths of his depression. His state of mind is also reflected in the seascape – the sea is flat, greyish calm and gives no hint of the underlying dangers and horrors. This sense of pointlessness and futility is combined with contempt for others. All other protagonists in the story are viewed with distaste and contempt. Helpful figures like Captain Giles, who wants to help him to get a command, are viewed with puzzled lack of understanding; in this situation of the doldrums, he contemplates throwing up his sea career and going home. Suddenly, with the help of Captain Giles, he gets command of a ship in Bangkok. Exultation replaces the doldrums. But he is no nearer understanding himself or others. He takes revenge on a steward who tried to deprive him of his chance by stealing a letter, by letting him believe that he had complained of him, though, in fact, he hadn't done so. When Captain Giles rushes to reassure the steward, the young man says contemptuously: 'He won't die out of fear.' And when Captain Giles tells him that he might well die of an overdose, the young man is uncomprehending. Suicide and despair are not within the realm of his comprehension.

He takes his command first on the wings of youthful enthusiasm and idealization. He falls in love with his ship at first sight: 'I knew that, like some rare women, she was one of those creatures whose mere existence is enough to awaken an unselfish delight. One feels that it is good to be in the world in which she has her being.' Sitting down in his cabin he thinks of the succession of captains who had sat in his chair: 'As if a sort of composite soul, the soul of command, had whispered suddenly to his mind.' Disillusion sets in slowly. He meets the first mate, Burns, who tells him horrible things about his dead predecessor – the previous captain who, according to Burns, gave himself to unrestrained dissolution and died mad, cursing the ship. Burns is convinced that his evil soul is out to destroy the ship and all its men. The young captain also realizes that Burns himself wanted the command. In the long wait while the ship is loading, in the oppressive port of Bangkok, men gradually fall sick, including Burns. The command begins to lie heavy on the young captain. But he still hopes that once under way, the fresh breeze of the sea will wipe out the sickness. This too, however, is an illusion. When the ship puts to sea, she is becalmed for eighteen days and 'she took the sickness with her'. One after another the men sicken and some of them die. Burns, too, is ill. He became ill while still in port but begged to be taken on, and he gets madder and madder. The previous captain's body was buried at sea at latitude 8°20' and Burns is convinced that they have to fight his evil spirit at that latitude. They cannot get past the island of Koh–ring:

> The island of Koh–ring – a great black upheaved ridge amongst a lot of tiny islets lying upon the glassy water like a Triton amongst minnows seemed to be the centre of the fatal circle. It seemed impossible to get away from it. Day after day it remained in sight. More than once in a favourable breeze I would take its bearing in the first ebbing twilight,

thinking it was for the last time. Vain hope. A night of fitful airs would undo the gains to temporary favour and the rising sun would throw out the black relief of Koh-ring looking more barren, inhospitable and grim than ever.

The nadir of his despair is reached when the captain discovers that the vials of quinine contain nothing but sand, the previous captain having sold the quinine. He experiences despair and guilt. He should have checked the medicine before starting. Courageously he faces his crew, admitting his responsibility. To his surprise he meets not with anger but comprehension and helpfulness. The ill and dying men do all in their power to keep the work going. But in the end there are only two men untouched by sickness. They are the captain and his curious double, the steward, Ransome. Ransome is always there, always helpful. But Ransome suffers from a heart illness. He is presented as a very ideal figure and yet there is something uncanny about him. The knowledge that he carries death within him produces an aura of uncanny anxiety surrounding him. While in the depths of despair the captain starts writing a diary. After eighteen days, they pass, in the storm, the fatal latitude 8°20′ and Burns, in his delirium, fights the ghost of the old captain. Then a breeze comes and at last the ship can sail to Singapore. The rite of passage has been accomplished. The captain returns to his point of departure in Singapore but he is a changed man. He feels old. He has crossed the shadow line. He meets Captain Giles again and for the first time is interested in his conversation. He is now stripped of some of his illusions but capable of understanding love and compassion.

What did the young captain have to face in crossing the shadow line? I think he had to face the despair and persecution in his inner world. The old captain, far from being an idealized figure, is seen as the vengeful ghost of a dead father. Burns partly represents a part of himself persecuted and maddened by the ghost, his nearly mad self. The captain at times feels identified with Burns's madness. But he also represents another aspect of father as well. The captain not only stepped into their dead captain's shoes. He also stepped over Burns to get his command. And keeping Burns alive, rescuing him, is an important preoccupation of the captain. He is extremely proud that Burns is the only one who can leave the ship on his own feet, having recovered. 'Take care of him,' he says when finally help arrives 'I am very proud of him; he is my only convalescent.' Ransome, his strange double, represents, I think, the captain's suicidal self and his terror of death. Ransome reveals this terror after the ship is in port. In order to come out of the green sickness of youth, the captain had to face the real horrors of the sea – representing the undying horrors of his internal world. And he does it through courage and love. Before taking his command, the young man has a moment of insight when he says: 'The sea was the only world that counted and the ship the test of manliness, of temperament, of courage and fidelity – and of love.'

Two other stories referring to the same period throw some more light on what the captain of 'The Shadow-Line' had to face. In 'The Secret Sharer' a young captain takes his first command and, as he takes the first watch on the ship, a man emerges from the sea and climbs aboard. He is a murderer: a young first mate of another ship who had killed a crewman and who has escaped. The captain hides him in his cabin. The murderer is his double. He recognizes himself in him in an almost hallucinatory way. Koh-ring again plays a large role in the story. It is near Koh-ring that the captain releases his murderous alter ego to reach the shore.

On the face of it the stories are very dissimilar. 'The Secret Sharer' in a way celebrates muscular action. The murderer is presented as having committed his murder in the necessary pursuit of his duty. He killed a rebellious sailor who was endangering the ship, and he leaves the captain's ship 'a free man, a proud swimmer striking out for a new destiny'. But that is only part of the story. In the description of how he kills the sailor 'hanging on to his neck 'till he was prised loose', he appears more as a homicidal maniac than an honourable killer in the course of duty.

The similarities between the stories are many. Both are stories of the first command. In each the captain has a double: in 'The Shadow Line', the dying man; in the 'The Secret Sharer', the murderer. Also the murderer, as he first emerges from the sea, is seen by the captain as a headless corpse. He could be the victim as well as the murderer. In both stories the captain is near madness. In 'The Secret Sharer' at one moment he says: 'I came as near madness as it is possible for a man to do without going over the brink.' In both stories at the end the captain says goodbye to his double. And both are dominated by Koh-ring. In 'The Secret Sharer',

> The black southern hill of Koh-ring seemed to hang right over the ship like a towering fragment of the everlasting night. On that enormous mass of blackness there was not a gleam to be seen, not a sound to be heard.

The captain sails much too near to Koh-ring and nearly destroys the ship. There is a hint of a recklessly suicidal action. I think in both stories Koh-ring represents death, the fear of which has to be faced and overcome. Koh-ring throws a shadow on the still waters of the sea (the shadow-line).

The third significant story, based on the experiences of the time Conrad's first book was written is the best-known one, though to my mind not the best – *The Heart of Darkness*. The story starts in an atmosphere of deadliness. In the Sepulchral City, Brussels, in an office in which two women knit black wool (echoes of Dickens' knitting ladies), Marlowe, the narrator, signs on for his trip to the Congo. As he reaches the Congo he is confronted with endless greed, envy, exploitation; the natives in a state of helplessness, disease and starvation – everything happening confusedly in the greenish gloom. If Marlowe had believed at all, and maybe he partly did, in the ideals of bringing civilization to Africa, the first sight of the Congo would brutally shatter any such belief. He keeps hearing about Kurtz, described variously as the best agent the Congo Company ever had, sending vast quantities of ivory to the station; as an idealist who went into the interior with great ideas of reform; or as a devil.

Sickened by the last outpost of civilization, the central station where he has to wait endlessly to get a ruined steamship mended, Marlowe is fascinated by stories he hears about Kurtz. Maybe in the interior there is something more alive, less corrupt. Eventually he is sent into the interior to collect Kurtz, reported to be dying (or is it to collect the ivory for the company?). The journey takes him to the heart of darkness, to unremitting savagery. Kurtz runs his own empire in the depths of the jungle. He is enormous, overpowering – but he is dying. Only his voice remains, powerful, hypnotic, and keeps Marlowe entranced. Kurtz has surrendered himself to the powers of darkness and become the prime devil among devils. His station is surrounded by stakes with heads impaled on them. He is supposed to have indulged all his appetites, particularly the vilest. He is also corrupted by megalomania. Marlowe is fascinated by his endless talk. On the trip back, before dying, Kurtz pours out his mad, deluded, megalomanic ideas and dies, saying, 'The horror, the horror'. He, too, is a kind of mirror image of Marlowe, representing the darkest, most primitive, unrestrained, unconscious self. Like the captains of the other stories, Marlowe touches madness and death. After Kurtz's death he is himself on the brink of dying, but recovers and returns to the Sepulchral City. But, unlike the captain of 'The Shadow-Line', we don't know what the experience did to him; 'it is one of Marlowe's inconclusive stories.'

I have spoken of these three stories in an order reversed to that in which they were written. *The Heart of Darkness* was written first in 1899. It is the story of almost unremitting destructiveness and despair. Idealism is either sheer hypocrisy, a cover for exploitation, or it is based on a complete delusion. Women seem capable of it, but only because they are completely cut off from realities.

> It is queer how out of touch with truth women are. They live in a world of their own and there had never been anything like it and never can be. It is too beautiful altogether. And if they were to set it up it would go to pieces before the first sun set.

Kurtz's intended, whom Marlowe meets after Kurtz's death, loves him with an ideal love, believing him to be a crusader for high ideals. And Marlowe has no heart to disillusion her. The idealism of the women in the story is a delusion – the pseudo-idealism of Western civilization's hypocritical cover for exploitation, megalomania and cruelty.

Kurtz writes a pamphlet, his *magnum opus*, for the International Society for the Suppression of Savage Cultures, and ends it saying, 'Exterminate the brutes.'

Western civilization is corrupt. Westerners are described as the 'flabby devils', greedy and reckless without courage. The savagery has something to be said for it. The crew of Marlowe's steamer are cannibals, and cannibalism seems to him cleaner and less corrupt. Twice he says, 'there is a choice of nightmares.' And of the two he prefers the darkness of the interior. Nevertheless, reaching the interior is also a descent into hell. Kurtz is almost pure destructiveness and he too is corrupt by megalomania.

There is a hint, though, of creativity in Kurtz. On returning to Brussels, Marlowe discovers that Kurtz may have been an artist. Some say, a writer; others, a musician. And there is his voice. Up to the moment of his death he talks, and Marlowe says: 'At least he had something to say.' But what he has to say offers no hope. Savagery wins and there is no relief. Insight can only lead to madness and despair.

> But his soul was mad. Being alone in the wilderness it had looked within itself, and by heavens, I tell you it had gone mad. I had, for my sins I suppose, to go through the ordeal of looking into it myself. No eloquence could have been so withering to one's belief in mankind as his final burst of sincerity.

And Marlowe at several points describes himself as having drawn back from the brink. The choice seemed to be between acknowledging the Kurtz part of himself – with subsequent madness or death – or withdrawing from the experience with a loss of potential. And on his trip to the Congo, Conrad nearly lost his manuscript. Marlowe, though a story teller, unlike Conrad is not an artist.

In 'The Secret Sharer' (1912), the captain comes to terms with his murderous double, but it nearly drives him mad and nearly makes him smash his ship against Koh-ring. So long as his double is there he remains completely cut off from his ship and his crew whilst hiding his guilty secret.

In 'The Shadow-Line' (1917), all those experiences are integrated. The captain faces the horrors, the destructiveness, his ghosts, his own guilt, the despair. He also touches madness and death. But, sustained by a mutual love between himself and his crew and his sense of personal responsibility, he comes out of the experience a man – not a youth. And in 'The Shadow-Line' the captain, at the height of his despair, begins to write a diary. He neither succumbs to the horror, like Kurtz, nor, like Marlowe draws back from the brink. He starts writing.

It is my contention that Joseph Conrad, who had a most traumatic childhood and carried a severe depression in his heart – like Ransome, 'who carried death within his noble breast' – came to the crossroads in his mid-life crisis. Up to his early thirties he could, despite a serious suicidal attempt when very young, manage to cope with his depression by youthful romanticism, risky adventure, action and an idealization of the ships, the sea and, curiously, the British Merchant Navy. Coming to mid-life crisis these defences began to fail him and 'the green sickness of late youth' overcame him. External action wasn't sufficient any more. He had to look within himself, come to terms with his inner world and attempt to restore it. He had to face the heart of darkness, his destructive, murderous and suicidal impulses, the destruction of his inner world. Love, given and received, courage and a sense of personal responsibility gave him some hope of coming out of the shadow. Kurtz looked into himself, went mad and destroyed himself. Conrad looked into himself, and though he was near the brink, he started writing. Proust says: 'I had to recapture from the shade that which I had felt, to reconvert it into its psychic equivalent. But the way to do it, the one I could see – what was it, but to create a work of art' (*Time Regained*). Faced with his mid-life crisis, Conrad had to succumb to madness or death, or make a heroic effort to restore his inner world in the process of writing.

Summary

Joseph Conrad, a professional seaman, published his first novel at the age of 37. The thesis of this paper is that his creativity was mobilized by Conrad's severe mid-life crisis and was a way of working through his deep depressive anxiety which came to a crisis at the approach of mid-life. The paper refers to my previous papers relating artistic creativity to the depressive position and Elliott Jaques' paper, 'Death and the mid-life crisis', in which he emphasizes the particular importance of the mid-life crisis in the creative life of artists. Three short stories of Conrad's, which describe experiences of the time he was writing his first book, illustrate his state of mind and the problems he was struggling with at the time of writing: 'The Secret Sharer', *The Heart of Darkness* and 'The Shadow-Line'. In 'The Shadow Line', in particular, he describes the 'crossing of the Shadow Line' between late youth and adulthood – the mid-life crisis.

Note

1   This paper has been published previously (Segal, 1984).

Salman Rushdie and the sea of stories:[1]
a not-so-simple fable about creativity

Zembla, Zenda, Xanadu:
All our dream-worlds may come true.
Fairy lands are fearsome too.

Salman Rushdie

Beauty is the beginning of terror that we are only just able to bear.

Rainer Maria Rilke

This paper was originally written for a symposium on the theme, What can Psychoanalysis Learn from Great Literature? Psychoanalysis and psychoanalysts can of course learn from any human experience and expression. A psychoanalytical viewpoint aims at achieving a state of mind in which we should be able to feel *nil humanum ad me alienum esse puto*. But what specifically can we learn from literature, or indeed in art? I have suggested (Segal, 1952) that an essential component of the aesthetic experience is our identification with the artist's creative process – what Dilthey called 'Nachehrleben'. This is true of all art. Unconsciously, we learn from it about the creative experience itself. Every work of art carries within it the story of its creation. It captures its experience.

Some artists are consciously preoccupied with the sources of their creativity and have an urge to explore it and communicate about it directly; for instance, the English romantic poets. Shelley's notebooks contained a project for scientific research on the subject, and many artists keep similar notes. Some incorporate the exploration of experience into their creative art, like Proust, in *Time Regained*, or Wordsworth, in *The Prelude*. Some tell us fables about creativity: for instance, Thomas Mann in *Dr Faustus* and *Felix Krull*.

And if we want to learn about creativity, who can tell us more about it than the artists themselves? I shall consider here a children's story.

133

There was once, in the country of Alitbay, a sad city, the saddest of cities, a city so ruinously sad that it had forgotten its name. . . . And in the depths of the city, beyond an old zone of ruined buildings that looked like broken hearts, there lived a happy young fellow by the name of Haroun, the only child of the story teller Rashid Khalifa, whose cheerfulness was famous throughout that unhappy metropolis, and whose never-ending stream of tall, short and winding tales had earned him not one but two nicknames. To his admirers he was Rashid the Ocean of Notions, as stuffed with cheery stories as the sea was full of glumfish; but to his jealous rivals he was the Shah of Blah. To his wife, Soraya, Rashid was for many years as loving a husband as anyone could wish for, and during these years, Haroun grew up in a home in which, instead of misery and frowns, he had his father's ready laughter and his mother's sweet voice raised in song.

Then something went wrong. (Maybe the sadness of the city finally crept in through their windows.) The day Soraya stopped singing, in the middle of a line, as if someone had thrown a switch, Haroun guessed there was trouble brewing. But he never suspected how much.

Thus starts Rushdie's tale for children, *Haroun and the Sea of Stories*.

The trouble was very great indeed. Soraya deserted her husband and son, and eloped with Mr Sengupta, who hated stories and storytellers. Rashid fell into a great depression and could tell stories no more. Haroun was bereft of his beloved mother and of his exciting storytelling father. He also felt very guilty over his father's disarray, because in the first flush of anger at Soraya's desertion he shouted to his father, 'What's the use of stories that aren't even true?' – just the kind of thing Mr Sengupta kept saying.

Rashid had often been asked to tell his stories at political rallies of the ruling party to cheer up the depressed people and make them work for the candidate. After Soraya left, he was asked to talk for a candidate in the Town of G, but he dried up and was able only to say, 'Ark, ark, ark'. After this disastrous performance he was told by the politicians to go to the Valley of K to perform for Snooty Buttoo. This was to be his last chance. It had to be cheerful stories: 'If you want pay, then just be gay.'

Haroun is desperate, and determined to save his father. After an adventurous journey to K, which I will write about later, they were put up in an elegant hotel, and neither of them could sleep. In the night Haroun hears strange noises in the bathroom. Going to explore, he finds a strange-looking creature who tells him that he is Iff, the Water Genie and the Plumber of the Ocean of the Streams of Story; and he has come to disconnect Rashid, who has stopped being a subscriber. When he asks how he could appeal against this decision, Iff tells him that on the Moon Kahani there is an Ocean from which all stories originate, and that the Controller of the Plumbing is the Walrus, who lives in Gup City, capital of Gup on Kahani, but he refuses to take Haroun there. Haroun manages to steal his Disconnecting Tool and tells him he will not give it back unless and until Iff takes him to Walrus to plead his case. The rest of the story is about Haroun's trip of rescue.

This story can be read on many levels: as an imaginative, rumbustious fairy-tale; about a hero fighting evil forces and triumphing; as a political parable, dealing with the artist's struggle not to be squashed by the repression of thought and art in dictatorial regimes. The last includes Rushdie's own problem. In an interview he gave to the BBC at the time of writing this book, Rushdie said that his greatest fear was that he would not be able to continue to write.

But one can also look at it – and I choose to look at it from this angle – as the struggle to resolve an inner conflict between creative and anti-creative forces in all artists, and in all circumstances – that is, as a parable about creativity.

Kahani, a moon invisible from Earth, to which Haroun journeys, could be seen as his unseen, his unconscious, his own inner world, in which the stories originate. Haroun, the child of Rashid the storyteller, and Rashid himself, could be seen also as one character. The names Haroun and Rashid came from the famous one name Haroun-al-Rashid, of *The Thousand and One Nights*, and it is the child part that takes the trip to Kahani. The child is closer, more in touch with the unconscious phantasies which are the Sea of Stories.

Haroun and Iff travel on the magic creature Hoopoe, part-bird, part-machine, who resembles the driver of the bus, Butt, who drove them from the Town of G to the Valley of K. He is often referred to as Butt the Hoopoe.

When they reach Kahani and the Ocean, Iff tries two ploys to get out of his commitment. First, they stop where the Wishwater is, and Iff advises Haroun to drink a glass, and just wish for the reconnection of Rashid. But this fails, because Haroun is assailed with contradictory wishes and he cannot select one wish. His plight is all the worse as, since his mother's departure, he cannot concentrate on anything for longer than eleven minutes. His mother left at 11, and Haroun broke the clock, and since that time eleven minutes was the limit of his capacity to concentrate. So he cannot resolve the conflict between his wishes in time; and sadly, he and Iff have to admit that simple wish fulfilment does not work.

The second ploy is to try at least to cheer up Haroun, and Iff and Hoopoe think that if he drank from a pure stream of a lovely story that at least would restore his spirits. Haroun dives into the simple Rapunzel Rescue Story. To begin with, he lives a wonderful story. But slowly things start going wrong. He turns into a spider. Rapunzel starts hacking him to bits. He is in desperate straits, but somehow Iff and the Hoopoe manage to rescue him. They are shocked to discover that the Ocean of Stories is completely polluted, and they say that means war, war with the Land of Chup. Haroun learns that Rashid is not the only one who may lose access to the Ocean of Stories: it may be a fate threatening the whole world. Iff and Hoopoe explain to him the situation on Kahani. The Eggheads of Gup have discovered a way to stop the moon rotating, which resulted in one half of the moon being in permanent sunshine and one in permanent darkness. Gup is in permanent light, and it is in Gup City that Walrus lives, and everything is cheerful and creative, where both Eggheads and Creators of Stories flourish. Chup is in permanent darkness, and it is ruled by Khattam-Shud.

Between the two countries, the Eggheads built a wall which they thought would be impenetrable. But apparently the Chupwalas had managed to get out, reach the Ocean, and start polluting the stories.

When they arrive at Gup City they are told that things are very bad. Khattam-Shud had installed a new idol, Bezaban. The Ocean is in danger. Pollution is everywhere. And, worst of all, the enemy is approaching the Old Zone, the original source of the oldest stories, which Guppees had somewhat neglected. Khattam-Shud has also kidnapped Batcheat, daughter of King Chattergee, and the Beloved of Bolo, who thinks her rescue should be the first task.

At some point Rashid joins the party, having found the way with some magic to do with his love for his son. A great armada is prepared to go to the Twilight Strip, the land between the Light (Gup) and the Dark (Chup), rescue Batcheat and the Ocean of Stories. Approaching the Twilight Zone, Haroun becomes very sad, and Hoopoe comforts him that anyone approaching the Twilight experiences a heart shadow at the approach of the Dark Side of Kahani. When they penetrate the Zone they see a strange creature dancing: the dance is a fight with his shadow.

They are at first frightened, but then recognize that he is also struggling to speak, and wants to communicate with them. Rashid understands that he communicates in the oldest of all languages, the language of gestures, Abhinaya. And he is trying to say, 'Mudra. Speak Abhinaya'; Rashid begs the others to listen, and he translates what he has to say.

Mudra says that he has become disgusted with excessive cruelty since Khattam-Shud introduced the tongueless idol, Bezaban. Many people and shadows want to rebel against the excesses. In Chup, people can get separated from their shadows and they are usually on good terms with them – one of the terrible things that happen now is that people had started quarrelling with their shadows. He also warns them that because of the separation from his Shadow, Khattam-Shud can be in two places at once. Now one of him is in the Citadel of Chup where he holds Batcheat; the other is in the Old Zone, where he aims finally to stop the sources of the streams. Haroun leads the advance party to the Old Zone, accompanied by Iff and Hoopoe. After many adventures, the three are captured by the Dark Ship, where Khattam-Shud resides.

Khattam-Shud removes the brain from Hoopoe's head and boasts to Haroun about how he polluted the Ocean, how he is about to plug the Source of Stories, and before the Sources dry up completely how he can stop them by a stream of anti-stories. The Dark Ship has no light – it is shadowy. Haroun remembers that the Eggheads gave him a little source of energy, called Bite-a-Lite, and he uses it as a weapon. As he produces his light, shadows begin to crumble, including Khattam-Shud, and he realizes that the Dark Ship is all manned by shadows.

But he does not have enough light to defuse them completely, and he decides that his first task is to unplug the Sources. So he dives deep, and at the bottom of the Sea he meets despair. He cannot achieve his task and he cannot stay for ever at the bottom of the Ocean as he would die. But when he is in the depth of despair he feels a little object in his pocket and remembers that he still has some of the Wishwater that he has not finished drinking. And he makes what he thinks is his last wish: that the Moon should start rotating again so that the sun shines on the Dark Side as well. He returns to the surface, to a shining sun, and the shadows melt and disappear. He eventually returns to the Citadel, which has also collapsed, after Khattam-Shud lost his shadow, and the war is at an end. But the end is not just the triumph of the Good over the Bad. Mudra is at the head of the liberators and is on his way to Gup to negotiate a just peace and future collaboration.

> The new government of the Land of Chup, headed by Mudra, announced its desire for a long and lasting peace with Gup, a peace in which Night and Day, Speech and Silence, would no longer be separated into Zones by Twilight Strips and Walls of Force.

Everything, as it should in a fairy-tale, ends happily. Rashid's gift is restored and Haroun and Rashid find themselves again in the Valley of K as though no time had elapsed. Haroun makes his performance, but the story he tells is about Haroun and the Sea of Stories. And the result is rather different from what Snooty Buttoo expected, because the people rise and chase him out of town. Haroun and Rashid return to their little town and find it very happy. And when they ask, 'What are you happy about?' the people say, 'Because we remember our name. Our name is Kahani.'

Soraya has returned. The clock moves again. And Haroun has received as a gift the little Hoopoe (presumably so he can again take trips with him).

So, as in all fairy-tales, in a way Good triumphs over Evil, and they are contrasted. 'It was a war between Love (of the Ocean, or the Princess) and

Death (which was what Cultmaster Khattam-Shud had in mind for the Ocean, and for the Princess, too).'

The Good is understandable. But what is the Evil, and what is the nature of the solution? In some ways this fable is not an ordinary fairy-tale. I think that the Evil in this story represents what Freud described as the death instinct. To begin with, if Kahani, whether on the Moon or on Earth, represents Salman Rushdie's inner world, the attack is on his own sources of creativity. The Dark Side of the Moon is ruled by Khattam-Shud, which means 'Death'. Haroun knew about Khattam-Shud from his father.

> 'Khattam-Shud', he said slowly, 'is the Arch-Enemy of all Stories, even of Language itself. He is the Prince of Silence and the Foe of Speech. And because everything ends, because dreams end, stories end, life ends, at the finish of everything we use his name. 'It's finished', we tell one another, 'it's over. Khattam-Shud: The End.'

It is silence, blackness, death – what Freud described as the return to the inorganic. Freud also speaks of the death instinct as being silent, as it works silently in the body. The attack is on all sources of love, communication, creativity. In the end it is an attack on life itself.

> In the old days the Cultmaster, Khattam-Shud, preached hatred only towards stories and fancies and dreams; but now he has become more severe, and opposes Speech for any reason at all. In Chup City the schools and law-courts and theatres are all closed now, unable to operate because of the Silence Laws. And I heard it said that some wild devotees of the Mystery work themselves up into great frenzies and sew their lips together with stout twine; so they die slowly of hunger and thirst, sacrificing themselves for the love of Bezaban.

What a perfect description of some mental conditions such as anorexia and catatonia!

So the conflict is between the forces of life and death. And what is the possible resolution? In this story, the first solution is splitting, denial and idealization. In Gup all is light, joy and love. But it is also a bit foolish. The King is called Chattergee, the daughter Batcheat, which means Chitchat. The place is full of chatter. Bolo and the Princess are the epitome of idealization: whereas Soraya sang beautifully and was beautiful, Batcheat shrieks and is horribly ugly. Nobody can stand her. But Bolo is oblivious of her ugliness. She, on the other hand, infuriates pages – which in the story are pages in both senses of the word (the king's servants and the pages of a book) – by replacing all names of heroes by the name of Bolo. It is also a bit dull. At the beginning of the story there is a beautiful lake called Dull. And Haroun is told that youngsters in Gup City get attracted to the Twilight Zone, however dangerous, because they get a little bored at home.

Also Rashid at the beginning of the story is rather blind. He tells only cheerful stories, apparently oblivious to the misery around him. He happily performs for people like Snooty Buttoo to cheat the people out of their misery. Buttoo says:

'My enemies hire cheap fellows to stuff the people's ears with bad stories about me, and the ignorant people just lap it up like milk. For this reason I have turned, eloquent Mr Rashid, to you. You will tell happy stories, praising stories, and the people will believe you, and be happy, and vote for me.'

And in Rashid's personal life he completely ignores his wife's misery, which leads to her deserting him for the enemy, the Man who Hates Stories. Maybe the hostile nickname, the Shah of Blah, was not unduly unjust. When he returns to the Valley of K the story he tells is very different: he has learned from his experience. The Egghead solution to stop the natural rotation of the moon was not a lasting one. Half of Kahani lived in a fool's paradise, in an as-if world (I was particularly touched by the Water Genie being called Iff, as I was in the process of writing something about the difference between an as-if world, which is fantasizing, and a what-if world, which is the world of imagination). The other half is deprived of all goodness, and therefore it is forever attacking and wanting to pollute the good side. The Wall between them, built by the Eggheads, proved not impenetrable.

So, keeping the two apart is not a creative solution. Theoretically speaking, it is a paranoid–schizoid solution, a wall between good and bad, idealizing the good and projecting the bad outside, the enemy, the Evil Empire of Chup. And the Wall is not as impenetrable as it was supposed to be.

Haroun discovers another solution in the Twilight. In this most imaginative tale Mudra is to me the most beautiful creation, and one of great depth. First of all, he is surprisingly beautiful.

There was a small clearing up ahead, and in this leafless glade was a man who looked almost like a shadow, and who held a sword whose blade was dark as night. The man was alone, but turned and leapt and kicked and slashed his sword constantly, as though battling an invisible opponent. Then, as they drew nearer, Haroun saw that the man was actually fighting *against his own shadow*, which, in turn was fighting back with equal ferocity, attention and skill. . . . Haroun began to think of their combat as a dance of great beauty and grace, a dance danced in perfect silence, because the music was playing inside the dancers' heads. . . . 'Isn't he *wicked, awesome, sharp*? – Mudra, I *mean*,' says one of the pages.

139

The death instinct has its own kind of dark beauty. Mudra can live with the dark side. Peace for the Chupwalas, he says, is to be at peace with their shadows. He is a representative of the death instinct, but a death instinct moderated by love and compassion. He is aware of it, and wants to moderate its excesses. I think he does it by expressing it in the dance. The struggle is on a non-verbal level. And only when he has mastered the dance can he start to speak.

In the tale there is a very subtle differentiation between the non-verbal and the anti-verbal. The forces derived from the death instinct are anti-verbal: they attack speech and thought (the removal of Hoopoe's brain). Verbalization is important. Iff says:

'To give a thing a name, a label, a handle; to rescue it from anonymity, to pluck it out of the Place of Namelessness, in short to identify it – well, that's a way of bringing the said thing into being.'

But Mudra's dance is not anti-verbal; it is pre-verbal; he speaks Abhinaya – Rashid explains that it is the oldest language, that of gestures. And it is Rashid, the storyteller, the poet, who translates it. The poet's words verbalize for us what is not otherwise verbalizable.

The Twilight Zone is to me full of meaning. Approaching it, Haroun experiences depression, a shadow on his heart, but he has to face it and venture into the dark side of his nature and face the power of destructiveness and death. This Twilight Zone makes me think of Joseph Conrad's beautiful story, 'The Shadow-Line'. In that story a ship is becalmed in the shadow of Koh-ring. (The rocky island of Koh-ring often in Conrad's stories represents death.) Its captain has to face his dying crew, his own guilt about his mistakes, and death. He emerges from this experience a mature man, and it is at the moment of reaching despair that he also starts to write. In Salman Rushdie's story, it is also in this Twilight Zone that speech develops. When Mudra first tries to speak, the Guppees think he is saying 'murder', and blind, besotted Bolo wants to kill him right away. But the poet knows that he has to be listened to. Integration has to be achieved.

'But it's not as simple as that,' he [Haroun] told himself, because the dance of the Shadow Warrior showed him that silence had its own grace and beauty (just as speech could be graceless and ugly); and that Action could be noble as Words; and that creatures of darkness could be as lovely as the children of the light. 'If Guppees and Chupwalas didn't hate each other so,' he thought, 'they might actually find each other pretty interesting. Opposites attract, as they say.'

This theme of having to integrate the forces of darkness and fear runs right through the book. On the way to Town G and the Valley of K, there is a beautiful landscape which can be seen only before sunset. Butt, the driver of the mail-coach, promises to get the coach there in time, come what may. Having promised to Haroun that he will get him there on time, Butt drives hell-for-leather. The drive is terrifying. Haroun feels many times the danger of death. He dreads that they will all be wiped out and it will all be his fault. But they do get there on time, after facing all terrors, and discover a view of extreme beauty. And it is on this ride that Haroun first hears from his father that Khattam-Shud means 'the end', death. This ride is like a short preview of what Haroun will have to do when he reaches Kahani to face death, the death instinct, guilt and terror. And it is facing this that is important. It is Bite-a-Lite, I think insight, a ray of light, which makes the shadow first less frightening, and finally defeated: they melt away.

But the story is far from simple. Haroun's constant companions are the Iffs and the Butts. There are apparent, possibly real, contradictions. For instance, Butt could express mania. On his mad rush he keeps saying, 'No problem, no problem'. Hoopoe is all speed. And yet it is Butt the Hoopoe who makes Haroun face death and depression. Butt the Hoopoe tells him that everyone experiences the shadow on the heart in the Twilight Zone.

The different meanings of this figure are ambiguous. It could mean that some manic drive is necessary to start the journey. Melanie Klein thinks that in the early stages of the depressive position some early manic defences are needed to enable one to face it at all. But it could also mean that Butt the Hoopoe is also the beginning of integration, and Hoopoe is more reflective than Butt, and more capable of words of wisdom. But could it also show something else, possibly a persistence of some manic trend in Rushdie himself, which, in my view, sometimes mars his writing?

The Eggheads are equally complex. They are Guppees, which is good; and it is their Bite-a-Lite that defeats the Shadows. And yet it is the Eggheads that started all the trouble by stopping the moon from rotating. In this story the Eggheads are presumably intelligence, which can be used wisely or stupidly. The Eggheads learn from experience. When Haroun has to face them after he has destroyed the machinery to stop the rotation of the Moon he dreads their punishment. But they admit their error and reward him richly. Does intelligence become wisdom when it can learn from emotional experience – listen to the inner child? The clever Eggheads learn from Haroun.

The Shadows are also complicated. They must be defeated and melt away. And yet we are told also that we must live at peace with our shadows. Mudra says that to the Chupwalas peace means also to be at peace with their Shadows. What is the meaning of the fact that the Shadow of Khattam-Shud has to be defeated; and only then the real Khattam-Shud and the Citadel easily fall? Could it be that the Shadows represent our fear of the death instinct, making it appear more dangerous than it really is? Or could it be that it is the split-off death wish and the terror associated with it that have to be defeated, while as much as can be integrated, like Mudra's shadow, is an essential component of experience?

Another contradiction is in the Wishwater. The first drink of the Wishwater Haroun takes does not work. Haroun is at the beginning of his journey. His wish is that things should be as though the catastrophe had never happened. It is a kind of naïve wish fulfilment, which I would call an as-if world. When at the bottom of the Ocean he drinks what remains of the Wishwater I think it is different. The facing of the conflict, and the destructive and self-destructive forces, mobilizes the life instinct, the wish to live in a real way, and the fulfilment of the wish is not a return to some ideal as-if state, but the finding of a state of integration – the moon rotates again.

There is also an Oedipal level to the story, in which Haroun, represented by Sengupta, destroys the parental couple, and Haroun, like Oedipus, searches for the Truth to defeat the plague that affected the Ocean. But, unlike Oedipus, he finds a resolution to the conflict and re-unites his parents.

I have mentioned a few of the unresolved ambiguities in the story. There are many more. And that too, I think, has a meaning. To many of Haroun's questions on Kahani the answer is an algebraic formula P2C2E, meaning Processes Too Difficult To Explain. What the writer tells us, I think, is that, however much we know about the unconscious and the creative processes, we have only some of the answers. The unconscious and the creative processes are inexhaustible.

Note

1 This chapter has been published previously (Segal, 1994c). It was presented at an International Psychoanalytical Association Conference on Literature, London, November 1992.

13

Silence is the real crime[1]

When we look soberly, however hard it is to do so at the moment, at the political situation and the threat of nuclear warfare, we observe a phenomenon that is more like a surrealist scenario, an unbearable nightmare or a psychosis, than a sane world. The Hiroshima bomb killed at one go 140,000 people and that does not include the many thousands who died from the after-effects or the zombie-like existence of the survivors so vividly described by R.J. Lifton in his studies (1982). 'But today, on average, each major city in the northern hemisphere is targeted by the equivalent of 2,000 Hiroshima bombs' (Barnaby, 1983).

The nuclear arsenal of either Russia or America is enough to blow up the world many times over. And still they both continue to develop and stockpile nuclear weapons and contend that this is needed for security. The foreseeable effects of what is genteelly known as 'nuclear exchange' between Russia and America are well studied and documented by scientists. The medical evidence is that there will be no meaningful survival. There is growing scientific evidence that the exploding of only part of that arsenal will bring about a nuclear winter which will engulf all the northern hemisphere, if not the whole planet. These facts are constantly put before the public. Nevertheless, the urgency of the threat to human survival does not seem to have led to a concerted effort to stop what is happening. Indeed, the way things are going, it seems likely that a nuclear war may be an inevitable consequence.

Many take the view, especially in governmental circles, that the threat to the human race posed by nuclear weapons is minimized by mutual deterrence that is maintained by remaining vigilant, well-armed and technologically active. In a world of changing technology, this means constant research and upgrading of weapons and more and more powerful and destructive systems: the nuclear arms race. At the moment we are seeing this extended into space: Star Wars, a method of trying to prevent

143

one's opponent having a deterrent capacity, one could say. I believe, contrary to the prevailing governmental view, that the arms race and the theory of deterrence that supports and justifies it is actually dangerous. Psychoanalytic understanding can help us to see that the theory of deterrence and its current practice may actually lead to our destruction. It is this argument I want to develop and explain in this paper as part of a plea to psychoanalysts urgently to participate in active efforts to halt what I consider a mad process.

The theory of deterrence as propounded by governments implies that it is the existence of nuclear weapons that has ensured peace so far and will do so in the future. 'They are too terrible', it is said, 'nobody would be mad enough to use them.' And yet the papers made available in England under the Thirty-year Rule reveal that in 1954 the Allies seriously considered dropping atomic bombs on China (*Guardian*, 9 January 1985). The report of a military conference of the Chiefs of Staff from the United States, Britain, France, Australia and New Zealand says:

> Should war with China be precipitated by Chinese Communist aggression in South-East Asia, air attack should be launched immediately, aimed at military targets. In the selection of these targets political considerations cannot be ignored. To achieve the maximum and lasting effect, nuclear as well as conventional weapons should be used from the outset.
>
> (Guardian, 8 January 1985)

No papers are available to reveal whether or not the USSR may have been planning in the same way.

The idea of deterrence is to be stronger so as to frighten the enemy – to deter him from aggression. As the 1950 US National Security Document NSC 68 states: 'The only deterrent we can present to the Kremlin is evidence we give that we may make any of the critical points in the world which we cannot hold the occasion for a global war of annihilation.' But the enemy's reasoning is likely to be the same. Hence, the doctrine inevitably leads to escalating anxiety and to the arms race. The nuclear arms race is the heir to the nuclear deterrence. The 'defensive' preparations to counter aggression in which both sides in an arms race engage must create unstable fear. The sort of thing that takes place has been described in a chilling statement by a former US Secretary of Defense, Robert MacNamara. Commenting in 1982 about the defence policy of the 1960s he said:

> [By 1962] the advantage in the US warhead inventory was so great vis-à-vis the Soviets that the Air Force was saying that they felt we had a first-strike capability and could, and should, continue to have one. If the Air Force thought that, imagine what the Soviets thought.

and

> Read again memo to President Kennedy. It scares me today to even read the damn thing. What that means is the Air Force supported the development of US forces sufficiently large to destroy so much of the Soviet nuclear force, by a first strike, that there would not be enough left to cause us any concern if they shot at us. My God! If the Soviets thought that was our objective, how would you expect them, to react? The way they reacted was by substantially expanding their strategic nuclear weapons programme.

(His implication is that we were rather lucky; they might have reacted by a pre-emptive strike.) Preparing for war on both sides promotes the likelihood of a pre-emptive strike out of fear, and the equilibrium of a system of mutual deterrence is inherently unstable. Hatred leads to fear and fear to hatred in an ever-increasing vicious circle. We are like lemmings, pursuing a path to racial suicide, blind to what we are doing.

Psychoanalysis is very familiar with vicious circles of hatred and fear. It teaches us that in an individual, destructive and self-destructive drives can only be modified when the individual can get some insight into their motives and visualize the consequences to others and to themselves of their action. But we know that powerful defences operate against such insights. I suggest that there is some evidence that such resistances to knowing are active in our public life. For instance – there is a reluctance to visualize actual consequences of a nuclear war. We hear now that the use of nuclear weapons can be strategic or minimal. At the same time, there is some evidence that the governments do not clearly visualize the consequences of nuclear war. The civil defence plans, at least in Britain, are a case in point. When the British Medical Association was asked by the government to prepare a report on civil defence, the report said that there could be no meaningful preparation, since after a nuclear blast, there would be no communications, probably no doctors or nurses and no edible food. The British Government's response was to try to suppress this report. Again, in November 1984, SANA (Scientists Against Nuclear Arms) organized scientific seminars, attended by prominent scientists, about the theory of a nuclear winter. They invited, among others, representatives of the Home Office. The Home Office spokesman replied that they knew nothing about the theory of nuclear winter and were not interested in the invitation. So governments both envisage a nuclear war and deny the reality of what it would entail.

This attitude involves the operation of denial. Close to denial, but not identical to it, is the turning of a blind eye. I think the mechanism here is of a particular form of splitting (described by Freud as disavowal, operating in perversions). In this split we retain intellectual knowledge of the reality, but divest it of emotional meaning. An example in public life is the fact that various opinion polls have revealed that the vast majority of people think that nuclear war is inevitable, and that probably there will be no survival. And yet the same vast majority live their lives in that shadow without taking active steps to change policy.

We wish to deny the consequences of our actions to others and to ourselves, and to deny any aggressive impulses or actions on our own part. Increases in armaments are often kept secret. Here the British Cabinet papers of the 1950s are again revealing. When Attlee started manufacturing the A-bomb it was in secret, not only from Parliament, but even from members of his own Cabinet. Similarly, when the Churchill Government undertook the manufacturing of the H-bomb, they avoided the substantial opposition they anticipated. The Cabinet Committee responsible disguised the extent of the atomic programme by hiding the cost under 'other current expenditure' and 'extra-mural research'. Similarly, neither the public nor Parliament were ever informed of the contemplated use of atomic bombs against China, which I mentioned earlier. The hallowed word is 'security', but the secrecy, as those Cabinet notes make clear, is hardly motivated by having to hide from the enemy. Sooner or later the powers know all about one another's research. A note prepared for the Cabinet Committee said that the publicity could damage the West's defence interests, not because the Russians might learn something new, but because of the effect on public opinion. In dictatorial regimes like the USSR, this secrecy is built into the regime.

When our own aggressiveness can be disguised and hidden from us 'for security reasons', projective mechanisms and subsequent paranoia are increased. The enemy is presented as the devil. Mrs Thatcher speaks of the Russians as our hereditary enemy, yet since the Crimean War in 1854 the Russians have been Britain's allies in two world wars. President Reagan speaks of the Russians as the 'evil empire'.

The reaction to the shooting down of the Korean airliner in 1984 illustrates the same splitting and projection. Ronald Reagan, in an interview with Robert Scheer, said: 'We have a different regard for life than those monsters do. They are godless. It is this theological defect that gives them less regard for humanity or human beings.' By contrast, when, a couple of years before, the Israelis shot down a civilian Libyan plane in exactly the same circumstances, both the American and British governments defended it as unavoidably necessary to protect secret military installations. I suppose the Russians cried 'inhuman beasts' at that time. Gradually, each side creates a picture of the others as bloodthirsty, evil monsters beyond the pale. To hide our own aggressive desires we have to project the evil into an enemy, real or imaginary – he must appear an inhuman monster.

In genocide another element is added – that of contempt. The victim of genocide must be presented as not only inhuman, but as subhuman. As far back as the Middle Ages some crusaders used to roast and eat Arabs as a demonstration that Arabs were not to be seen as human. The Nazis called the Jews *Untermensch* – subhuman. The American soldiers called the Vietnamese Gooks. In the last war the Japanese called the Americans white devils – inhuman monsters. But when they exercised the utmost cruelty by practising vivisection on their prisoners, they called them logs – totally non-human, not even animal. To maintain a sufficient degree of paranoia and to deny the consequences to ourselves, we may have to dehumanize ourselves. In MacNamara's memorandum to President Kennedy, he states that the Air Force considers the loss of 50 million American lives, in case of a Russian counter-strike to the first strike, to be acceptable.

This kind of functioning has been described in the individual as a regression from the depressive position, characterized by a capacity to recognize one's own aggression, and to experience guilt and mourning, and a capacity both to function in reality and to make reparation. The regression is to the paranoid-schizoid position, characterized by the operation of denial, splitting and projection. I am speaking here of mechanisms familiar in the individual (Klein, 1946, 1948). It could be argued that we cannot transfer such knowledge directly to behaviour of large groups. Nevertheless, such mechanisms can be seen in group behaviour. Fornari (1975) has described wars as a paranoid defence against depressive anxiety. Indeed, in groups such mechanisms may be increased.

Psychoanalytic insight can throw important light on group behaviour. Co-operative groups were formed, as Freud pointed out in *Civilization and its Discontents* (1930), not only to combat forces of nature, but also to combat psychological dangers – primarily to bind the destructiveness of man against man. He commented that we can love one another in a group provided there are outsiders whom we can hate. Subsequently, a school of psychoanalytical thinking about the behaviour of groups elaborated the related idea that groups also bind and contain psychotic phantasies, anxieties and defences (Bion, 1952; Jaques, 1965; Menzies, 1970).

Groups can have features which, if present and acted on in an individual, would qualify that individual as mad or psychotic. Groups are usually narcissistic, self-idealizing and paranoid in relation to other groups. Conflict within the group and guilt about aggression can be dealt with by projection onto an outside group. In our private lives we have to contend with a superego which puts a check on destructiveness. If we vest the individual superego in a joint group superego, we can apparently guiltlessly perpetrate horrors which we couldn't bear in our individual existence. I think that the degree of dehumanization we encounter in such group practices as genocide we would see in an individual only in the

147

psychotic or the criminal psychopath. When such mechanisms get out of hand, the groups, instead of containing psychotic functioning, put it into practice and we get such irrational behaviour as wars and genocide. A perfect example of such irrational war was the 1914–18 War. Lloyd George said: 'We muddled into it.' According to numbers of historians the arms race was a significant, if not the most important, factor in this 'muddle' (Taylor, 1963).

According to Bion, a group may have the features of a 'work group' which is reality-orientated, and features of a 'basic-assumption group'. When the work group predominates we get a reality-orientated attitude (like Freud's idea that we form groups to combat the forces of nature). It also realistically contains and modifies the psychotic elements (basic-assumption). But in situations of excessive anxiety, the basic assumption type of group dominates. And the group can then behave in a destructive and self-destructive way which, in an individual, would be psychotic. Russell (1940) speaks of the loyalty to the state as having positive and negative motives: 'There is an element which is connected with love of home and family.' But he says later:

> No other organisation arouses anything like the loyalty aroused by the national state. And the chief activity of the state is the preparation for large-scale homicide. It is loyalty to this organisation for death that causes man to endure the totalitarian state and to risk the destruction of home and children and our whole civilisation.

Groups can hold views which in an individual could be named mad. A particularly worrying example of this group phenomenon in our time are the views of some Born Again Christians. They actually look forward to a nuclear war as Armageddon, which will cleanse the earth from evil, represented by Soviet Russia. The magazine *Family Weekly* noted that many believe that the social order is collapsing, with Armageddon just around the corner. However, the approach of Armageddon should not be a cause for fear, but for real hope! Why? Because Armageddon is God's war to cleanse the earth of all wickedness, paving the way for a bright, prosperous new order! The Bible explains that the righteous 'will possess the earth, and they will indeed find their exquisite delight in the abundance of peace' (Psalm 37:11). With bad conditions forever gone, every day of life then will be a delight. Not even sickness or death will mar the happiness of the people. God will 'wipe out every tear from their eyes, and death will be no more, neither will mourning nor outcry nor pain be any more' (Revelations 21:4, cited in circular from Jehovah's Witnesses, 1982).

It is astonishing that some of the leaders of the Western world seem, at least partly, to share those religious views:

I do not know how many future generations we can count on before the Lord returns.

> (James Watt, US Secretary of State for the Interior; (Franklin, 1982)

Jerry, I sometimes believe we're heading very fast for Armageddon right now.

> (President Reagan; Franklin, 1982)

I have read the Book of Revelation and, yes, I believe the world is going to end – by an act of God, I hope – but every day I think that time is running out. . . . I think of World War II and how long it took to prepare for it, to convince people that rearmament for war is needed. I fear we will not be ready. I think time is running out . . . but I have faith.

> (Caspar Weinberger, US Secretary of Defense; interview, *New York Times*, 23 August 1982)

A report in the British newspaper, the *Guardian*, estimates that 35 million Americans are registered as Born Again Christians. I am not implying here that 35 million Americans are mad. I don't know how many Mohammedans believe that if they die in a Holy War they will go straight to heaven. As individuals they are not all mad. But it is in the nature of groups that they can maintain corporately such mad beliefs.

In this situation leaders are very important. We like to trust them. That's part of feeling safe in a group. But according to Bion, when the basic assumption, a psychotic constellation of impulses, phantasies and defences, dominates, the group throws up leaders which best represent that psychotic element. Hitler would be the outstanding example. There is also some evidence that Stalin was openly psychotic towards the end of his life.

As I see it, we now live in a world situation producing great anxiety and defences against it, which, because of the very existence of atomic weapons and the arms race, are massively increased. For the first time humanity has in reality the power of complete annihilation and self-annihilation. Glover wrote in 1933:

> The first promise of the atomic age is that it can make some of our nightmares come true. The capacity so painfully acquired by normal man to distinguish between sleep, hallucination, delusion and the objective reality of wakened life has for the first time in history been seriously weakened.

In this not quite sane situation, the lure of omnipotence is increased and so is the lure of death. I speak of the lure of death because, in my view, beliefs such as are held by Born Again Christians, and similar groups, reveal almost nakedly the death instinct – the welcoming of Armageddon, idealized as the will of God and a prelude to eternal bliss. Universal death is seen as universal salvation – the aspect of nirvana of the death instinct, as described by Freud. In this situation of a reactivation of the death instinct, and seeing its possible final embodiment in the prospect of atomic war, we are, I believe pushed into what I would call the world of the schizophrenic.

I think the existence of atomic weapons mobilizes and actualizes this world of the schizophrenic. The obliteration of boundaries between reality and phantasy, as described by Glover, characterizes psychosis. Omnipotence has become real, but only omnipotent destruction. We can, at the push of a button, annihilate the world. In this world of primitive omnipotence, the problem is not of death wishes and a fear of death which pertain to the depressive and Oedipal world, it is governed by wishes for annihilation of the self and the world, and the terrors associated with them.

Lifton (1982) makes the point, very convincing to me, that atomic annihilation destroys the possibility of symbolic survival. In natural death or even in conventional war, people die, or at least those who have acquired some maturity die, with some conviction of symbolic survival in their children, grandchildren, in their work or in the civilization itself of which they were part. Coming to terms with the prospect of one's own personal death is a necessary step in maturation and in giving full meaning to life (Jaques, 1965; Segal, 1952, 1958). The existence of nuclear weapons and the prospect of nuclear war makes difficult a growing acceptance of death and symbolic survival. The prospect of death in atomic warfare leaves an unimaginable void and produces terror of a different kind. Those of us who work with psychotics get an inkling of this kind of terror. In normal development, as Freud has described, and Klein elaborated further, Eros, the life forces, succeed in integrating and taming destructive and self-destructive drives and convert them into life-promoting aggression.

In the depths of our unconscious, however, such unintegrated wishes and terrors still exist. We are all only partly sane, and such circumstances as prevail now mobilize the most primitive parts of ourselves. Einstein said that, with the advent of atomic power, everything has changed except our way of thinking. And in a way he is of course right. It has not changed it for the better. We have not come to realize that the advent of the atomic weapons made meaningless the idea of a just war, or the defence of civic values, since the war would destroy all values. It has not changed our thinking in the direction of realizing that our national, racial, religious or political narcissisms are not only paltry, but lethal, and that our concern should be with the survival of the human race. But I am afraid that the atomic bomb may have changed our thinking for the worse. Confronted with the real terror of annihilation, our schizoid defences are increased, denial – 'It won't happen, or it won't be that bad' – the turning of a blind eye, and splitting and projection are increased. There is also a regression to part-object relationships, which exclude empathy, compassion and concern. The distortion of language, present in all wars, has reached an Orwellian degree of absurdity in the terms used to describe nuclear warfare – Nukespeak. The code signal for the dropping of the bomb on Hiroshima was 'Baby is born'. The bomb itself was called 'Little Boy'. The bomb thrown on Nagasaki was called 'Fat Man'. Recently, nuclear has become 'nuke'. All these words cover up the utter destructiveness of what is being done and make it sound manageable, unaggressive, even cute. At the height of the Falklands conflict some youngsters in England wore T-shirts showing 'Nuke Buenos Aires'. I doubt if those same youngsters would wear a badge saying 'Annihilate several million people'. To 'nuke' sounds so innocent. Even 'nuclear exchange', often discussed, hides the lethal nature of the exchange.

The worst linguistic deception is perhaps the word 'deterrence' itself. Over the years it has completely changed its meaning. The first idea of deterrence was that the Americans had the A-bomb and could use it to deter Russia from invading Europe. Soon, of course, the Russians had the bomb as well, and deterrence changed its meaning. It came to mean 'to deter the other party from the use of nuclear weapons'. This seemed to make some sense. Since the bomb was dropped by a country possessing the bomb on a country which did not, it made some kind of sense to think that if the big powers were both armed, each would deter the other from the nuclear initiative. Even at the time, the reasoning was not very sound on how to prevent other countries from acquiring nuclear weapons, how to maintain a balance of terror as a basis for co-existence, since such balance of terror would inevitably increase the paranoia. With the increasing arms race, the system came to be known as MAD (Mutual Assured Destruction).

Then in the last few years, deterrence changed its meaning again. It became, more like the original meaning, the threat of the use of atomic weapons should Russia be in any conflict with its neighbours which might be seen as a threat to the United States. This change in the United States became more explicit in the 1960s and 1970s. That is when we started hearing that nuclear war could be won – that we must start to think of 'a rational nuclear war'. 'The US must possess the ability to wage nuclear war rationally' (a US defence adviser, 1982). Again, distortions of language are used to hide a change from purely defensive to aggressive warfare. The notion of a 'flexible response' was introduced; another attractive phrase invented to cover this change from a defensive to an aggressive posture. 'Flexible response' means that in the case of a conventional conflict between Russia and its neighbours, so-called strategic nuclear weapons would be used. In 1981, in an interview in the *Daily Telegraph*, Caspar

Weinberger, US Defense Secretary, said: 'The simple fact of the matter is that, unfortunate and awful as it would be for the world, it is possible that with nuclear weapons, there can be some use of them in a limited, or in connection with what is up to that time a war solely within the European theatre.' The confused English does not disguise the meaning. But how limited is limited? 'Little Boy' dropped on Hiroshima had a yield of about 13 kilotons, but the modern Polaris has a yield of 60 kilotons; the Cruise missile of 200 kilotons. How many Hiroshimas for a little strategic limited war in Europe? Unsurprisingly, the Europeans didn't relish the idea.

The term 'Strategic Defence Initiative' (SDI), to describe the latest escalation of the arms race, sounds fine. It is defensive, not offensive. But it conceals the fact that a fool-proof defence would put the side which had it in an incontestable first strike position. In fact, Henry Kissinger argues that if America could be fully protected by the Strategic Defence Initiative 'that would be in the European interest, because it would increase our willingness to use nuclear weapons in Europe's defence' (Kissinger in an interview for *Stern* magazine). Such a stand would inevitably lead the Russians in turn to increase their offensive arsenal – a new hotting up of the arms race. The alternative term, 'Star Wars', is even more misleading. It has a heroic science fiction sound. It conjures up the picture of a war among the stars – not affecting the earth.

All this Nukespeak is a distortion of language to disguise from ourselves and others both the full horror of a nuclear war and our own part in making it possible or more likely. Everything is presented as defensive by both superpowers. One's own destructive wishes and activities are always blamed on the others. Fragmentation, characteristic of this schizophrenic process, has increased with the nuclear arms race. In particular, there is a fragmentation of responsibility – with a resulting lack of clear accountability. One consequence is that the military industrial complex increasingly acquires its own dynamic. There is a view that dropping of the bomb on Hiroshima, and particularly on Nagasaki when Japan was already disintegrating, was pushed by the military wishing to test a new weapon. According to the Oxford Research Group (1986), the nuclear weapons policy is 'at best a post rationalisation for the development of the weapon systems whose *raison d'être* has become institutionalised'.

This is particularly so in the case of nuclear weapons, which take up to twenty years to develop. The Government is not accountable, as it has inherited tentative decisions on research taken years ago which have now acquired their own momentum. The contracts the Europeans are making now for the SDI will be hard to reverse, should the government's policy change. They contain provision for quite swingeing compensation in the event of cancellation. The expenditure on nuclear weapons apparently is not accounted for in any way. For instance, the development of the

Chevaline warhead for Polaris was carried on through four changes of government and completion in the early 1980s with no public debate, and the first mention of Chevaline in Parliament was by Defence Secretary Pym in 1980. The overall estimated cost of the programme was then £1,000 million. It had originally been estimated at £7.5 million. According to the Oxford Research Group, in the West, the least degree of accountability to Parliament, or even to government, is in Great Britain. But their research in five countries comes to the conclusion that the situation is very similar in other countries. We could be led to believe that the position is different in Soviet Russia and that the Politburo has absolute power. But according to the Oxford Research Group, the situation there is practically the same. Galbraith, in a number of his works, shows the structural similarities of the capitalist and Soviet systems:

> Q: Does the technological structure have a similar existence in both public and private corporations? *A*: Oh, yes. And in both, it requires independence. As I have said, the technological structure cannot suffer the uninformed intrusion of either stockholders or politicians.
>
> (Galbraith and Salinger, 1981)

So we have a near-autonomous existence of continuing increase and proliferation of nuclear weapons.

There is also fragmentation and lack of accountability in the provisions for using nuclear weapons. In an extremely important American book, *The Command and Control of Nuclear Forces*, Paul Bracken (1984) describes the fragmentation of command centres such that, should an atomic war happen, and should there be survivors, it would be impossible to trace who had started it. This fragmentation is also in evidence in a minor way in non-nuclear conflicts now. Who gave the order to sink the *Belgrano* – and on what information? The Government says the commanders in the field must decide. The commanders say they had Government orders. Similarly, the Russians could never trace satisfactorily who bears responsibility for the shooting down of the Korean plane.

Another aspect of fragmentation and lack of accountability is evidenced in the spread of nuclear weapons, which I think now concerns the United States and Russia. The split-off fragments of their nuclear know-how and materiel are now spread throughout the world and out of their control. Any of those fragments may start a general flare-up.

The growth of technology is also used for a typically schizoid dehumanization and mechanization. There is a kind of prevailing depersonalization and de-realization. Pushing a button to annihilate parts of the world we have never seen is a mechanized, split-off activity. Bracken contends that the war is likely to happen through our machines getting out of control. Everything is so automated that over-sensitive machines could

153

start an unstoppable nuclear exchange. The MIT computer expert Joseph Weizenbaum comes to the similar conclusion: that modern big computers are so complicated that no expert can see through and control them. The whole nuclear early warning system is based on these machines – perhaps the worst danger if the paranoid international tensions reach a high level. Since one effect of nuclear explosion is a disturbance in communication systems, it might not be in the powers of governments to stop an escalation even if they wish to. But the fact that we can even think that 'machines will start the war, not us' shows the extent of the denial of our responsibility. We seem to live in a peculiar combination of helplessness and terror and omnipotence – the helplessness and omnipotence increasing each in a vicious circle. This helplessness which lies at the root of our apathy is partly inevitable. We are faced with a horrifyingly threatening danger. But partly it is self-induced and becomes a self-fulfilling prophecy. Confronted with the terror of the powers of destructiveness, we divest ourselves from our responsibilities by denial, projection and fragmentation.

The responsibility is fragmented and projected further and further away – into governments, army, scientists and, finally, into machines beyond human control. We don't only project into our so-called enemies. We also divest ourselves from our responsibilities by projecting them into governments. They in turn can't bear such responsibility and they project into us, the people, public opinion, and so on, as well as fragmenting their responsibility, as described above. When we project into governments, we become truly helpless. We are in their hands. Then we can either become paranoid about the government's or Reagan's doings, or Thatcher's or the Kremlin's. Or, we idealize our governments and leave the responsibilities in their hands – they are the experts. And then we make ourselves truly helpless. And the governments offer us the escape of megalomania. We like to feel big and powerful and think we can frighten our enemy. But we forget how dangerous a frightened enemy can be.

If all that is a result of unbound, split-off and denied operation of what Freud called the death instinct, does it make it hopeless? I do not think so. In the individual analyses of patients we find that the hopeless situations are due not solely to the power of the instincts, but largely to the vicious circles between impulses and defences. In normal development, self-preservation and love (Eros) can integrate the death instinct and turn it into useful life-promoting aggression. But in situations of acute anxiety, vicious circles between the death instincts and the defences against it preclude such integration.

The fateful question for the human species seems to me to be whether and to what extent their cultural development will succeed in mastering the disturbance of their communal life by the human instinct of aggression and self-destruction. It may be that in this respect precisely the present time deserves a special interest. Men have gained control over the forces of nature to such an extent that with their help they would have no difficulty in exterminating one another to the last man. They know this, and hence comes a large part of their current unrest, their unhappiness and their mood of anxiety. And now it is to be expected that the other of the two 'Heavenly Powers', eternal Eros, will make an effort to assert himself in the struggle with his equally immortal adversary. But who can foresee with what success and with what result?

(Freud, 1930: 145)

This was written in 1930 (with the last sentence added in 1931). It is more than ever applicable today. We are at a crossroads. We must try to find means to mobilize our life forces against the destructive powers. To do that we must confront those powers and dangers without denial, hoping that the realization of what we are about to do to ourselves will mobilize our life forces and our reality sense.

What role can we, as analysts, play in this tragic drama? I think first we must look into ourselves and beware of turning a blind eye to reality. We are like other humans, with the same destructive and self-destructive drives. We use the same defences. We are prone to the same denials and, moreover, we can hide behind the shield of psychoanalytic neutrality. We know that, as psychoanalysts, we should be neutral and, for instance, not take part in political debates as psychoanalysts, whatever our own political convictions, which we can pursue as individuals. But there are situations in which such an attitude can also become a shield of denial. To be acquainted with facts and recognize psychic facts, which we of all people know something about, and to have the courage to try to state them clearly, is in fact the psychoanalytic stand. We must face our fears and mobilize our forces against destruction. And we must be heard.

There has been a change in the nature of the movement opposed to the nuclear arms race. Today it is largely led by informed opinion. I do not mean to imply that all informed opinion is necessarily part of that movement, but that in the forefront of the movement opposing nuclear weapons are doctors, scientists, historians, teachers, lawyers – all those used to looking objectively at facts. There are some signs that the clear message is beginning to get through a little. We belong with them. We are also scientists – looking at psychic facts. We must add our voice clearly to their voices.

Secondly, I think we have a specific contribution to make. We are cognizant of the psychic mechanisms of denial, projection, magic thinking and so on. We should be able to contribute something to the overcoming of apathy and self-deception in ourselves and others. When the Nazi phenomenon was staring us in the face, the psychoanalytic community outside Germany was largely silent. This must not be repeated. Nadezhda Mandelstam said: 'Silence is the real crime against humanity' (*Hope against Hope*, 1971).

We psychoanalysts who believe in the power of words and the therapeutic effect of verbalizing truth must not be silent.

Summary

This paper aims to show that psychoanalysts have a meaningful and specific contribution to make to the understanding of psychological causes and effects of the nuclear arms race. It examines some of the psychoanalytical ideas about wars in general – in particular, the importance of the regression from the depressive position and the mobilization of paranoid-schizoid mechanisms, splitting and projection – present in all wars. But it emphasizes that the very existence of nuclear weapons mobilizes those mechanisms to a far greater extent because of the threat of total annihilation.

In my view, the blurring of the border between reality and phantasy mobilizes infantile omnipotence and the death instinct and destructive psychotic defences against the threat of total annihilation. A vicious circle between the death instinct and the defences against recognizing it produces a situation in which we are not facing the consequences of an unbridled arms race. Denial and apathy in the face of the threat are phenomena understandable to analysts who, according to me, should make their views known.

Note

1 This chapter has been published previously (Segal, 1987). It was first given in Hamburg in 1985, in the wake of the IPA Congress, at the inaugural meeting of the International Psychoanalysts Against Nuclear Weapons. The phrase 'Silence is the real Crime' comes from N. Mandelstam, *Hope against Hope* (1971).

14

From Hiroshima to the Gulf War and after: socio-political expressions of ambivalence[1]

It is often contended that psychoanalysts can only speak authoritatively of their work in the consulting room and of individual psychology. Socio-political phenomena should therefore be left to specialists in other spheres, economists, sociologists, politicians and, in the area of war, even generals. But I contend that psychoanalysis has as its field the manifold aspects of the human mind and its activities and that therefore the exploration of its social aspects is a legitimate field of psychoanalytic inquiry. Moreover, I think that psychoanalysis has a unique contribution to make to the understanding of these phenomena; in particular, because of our experience of the conflicts between constructive and destructive attitudes in the individual we are able to shed light on some of the destructive forces we have to deal with socially. I will therefore begin by discussing the nature and development of ambivalence as we have learned to understand it in psychoanalysis and then make some remarks about the knowledge we have acquired in the study of groups. Finally, I will apply such considerations to the wider area of the handling of aggression in social situations and its mishandling in our failure to prevent wars and above all to make the world safe from nuclear catastrophe.

In the 1920s, in his final theory of instincts, Freud posits a conflict between the instincts of life and death. He believed that this conflict and the ambivalence that results from it underline all other conflicts and are reflected not only in pathology or dreams but in all human individual and group behaviour. This conflict between the life and death instincts is expressed as ambivalence towards primary objects, which is not necessarily pathological, and indeed is a part of human nature.

In 'Mourning and melancholia' (1917) Freud gives perhaps the best description of the central role of ambivalence. This is the paper which foreshadows his description of the superego and his theory of the life and death instincts. He differentiates between mourning the loss of an object,

157

which necessitates a gradual detachment of the libido from the lost object, and the state of melancholia. In melancholia the work of mourning is impeded by an ambivalence towards the object, an ambivalence that continues in relation to this object even after it has been internalized, and results in a painful mutual hatred between this internal object and the ego that is in conflict with the love which also exists between them. That paper brings to light more vividly than any of the preceding ones the importance of ambivalence towards an internal object. The Oedipus complex, with the simultaneous expression of love and hate toward both parental objects, is a major focus of ambivalence and it is the introjection of those ambivalently loved figures which forms the core of the superego.

In *Beyond the Pleasure Principle*, Freud (1920) described how the life instinct, which desires and aims at life, love, integration and growth, is in conflict with the death instinct, which Freud considered to be a desire to return to an inorganic state. Freud assumes that the 'organism', in order to avoid death, deflects the death instinct outwards and in this way it becomes aggression against objects. He comments that in clinical practice we never observe the death instinct directly – its work being done silently within the organism – but we see it when it is fused with libido. However, we now recognize that at least in the case of psychosis, severe neurosis and sadistic perversions, we can observe defusion of the two instincts which allows the death instinct to be recognized almost in its naked form.

Melanie Klein, starting work in the 1920s, held the view that the conflict between loving and destructive impulses was experienced from the beginning of life in relation to objects, primarily the maternal breast. In her view, it is the rudimentary ego that deflects the death instinct, and that from birth onwards this deflection functions as a defence mechanism. She sees this deflection as projection into an object as well as an aggression directed against the object. This projection creates a 'hateful' object, which is perceived to be full of hatred as well as being hated. And split off from this, the life instinct searches for the object of need and partly also creates one by projection. Bad experiences attach themselves to, and are attributed to, the bad object, and good experiences to the good one. Klein called this early stage 'paranoid–schizoid' because of the paranoid anxiety in relation to a bad object imbued also with the infant's projected destructiveness, and because of the schizoid split existing between idealized and persecutory experiences. Those of course are not the only characteristics of the paranoid–schizoid position, but are the main ones in relation to dealing with ambivalence.

As those projections get gradually withdrawn, and a more realistic picture is formed of the object, and of itself, the infant has to experience his or her own ambivalence. Infants begin to perceive their mother as a whole object – that is, not split into two or fragmented into parts, but as one person both gratifying and frustrating. And infants also realize that they are one person with conflicting feelings and that their mother is one person whom they both love and hate.

This stage, when the infant recognizes the mother as a whole person, Klein called 'the depressive position' because the realization of ambivalence brings with it the threat of the loss of the object and the depressive feelings associated with it. Looked at from that angle, the capacity to experience ambivalence is a fundamental achievement, a major step in development. It is essential to integration of split objects and feelings, and to the recognition of reality, which is both gratifying and frustrating. It also brings with it a new range of feelings, such as fear of loss and guilt. Guilt replaces persecution, and this is of great importance because persecution has no resolution; hatred brings persecution and persecution brings hatred. On the other hand, when ambivalence is recognized, aggression is felt as damaging an object that is also needed and desired, and brings in its wake not more hatred but, on the contrary, a mobilization of loving impulses and the wish to repair and restore. This, in Klein's view, is the basis of constructive sublimation. However, the recognition of the ambivalence, guilt and fear of loss is extremely painful, and powerful defences can set in, manic defences, paranoid defences and others, all necessitating some degree of regression to more primitive forms of functioning.

The depressive position brings about a fundamental re-orientation to reality. With the withdrawal of projections the object is perceived more in accordance with the reality principle and so is the self. We begin to take responsibility for our own impulses and the achievement of ambivalence can be seen as a major developmental step. Moreover, a flight from ambivalence brings about a regression to the primitive mental mechanisms of the paranoid-schizoid position of denial, splitting, projection and fragmentation.

I think it is essential to differentiate the fact of the existence of ambivalence, which is there from the beginning, from the achievement of knowing one's ambivalence, accepting it and working through it. Such working through is accomplished primarily through the recognition of guilt and of loss brought about by ambivalence which leads to the capacity to mobilize restoration and reparation. This does not mean that aggression is absent; but it becomes proportional to the cause, as does the guilt attached to it.

From my description, it sounds as though I were ignoring problems of environment. This is not the case. The environment helps or hinders the resolution of the ambivalent conflict. Obviously, good experiences increase love and bad experiences hinder it. And furthermore, how the parental objects deal with the infant's destructiveness or self-destructiveness is of fundamental importance in modulating it. This fact is of course crucial in psychoanalysis used as a therapeutic tool. The patient brings their infantile impulses and their internal objects to be re-examined in a different way, a different environment.

I have dealt so far with individual psychology only, but the conflicts described are also expressed in our group behaviour. Humans are social animals and this is life-promoting. We form groups to help one another and to face problems together. But at the same time groups contain and give expression to death drives which are a danger to themselves and to other groups.

In relation to the socio-political field, it is clear that the baby and the child relate from the beginning to other people, primarily the parents, and that the family is the prototype and the nucleus of all other social engagements. At first the baby relates to and depends on the breast as a part-object. Then, when they start to perceive their mother as a whole person, they realize that she has other relations as well, and start to relate to their father and the family as a whole. Very soon this extends to groups such as neighbours and school companions. We all belong to a variety of groups, some of which are chosen, some that we are born into, such as a nation, and sometimes a religion. The analyst's concern is not just with the individual, but with the interaction between the individual and their environment, starting with the family group in infancy and extending later to larger groups.

One reason why psychoanalysis has a particular contribution to make to the understanding of social phenomena arises from the fact that group behaviour is very often very irrational. For society to behave in such irrational ways, evident in our destructive activities to the planet we depend upon, in particular the destruction of our own habitat by greedy exploitation and pollution, and the continuation of the insane nuclear arms race, it is necessary to assume that powerful unconscious forces are at work.

In his writing on groups, Freud contends that they are established under the aegis of the libido, which functions as a force towards the achievement of harmony within the group in order to enable it to carry out tasks. But this process is disturbed by the continual disruptions caused by impulses and phantasies derived from the death instinct.

> In all that follows I adopt the standpoint, therefore, that the inclination to aggression is an original, self-subsisting instinctual disposition in man, and I return to my view that it constitutes the greatest impediment to civilisation. At one point in the course of this enquiry I was led to the idea that civilisation was a special process which mankind undergoes, and I am still under the influence of that idea. I may now add that civilisation is a process in the service of Eros, whose purpose is to

combine single human individuals, and after that families, then races, people and nations, into one great unity, the unity of mankind. Why this has to happen, we do not know; the work of Eros is precisely this. These collections of men are to be libidinally bound to one another. Necessity alone, the advantages of work in common, will not hold them together. But man's natural aggressive instinct, the hostility of each against all and of all against each, opposes this programme of civilisation. This aggressive instinct is the derivative and the main representative of the death instinct which we have found alongside of Eros and which shares world-dominion with it.

(Freud, 1930: 122)

Freud was not the only person to try to apply the insights derived from the couch to observations of group behaviour and social phenomena. But despite all this work, somehow psychoanalysis did not seem to throw much light on actual contemporary phenomena. It is amazing to think that, while many psychoanalysts played a heroic role in combating National Socialism, the organized body of psychoanalysts, the International Psychoanalytical Association, had nothing to say on the subject, and there were no major scientific papers dealing with the Nazi phenomenon or giving a warning about its meaning, though Freud makes a passing reference to the growth of Nazism in his letter to Einstein.

It was different after the Second World War, when a number of outstanding papers and books appeared on the subject of war and fascism (Glover, 1947; Fornari, 1966; Money-Kyrle, 1978). I think this change after the war came about partly because analysts were beginning to work directly with groups and partly because of the advance in our understanding of psychosis. Group functioning is often basically influenced and disrupted by psychotic phenomena. Freud said that we form groups for two reasons: one, to 'combat the forces of nature'; and the other, to bind 'man's destructiveness to man'. Groups typically deal with this destructiveness by splitting, the group itself being idealized and held together by brotherly love, and collective love of an ideal, while destructiveness is directed outwards to other groups. Generally we tend to project into the group parts of ourselves which we cannot deal with individually, and since it is the most disturbed, psychotic parts of ourselves which we find hardest to deal with, those tend to be projected primarily into groups.

Group defence mechanisms are mainly directed against psychotic anxieties which individuals cannot contain in themselves, and they use mechanisms in a way that if used by an individual would be considered psychotic. In normal circumstances constructive and realistic functioning predominates and psychotic features are kept under control. Even so,

161

however, groups behave in a way which in an individual would be considered mad; for instance, almost invariably groups are self-idealizing, grandiose and paranoid, and they can free themselves of guilt by allowing the group to sanction aggression which in the individual would be unforgivable.

Wilfred Bion (1961) has extended Freud's hypothesis about the functions of the group. According to him, a group fulfils two functions. One he called the 'work group', in which the group is able to function at a realistic level and to carry out its task. The other he called the 'basic-assumption group', in which the group function relies on a psychotic premise. Such psychotic premises underlie, for instance, our sense of superiority to other groups, our unjustifiable hostility or fear of them and so on. Our psychotic parts are merged into our group identity, and we do not feel mad since our views are sanctioned by the group. If the work function predominates in the group the psychotic elements are kept in check and our crazy assumptions may be expressed in a fairly innocuous way.

A large group, such as a state or nation, can also delegate such psychotic functions to sub-groups which are kept under control by the group as a whole – such sub-groups as, for instance, the Army, in which the military mind and military training are based on paranoid assumptions. Similarly, our sense of dependence on omnipotence and our messianic, grandiose delusions can be vested in the Church and in religion in general.

This type of delegation of a function to a circumscribed group fails if the group becomes too powerful. A political grouping, such as Fascism or Communism, can combine the Army mentality with religious mentality, bringing about guiltless destruction. The same can happen when the group called the nation gets ruled by nationalism.

Members of a group brought together by work of whatever kind have a common individual and group interest, and in this case the security of both the individual and their group is bound up with the success of the work. Rivalries are unavoidable, but tempered by the need for survival and success of the group. Like a child in a family, the group itself can face rivalry with other groups, and this too can take a sane form – for instance, involving competition and emulation – or, on the other hand, become an insane, destructive force which threatens to destroy both parties.

The predominance of psychotic processes over work orientation in a group is a particular danger of *political* groupings, whether national or ideological. This may be so because the national or political group's work is less well defined. If a group of scientists and other workers in a laboratory was dominated not by the work function but by psychotic assumptions, the actual work could not be performed. This is not so in political groupings, which seem to embody most easily feelings of superiority, messianic missions, and convictions of rightness and paranoia about others. It may be also because political groupings have to do with the search for power, which in itself is a primitive aim.

Actually, politics are involved in any sizeable groupings. It is an unrealistic ideal to think that one can have an organization or society without politics. There will always be different views about policies to be pursued, giving rise to political tensions, and there will also be more destructive tensions due to rivalries and search for power. But, in an ordinary, well-functioning group, such destructive tensions will be subjected to the work function of the group – just as in a well-functioning family, love and goodness can contain and modify violence and hatred. One could say, 'Too much politicking will not be tolerated because it will disrupt the work.' Not so in a political grouping, which has no other task but politics. The group chooses its leader according to its orientation. Groups under the sway of psychotic mechanisms tend to select or to tolerate leaders who represent their pathology. But not only do those groups choose unbalanced leaders; they also affect them. The groups thrust omnipotence onto their leaders, and push them further into megalomania. There is a dangerous interaction between a disturbed group and a disturbed leader, increasing each other's pathology.

A political group may be an organization, such as a state or a political party within a state. But there is a larger, undefined political group which is in fact all of us. Everybody does some political thinking, unavoidably, even those who do not bother with political parties. And our political thinking is largely controlled by the group, whether it is based on race or religion or nation. Unthinkingly, we adopt the mental posture of the group to which we belong, a posture which may be quite irrational and dangerous for our survival.

I have previously argued [for example, in Chapter 13] that the very existence of nuclear weapons has given a new dimension to problems of war and peace. My own interest in trying to apply psychoanalytical understanding to the socio–political scene was stimulated by my awareness of this situation, which led me to address myself to the problem of the lure of destructive and self-destructive omnipotence, and the terror they induce. I argued that the very existence of the bomb arouses the most primitive psychotic anxieties about annihilation, and mobilizes the most primitive defences. I will not repeat this argument except to emphasize one of the points I made there; namely, that, in the social problem of destructiveness, a new element enters with the creation of nuclear weapons.

I think the existence of atomic weapons mobilizes and actualizes what I would describe as the world of the schizophrenic in which there is an obliteration of boundaries between reality and phantasy which characterizes psychosis. Omnipotence has become real, but only omnipotent destruction. We can in reality annihilate the world at the push of a button, but while in phantasy we can also omnipotently reconstruct it, we cannot do so in reality. In this world of primitive omnipotence, the problem is not of death wishes and a fear of death, which pertain to the more mature depressive and Oedipal world, but rather one governed by wishes for annihilation of the self and the world, and the terrors associated with it.

It is here that Lifton's point is so very convincing. He describes (Lifton, 1982) how atomic annihilation destroys the possibility of symbolic survival. In natural death, or even in conventional war, people face death while retaining a conviction of symbolic survival in their children, grandchildren, in their work or in the civilization itself of which they are part. As a result of their death, mourning, reconciliation, and reparation can eventually take place. Coming to terms with the prospect of one's own personal death is a necessary step in maturation and in giving full meaning to life. The existence of nuclear weapons and the prospect of nuclear war makes such an acceptance of death and symbolic survival impossible. The prospect of death in atomic warfare leaves an unimaginable void and produces terror of a different kind. Those of us who work with psychotics get an inkling of this kind of terror. In normal development, as Freud has described and Klein elaborated further, Eros, the life force, succeeds in integrating and taming destructive and self-destructive drives, and converts them into life-promoting aggression. But in the depths of our unconscious, such unintegrated wishes and terrors still exist. We are all only partly sane, and such circumstances as prevail now mobilize the most primitive parts of ourselves. The lure of omnipotence is powerful; and so is, at some level, the lure of death.

Against the anxieties and guilt about those destructive drives most powerful defences are mobilized. Splitting and projection have to be increased, creating evil empires. That in turn increases both irrational anxiety and realistic fears. Then megalomania has to be increased as a defence, and it becomes vested in the omnipotence of the bomb. Dehumanization of the enemy has to take place, making the enemy either a monster or an object beneath contempt. But not the enemy only; we also dehumanize ourselves and our allies.

[This theme has been further elaborated in Chapter 13, where the way the language is misused to deny the reality of nuclear catastrophe is described. I argue that this led to a kind of thinking which was of course active on both sides of the East–West divide, producing an unstable equilibrium based on insane premises and paranoid-schizoid defences.]

In this chapter I want to look at the way the system has been undermined by perestroika, following which the paranoid system, since it requires an enemy, could not be maintained. Perestroika was a time of hope, because of the possibility that it might lead to a change of attitude.

But it was also a time of new dangers associated with a search for a new enemy.

This was a particular problem for the NATO powers, which needed a new enemy to justify its continued military power. Despite the disappearance of the supposed Soviet threat, our apparent reason for keeping a nuclear arsenal, the Western countries could not tolerate the idea of nuclear disarmament or conceive of a world without the atom bomb. It was like an addiction. And though apparently much had changed with perestroika, one thing had not changed. Nuclear fire-power was constantly increasing, in the process of so-called modernization.

So what was going on? Clinically, we are familiar with those moments of hope when a paranoid patient begins to give up their delusions, or when an addict begins to give up the drug and get better. The improvement is genuine. But as they get better they have to face reality. With the diminishing of omnipotence they have to face their dependence, possibly helplessness, and the fact that they are ill. With the withdrawal of projections they have to face their own destructiveness, their inner conflicts and guilt: they have to face their internal realities. Moreover, they often have to face very real losses and damage brought about by their illness, in external reality. Formidable manic defences can be mobilized against this depressive pain, with a revival of megalomania and in its wake a return of paranoia.

Similarly, in the social domain, when we stopped believing in the evil empire we had to turn to our internal situation and we had to face our social problems: economic decline, unemployment, guilt about the Third World. In Britain and the United States in particular, we had to face the effect of our mismanagement of resources and we had to face the guilt about the waste of resources on excessive, unnecessary, mad nuclear armaments against a non-existent danger – resources which should have been turned to education, health, industrial infrastructure and so on. One of the factors in the prosperity of Germany and Japan was the fact that they were not allowed to develop weapons.

Since a very important function of the group, one of the first ones observed by Freud and amply confirmed both by observation and clinical experience of groups, is to defend individuals against their guilt feelings, groups find it almost impossible to face collective guilt. This is a point made by Fornari (1966), who argued that wars are often started as a defence against guilt about previous wars. In the case of the United States, the guilt over the Vietnam War, both for the damage done to the enemy and for the humiliation and failure to the United States itself, was, until recently, not recognized and is only now partially being faced. This unacknowledged guilt was one of the factors making the Gulf War necessary; it was intended to wipe out the depression about Vietnam.

At the time of perestroika, rather than face guilt we turned to manic defences: in particular to triumphalism. Perestroika was felt to be the triumph of our superior system and power, and our nuclear mentality did not change. The megalomaniac search for power and the addiction to the bomb was bound to create new enemies to replace Soviet Russia – first, because megalomania does in fact create new enemies, and, second, because we need a new evil empire to justify the arrogant aggression which we project into it.

Einstein said that, with the advent of atomic power, everything has changed except our way of thinking. And in a way he is of course right. It has not changed for the better. We have not come to realize that the advent of the atomic weapons made the idea of a just war and the military defence of civilized values meaningless, since such a war would destroy all values. It has not changed our thinking in the direction of realizing that our national, racial, religious or political narcissisms are not only paltry, but lethal, and that our concern should be with the survival of the human race. But I am afraid that the atomic bomb may have changed our thinking for the worse, producing a nuclear-mentality culture based on fears of annihilation and increasing schizophrenic defences. This mentality survived the end of the Cold War, and prevented us from using constructively the collapse of the 'Evil Empire'.

I and my colleagues of the PPNW,[2] in a number of mostly-unpublished papers presented to various audiences, warned about the dangers inherent in the post-perestroika situation. But numbness and apathy had set in. Anti-nuclear war organizations lost much of their membership. Public meetings were poorly attended. There was a feeling of great relief, and a wish to believe that all was well now – and increasing denial of the dangers that were still there. Specifically, we warned that unless attitudes to the whole problem changed we were in danger of finding a new enemy.

The Gulf War was a striking instance in which an enemy was found or created to fill this vacuum. We found a new enemy in Iraq and Saddam Hussein, who had been, almost to the outbreak of the war, supported by both East and West. His naked aggression to Iran, and his tyranny at home, did not prevent both power blocs from supplying him with sophisticated weapons. Then overnight he became a monster, and he readily accepted the role since he, like the West, had lost an enemy and needed one to replace it. The enormous destructive power used in that war gave the West the triumph it demanded, and it seems likely that had it been necessary to deploy nuclear weapons to achieve that superiority they would have been used.

The Gulf War, in turn, is forgotten as though it is ancient history. There is a universal denial of what we have done and what the consequences are. The countless victims, the devastation of the whole area and the continuing human and ecological disaster is ignored. The guilt remains unacknowledged and the dangers of such a stance remain with us. Those who do not remember their history are bound to repeat it, but facing the reality of history exposes us to what is most unbearable. This is particularly difficult in groups where the task is one of admitting that we made a mistake of vast proportions and have to take responsibility for the consequences. But unless we do that, our manic and schizoid defences will make us blind to these realities and lead us to further disasters.

To go back to my theme of the 'nuclear mentality'. The dangers of nuclear war are no fewer than they were during the Cold War and have possibly increased. The dangers I was concerned with then still exist, and I think now new dangers are added through an increasing fragmentation of the nuclear know-how and nuclear resources since the fragmentation of the Soviet Union. To look at the situation soberly, I think we would have to face, in addition to the guilt of the whole nuclear-mentality attitude, the specific guilt of the various wars we have engaged in, most particularly the Vietnam War and the Gulf War and its consequences. Unless we can admit our part in those devastating events, the old way of paranoia and fragmentation will increase all the dangers.

I have tried to summarize the psychological constellations as I saw them developing after Hiroshima through the Cold War and perestroika, leading to the inevitability of further wars. What can psychoanalysis possibly offer in such a situation? I think it has something unique to contribute and that this arises from our understanding of the mental processes we observe in the clinical situation in which we work with our patients. It is here that the study of ambivalence, and the need to accept and face what has happened despite the enormous guilt involved is of prime importance. I think the only remedy we can possibly offer is to argue that it is not always necessary to swallow lies, and that circumstances do arise when we can look at the facts. These facts include the psychological motivations which underlie ambivalence, and an understanding of them can help in the struggle for glimmers of insight and sanity.

I, and others, have been accused of being partisan – not just personally, which it is our right to be, but involving psychoanalysis and speaking as analysts. I do not agree with this viewpoint. I think psychoanalytical neutrality must not be confused with an ethical neutrality which would allow us to be neutered. I think we should speak, not so much of the analyst's neutrality as of their objectivity. The analyst's task is to try to understand and objectively assess the situation, and communicate this understanding to others. And there can be no neutrality, say, as between Hitler and his victims. One can only strive for the understanding of factors that produce certain situations, and we are entitled, and indeed ethically bound, to make known our views know about the dangers we foresee. 'Qui tacet consentire videtur'![3]

We have also been accused of idealism. This I do not entirely refute, but I do not consider that it is 'un-analytic'. One has to distinguish between idealization and having ideals. Idealization is a a distortion of realities and is a dangerous stance, since it is invariably accompanied by splitting and projection – idealizing oneself and one's ideas or groups at the expense of paranoid attitudes to others. Having ideals is very different: it is not pathological to hope for a better future – for instance, for peace – and to strive for it, while recognizing how hard it is to attain, and that the opposition to it comes not only from others but also has its roots in ourselves.

Notes

1 This chapter combines material from two papers: 'The achievement of ambivalence' (Segal, 1992) and 'Hiroshima, the Gulf War and after' (Segal, 1995). It also includes some material from unpublished papers and talks. There is therefore some repetition of themes discussed in chapter 13.
2 The PPNW (Psychoanalysts for the Prevention of Nuclear War) was founded in 1983 by Dr Segal together with Dr Mo Laufer. It functioned both as a political pressure group within the British Psycho-Analytical Society, and as a forum for the study of nuclear war and its prevention by psychoanalysts and others. Subsequently, in 1985, an international association was founded.
3 He who is silent appears to give consent.

References

Abraham, K. (1924) 'A short study of the development of the libido viewed in the light of mental disorders', in *Selected Papers of Karl Abraham*, London: Hogarth Press (1927), pp. 418–501.

Anderson, R. (ed.) (1991) *Clinical Lectures on Klein and Bion*, Routledge: London, New York.

Barnaby, F. (1983) *Peace Studies Paper No. 4*, Bradford: University of Bradford.

Bion, W.R. (1952) 'Group dynamics: a re-view', *International Journal of Psycho-Analysis* 33: 235–47; also in *New Directions in Psychoanalysis*, Tavistock: London (1955).

—— (1956) 'Development of schizophrenic thought', *International Journal of Psycho-Analysis* 37: 344–6; reprinted in *Second Thoughts*, London: Heinemann (1967).

—— (1957) 'Differentiation of the psychotic from the non-psychotic personalities', *International Journal of Psycho-Analysis* 38: 266–75; reprinted in *Second Thoughts*, London: Heinemann (1967).

—— (1961) *Experiences in Groups*, London: Tavistock Publications.

—— (1962) *Learning From Experience*, London: Heinemann.

—— (1963) *Elements of Psycho-analysis*, London: Heinemann.

Bracken, P. (1984) *The Command and Control of Nuclear Forces*, New Haven, CT: Yale University Press.

Britton, R.S. (1989) 'The missing link: parental sexuality in the Oedipus complex', in R.S. Britton, M. Feldman and E. O'Shaughnessy, *The Oedipus Complex Today*, London: Karnac Books, pp. 83–101.

—— (1991) 'Keeping things in mind', in *Clinical Lectures on Klein and Bion*, R. Anderson (ed.), London, New York: Routledge.

Britton, R. S., Feldman, M. and O'Shaughnessy, E. (1989) *The Oedipus Complex Today*, London: Karnac Books.

Bychowski, G. (1966) 'Obsessive-compulsive façade in schizophrenia', *International Journal of Psycho-Analysis* 47: 189–97.

Chomsky, N. (1968) *Language and Mind*, New York: Harcourt, Brace & World.

Conrad, J. (1896) *Almayer's Folly*, in *The Collected Works of Joseph Conrad*, London: J.M. Dent & Son.

—— (1896) *An Outcast of the Islands*, in *The Collected Works of Joseph Conrad*, London: J.M. Dent & Son.

169

—— (1912) 'Secret Sharer', in *The Collected Works of Joseph Conrad*, London: J.M. Dent & Son.

—— 'The Shadow-Line', in *The Collected Works of Joseph Conrad*, London: J.M. Dent & Son.

—— (1947) *The Collected Works of Joseph Conrad*, London: J.M. Dent & Son.

Fornari, F. (1966) *Psychoanalysis and War*, Bloomington: University of Indiana Press.

—— (1975) *Psychoanalysis of Nuclear War*, Bloomington: University of Indiana Press.

Franklin, J.L. (1982) 'The religious right and the new Apocalypse', *Boston Globe*, 2 May.

Freud, S. (1910a) 'Leonardo da Vinci and a memory of his childhood', *SE* 11, 59–137, *Standard Edition of the Complete Psychological Works of Sigmund Freud*, London: Hogarth Press (1950–74).

—— (1910b) 'The future prospects of psychotherapy', *SE* 11, 141–51.

—— (1911a) 'Formulation on the two principles of mental functioning', *SE* 12, 215–26.

—— (1911b) 'Psycho-analytic notes on an autobiographic account of a case of paranoia (dementia paranoides)', *SE* 12, 3–82.

—— (1917) 'Mourning and melancholia', *SE* 14: 237–58.

—— (1920) *Beyond the Pleasure Principle*, *SE* 18.

—— (1923) *The Ego and the Id*, *SE*, 19.

—— (1924a) 'Neurosis and psychosis', *SE*, 19, 149–53.

—— (1924b) 'The loss of reality in neurosis and psychosis', *SE*, 19, 183–7.

—— (1926) *Inhibitions, Symptoms and Anxiety*', *SE*, 20, 77–172.

—— (1930) *Civilization and its Discontents*, *SE*, 21, 59–145.

Galbraith, J.K. and Salinger, N. (1981) *Almost Everyone's Guide to Economics*, London: Pelican Books.

Glover, E. (1933) *War, Sadism and Pacifism*, London: George Allen & Unwin.

—— (1947) *War, Sadism and Pacifism: Further Essays on Group Psychology and War*, Edinburgh: Hugh Paton & Sons.

Grinberg, L. (1962) 'On a specific aspect of countertransference due to the patient's projective identification', *International Journal of Psycho-Analysis* 43: 436–40.

Isaacs, S. (1948) 'The nature and function of phantasy', *International Journal of Psycho-Analysis* 29: 73–97; also in *Developments in Psycho-analysis*, J. Riviere (ed.), London: The Hogarth Press.

Jaques, E. (1955) 'Social systems as a defense against persecutory and depressive anxiety', in *New Directions in Psychoanalysis*, ed. M. Klein *et al.*, Tavistock: London.

—— (1965) 'Death and the mid-life crisis', *International Journal of Psycho-Analysis* 46: 502–14.

Jones, E. (1916) 'The theory of symbolism', in E. Jones, *Papers on Psycho-Analysis*, London: Ballière, Tyndall & Cox (1918).

Joseph, B. (1982) 'Addiction to near death', *International Journal of Psycho-Analysis* 63: 449–56; reprinted in *Psychic Equilibrium and Psychic Change: Selected Papers of Betty Joseph*, M. Feldman and E. Bott Spillius (eds), London: Routledge (1989).

King, P. and Steiner, R. (1991) *The Freud–Klein Controversies 1941–45*, London: Routledge.

Klein, M. (1930) 'The importance of symbol formation in the development of the ego', *International Journal of Psycho-Analysis* 11; reprinted in *The Writings of Melanie Klein*, London: The Hogarth Press, 1: 186–98 (1975).

—— (1935) 'A contribution to the psychogenesis of manic-depressive states', *International Journal of Psycho-Analysis* 16: 145–74; reprinted in *The Writings of Melanie Klein*, London: The Hogarth Press, 1: 262–89 (1975).

—— (1946) 'Notes on some schizoid mechanisms', *International Journal of Psycho-Analysis* 27: 99–110; reprinted in *The Writings of Melanie Klein*, London: The Hogarth Press, 3: 1–24 (1975).

—— (1948) 'On the theory of anxiety and guilt', *International Journal of Psycho-Analysis* 28; reprinted in *The Writings of Melanie Klein*, London: The Hogarth Press, 3: 25–42 (1975).

—— (1952) 'The origins of transference', *International Journal of Psycho-Analysis* 33; reprinted in *The Writings of Melanie Klein*, London: The Hogarth Press, 3: 48–56 (1975).

—— (1957) *Envy and Gratitude*, London: Tavistock, reprinted in *The Writings of Melanie Klein*, London: The Hogarth Press, 3: 176–235 (1975).

—— (1961) *Narrative of a Child Analysis*. London: The Hogarth Press; reprinted in *The Writings of Melanie Klein*, 4 (1975).

Lifton, R.J. (1982) *Nuclear War's Effect on the Mind*, London: Faber & Faber.

London, J. (1967) *Martin Eden*, London: Arcol and Penguin.

Mandelstam, N. (1971) *Hope against Hope*, London: Collins.

Meltzer, D. (1966) 'The relation of anal masturbation to projective identification', *International Journal of Psycho-Analysis* 47: 335–42.

Money-Kyrle, R. (1968) 'Cognitive development', *International Journal of Psycho-Analysis* 49: 691–8; reprinted in *The Collected Papers of Roger Money-Kyrle*, Perthshire: Clunie Press, 416–33 (1978).

Menzies, I. (1970) *The Functioning of Social Systems as a Defence against Anxiety*, London: Tavistock Institute of Human Relations.

Oxford Research Group (1986) *How Nuclear Weapons Decisions are Made*, S. McLean (ed.), London: Macmillan.

Rodrigue, E. (1955) 'The analysis of a three-year-old mute schizophrenic', in *New Directions in Psychoanalysis* M. Klein, P. Heimann and R. Money-Kyrle (eds), London: Tavistock.

Rosenfeld, H.A. (1964) 'On the psychopathology of narcissism: a clinical approach', *International Journal of Psycho-Analysis* 45: 332–7; reprinted in *Psychotic States*, London: The Hogarth Press (1965).

—— (1971) 'A clinical approach to the psychoanalytic theory of the life and death instincts: an investigation into the aggressive aspects of narcissism', *International Journal of Psycho-Analysis* 52: 169–78.

Rushdie, S. (1990) *Haroun and the Sea of Stories*, London: Granta Books/Penguin.

Russell, B. (1940) *Power*, New York: Basic Books.

Sandler, J. (1976) 'Countertransference and role-responsiveness', *International Review of Psycho-Analysis* 3: 43–7.

Segal, H. (1952) 'A psycho-analytical approach to aesthetics', *International Journal of Psycho-Analysis* 33; reprinted in *The Work of Hanna Segal*, New York: Jason Aronson (1981).

—— (1956) 'Depression in the schizophrenic', *International Journal of Psycho-Analysis* 37: 339–43; reprinted in *The Work of Hanna Segal*, New York: Jason Aronson, 121–30 (1981).

—— (1957) 'Notes on symbol formation', *International Journal of Psycho-Analysis*, 38: 391–7; reprinted in *The Work of Hanna Segal*, New York: Jason Aronson, 49–65 (1981).

—— (1958) 'Fear of death: notes on the analysis of an old man', *International Journal of Psycho-Analysis* 39: 187–91; reprinted in *The Work of Hanna Segal*, Jason Aronson, 173–82 (1981).

—— (1964) *Introduction to the Work of Melanie Klein*, London: The Hogarth Press.

—— (1972) 'A delusional system as a defence against the re-emergence of a catastrophic situation', *International Journal of Psycho-Analysis* 53: 393–401.

—— (1978) 'On symbolism', *International Journal of Psycho-Analysis*, 55: 315–19.

—— (1979) *Klein*, London: Fontana.

—— (1981) *The Work of Hanna Segal*, New York: Jason Aronson.

—— (1982) 'Early infantile development as reflected in the psychoanalytical process: steps in integration', *International Journal of Psycho-Analysis* 63: 15–22.

—— (1983) 'Some clinical implications of Melanie Klein's work: emergence from narcissism', *International Journal of Psycho-Analysis* 64: 269–76.

—— (1984) 'Joseph Conrad and the mid-life crisis', *International Review of Psycho-Analysis* 11: 3–9.

—— (1987) 'Silence is the real crime', *International Review of Psycho-Analysis* 14: 3–12.

—— (1988) 'Sweating it out', *Psycho-analytic Study of the Child* 43: 167–75.

—— (1989) 'Political thinking: psychoanalytic perspectives', in: L. Basnett and I. Leigh, *Political Thinking*, London: Pluto Press.

—— (1991a) 'Imagination, play and art', in *Dream, Phantasy and Art*, London: Routledge, pp. 101–9.

—— (1991b) *Dream, Phantasy and Art*, London: Routledge.

—— (1991c) 'Psychanalyse et thérapeutique', *Revue Française de Psychanalyse* 2: 366–76, 265.

—— (1992) 'The achievement of ambivalence', *Common Knowledge* 1: 92–104.

—— (1993) 'On the clinical usefulness of the concept of the death instinct', *International Journal of Psycho-Analysis* 74: 55–61.

—— (1994a) 'Phantasy and reality', *International Journal of Psycho-Analysis* 75: 359–401.

—— (1994b) 'Paranoid anxiety and paranoia', in *Paranoia – New Psychoanalytical Perspectives*, J.M. Oldham and S. Bone (eds), Madison: International Universities Press.

—— (1994c) 'Salman Rushdie and the sea of stories', *International Journal of Psycho-Analysis* 75: 611–18.

—— (1995) 'Hiroshima, the Gulf war, and after', in A. Elliott and S. Frosch (eds), *Psychoanalysis in Contexts: Paths between Theory and Modern Culture*, London: Routledge.

Sohn, L. (1985) 'Narcissistic organisation, projective identification and the formation of the identificate', *International Journal of Psycho-Analysis* 66: 201–14.

Spillius, E. Bott (1988) *Melanie Klein Today*, 1, *Mainly Theory*, London: Routledge.

Steiner, J. (1993) *Psychic Retreats: Pathological Organisations of the Personality in Psychotic, Neurotic and Borderline Patients*, London: Routledge.

Taylor, A.J.P. (1963) *The First World War*, London: Hamilton.

Vellacott, P. (1991) *An English Reader's Guide to the Oresteia*, Monophron Press: Cambridge.

Wollheim, R. (1984) *The Thread of Life*, Cambridge: Cambridge University Press.

Name index

Subject index

acting out: and transference 75, 84; by the analyst 22
actions 36, 38
actualization 112, 150
aggression: as deflection of the death instinct 18, 23, 158; guilt about 147; in the service of the life instinct 23, 150, 154, 164; sanctioned by group 162
Alpha elements 91; transformation from Beta elements 91, 92, 99, 102, 115
ambivalence 157–168; and reparation 159; and the death instinct 157; and the depressive position 159; in borderline patients 37; in mourning 157
annihilation: and psychotic anxieties 163; and symbolic survival 150, 164; fear of in paranoid-schizoid position 76; in nuclear war 149; of self to avoid pain 24
as-if world 38, 139, 142

Beta elements 102; and the move to the depressive position 68; and delusional states 38; and symbolism 99; conversion into Alpha elements 47
bizarre object 45, 97, 98
Born Again Christians 148, 149, 150

concrete symbolism 34–8, 43, 45, 47, 99

concrete thinking 37; and Beta elements 90
Conrad and the mid-life crisis 123–132
countertransference 111–119; and transference 116; and projective identification 112; and receptive disposition 116; and the death instinct 21; as a clue to patient's state of mind 119; as servant or master 119; dangers of 111, 117, 119; Klein's view of 117; uses and abuses of 111–119
countertransference disposition 116
creativity: in writers and artists 123, 125, 133; and the depressive position 132, 141

death instinct 17–26; and aggression 23; and ambivalence 157; and attacks on reality 39; and envy 23; and evil 138; and experience of pain 22, 23; and guilt 22; and hopelessness 154; and melancholia 18, 157; and narcissism 78, 79, 80, 84; and phantasy 156; and the environment 25; and Armageddon 150; beauty of 140; conflict with life instinct 158; defences against 25; deflection of 21, 158; Freud's view 18; fusion with life instinct 18; integration of 39; Klein's view of 24, 158; moderated by love 140; operating silently 138; pull of self destructive forces 25

175

176